Education in Democracy

Education in Democracy

EDUCATION'S MORAL ROLE
IN THE DEMOCRATIC STATE

Robert D. Heslep

IOWA STATE UNIVERSITY PRESS/AMES

Robert D. Heslep is Professor of Education at the University of Georgia, Athens.

© 1989 Iowa State University Press, Ames, Iowa 50010

Manufactured in the United States of America

First edition, 1989

Library of Congress Cataloging-in-Publication Data

Heslep, Robert D.
   Education in democracy: education's moral role in the democratic state / Robert D. Heslep.— 1st ed.
     p.   cm.
   ISBN 0-8138-0171-0
   1. Education—United States—Aims and objectives.   2. Moral education—United States.
3. Democracy.   4. Education—United States—Moral and ethical aspects.   I. Title.
LA217.H48   1989
370'.973—dc19   89-1754

Contents

Preface

THIS WORK IS AN EFFORT TO FILL an important void that has existed in educational literature during recent decades. Beginning in the eighteenth century, when Thomas Jefferson and others wrote about education in democratic society, and continuing well into this century, as the writings of John Dewey testify, commentators on schools and other academic institutions of the United States and other democracies often approached their subject by asking, What is education's role in the democratic state? In asking the question, they were not seeking to discover merely what education as a matter of fact does in actual democratic society; nor were they trying to find out just what education should do in order to help a democratic society fulfill its political principles. Instead, they were attempting to determine, beyond those things, what education ought to do in a democracy according to moral belief. They perceived that mere reports about education in democracy would not provide guidance for making policies, programs, and plans; and they saw that any claims about what education should do for political reasons would be liable to challenge on moral grounds. Of those discussing the issue of education's moral role in the democratic state, some made use of theoretical frameworks within which to conduct their inquiries; for they recognized that such frameworks could provide the principles required for investigating the issue. A framework that was adequate for an inquiry into the issue necessarily had to be complex; it had to include a theory of morality, of democracy, and of education.

Since World War II critics of education in America and elsewhere have continued to talk about education in democracy, but they have less and less frequently looked at the subject as a question of education's moral role in the democratic state. Some have confined themselves to providing mere descriptions of what education does in actual democracies, and others have restricted themselves to arguing the matter in purely political and educational terms or in moral and educational terms. Moreover, the theoretical frameworks within which they have analyzed the subject have not been suitable for understanding the role. Some, to be sure, have used frameworks consisting of political and educational theories; and others have supplemented their political and educational theories with indications of moral commitments. None, however, has employed a framework containing a moral as well as a political and an educational theory. So, the numerous criticisms and recommendations that have appeared since the Second World War about what education should be doing in this and other democratic nations have lacked adequate theoretical foundations; they have lacked principles whereby they fully may be explained and justified. It is the purpose of this work to analyze education's moral role in the democratic state on a basis of moral, political, and educational theories.

The principles unifying the several theories of the foundation come from the concept of voluntary action. The theory of morality is a critical modification of Alan Gewirth's theory. The theory of the democratic state is one of traditional liberalism. And the theory of education closely resembles those theories developed by analytic philosophers of recent decades. While this inquiry necessarily is abstract and complicated as its foundations are laid, it becomes specific as education's moral obligation in democratic society is discussed. Not only does the inquiry provide a general formulation of that duty, but it also applies the formulation to various specific aspects of the role. It addresses questions of curriculum, equality, moral education, and participatory decision making about education. Moreover, the investigation seeks clarification by comparing and contrasting some of its claims with those taken by other writers, contemporary as well as ancient.

In presenting this inquiry, I frequently make use of the pronoun *we*. This is not done to disguise direct references to myself. It is done, rather, because the investigation is a joint undertaking between the reader and me. To be sure, the inquiry has been initiated and developed by me; but it has not been directed from a private standpoint. It has been conducted according to canons of thought and language that are commonly shared. These canons are, among others, the standards and rules of deductive and inductive logic and the standards and rules of ordinary discourse. In setting forth the investigation, therefore, I assume that the reader will follow it according to the canons of thought and language I have used and in that respect will participate in it. Hence, the use of *we* recognizes the reader's and my joint participation in the inquiry.

Acknowledgments

Of the persons who have supported me in this project, several deserve a special thanks. To Professor James E. Giarelli of Rutgers University, who read most of the manuscript very closely when it was in an early draft, I am indebted for suggestions that led to improvements in the work. That he was unable to save me from all my errant ways was no fault of his. To my graduate assistant at the University of Georgia, Kay Mahar, who helped edit the final draft, I am grateful for meticulousness and concern with the clarity of this work. To Anne Howe, who faithfully and patiently typed and retyped the various drafts of the manuscripts, I am very thankful. To my wife, Joelyn, who tolerated with good humor my hours in the study, and to our children, Jonathan and Sarah, who did not have all the attention that they might have needed from their father, I am indebted for a home that has been congenial to this undertaking.

I am also grateful for permission to use previously published material.

The University of Chicago Press has graciously given permission to quote passages from Alan Gewirth, *Reason and Morality* (1978), pp. 134–35.

Philosophy Research Archives has graciously granted permission to paraphrase large portions of my article "Gewirth and the Voluntary Agent's Esteem of Purpose," *Philosophy Research Archives* 11 (1986): 379–91.

Educational Theory has graciously given permission to paraphrase large portions of my article "Political Theory and Education's Role in the United States," *Educational Theory* 14 (Summer 1964): 174–81.

Education in Democracy

The Context of the Inquiry

I

AMERICA'S EDUCATIONAL INSTITUTIONS have been subjected to steady criticism since World War II. In the 1950s they were held to be overly permissive as well as responsible for certain shortcomings in the fields of science and technology. In the 1960s they were charged with being factorylike, irrelevant, unacceptable, and in league with the establishment. In the 1970s they were accused of failing to teach adequately the academic basics and of neglecting to provide instruction in morality and religion. In the 1980s they have been blamed for the nation's weakened position in the world's economy, for the erosion of scores on standardized academic tests, for the decline of general education, for the disappearance of patriotism, and for other matters. The objections have not been raised merely for the sake of being critical; rather, they have been posed with a view to determining proposals for what should be done about the nation's schools, colleges, and universities. Recommendations have ranged from organizing curricula according to the scholarly disciplines to organizing them according to student interests, from deschooling America to student participation in academic governance, from a return to the academic basics to a reinstitution of prayer and Bible reading in classrooms, from a reemphasis upon the humanities to additional coursework in mathematics and the sciences, and from a reconstruction of civic education to the use of merit pay for school teachers.

For many of those who have followed the course of these debates and discussions, there have been conflict and confusion. Conflict has arisen because the criticisms and proposals have been at odds with one another at times. For instance, the position that the nation's scholastic institutions should not be tools of the military-industrial complex has been opposed by the belief that they are

3

not serving the nation's military and economic needs well enough. And the contention that students should pursue their studies according to their interests has been opposed by pleas for increasing coursework in the humanities, mathematics, and the sciences. Confusion has arisen partly because of the vast array of positions taken and partly because of the conflicts among them. School officials and the general public have found it difficult to choose among the great variety of positions. And they have been bewildered by the conflicts: no sooner, it seems, have they accepted and acted in good faith on one set of criticisms and proposals than they have been told to follow another set. It is not surprising, then, that some have become jaded and regard all efforts to improve the nation's academic institutions as faddish, while others have become cynical and view such efforts as little more than promotions of vested interests.

There is nothing endemically wrong with the persistence of arguments about the nation's academic institutions. Times change, and institutions need to be reexamined with respect to new conditions. Moreover, America is committed to democracy, and disputes over the nation's academic institutions are indicative of the presence of a democratic decision-making process. While conflict and confusion occasionally are by-products of democracy, they are not necessarily so; and when they do result from the free exchange of ideas, they may mean not that debates about the problems of democratic society should be abolished but that such debates should be scrutinized.

In examining the arguments about America's educational institutions, one is struck by the fact that they have ignored a question that is fundamental for any inquiry into these institutions: What is education's moral role, or moral duty, in the democratic state? In other words, what should education be doing in democratic society according to some body of moral beliefs? This issue is basic for several reasons. Even though the United States has some features commonly thought to be undemocratic, it has many important ones—such as its ideals of liberty, equality, and representative government—that constitute it by and large as a democratic state, albeit an imperfect one. Thus, to understand the nation's academic institutions fully is to recognize them as operating within a democracy. It follows that proposals concerning the institutions may be justified or criticized insofar as they are or are not in keeping with democratic ideals. While the nation's schools, colleges, and universities have multiple functions, they do have one that supposedly is central: to educate their students. They came into existence mainly to educate their students, and they assumed their other functions as secondary to this one. Moreover, they commonly are called "educational institutions." It is because education presumably is central to our academic institutions, as well as because these are the most obvious educational institutions in the nation, that Americans tend to identify education with schooling despite the latter's noneducational functions. At any rate, recommendations about our scholastic institutions may be defended or rejected to the extent that they encourage or oppose education. When a person talks about what education should or should not be doing in a political society, he may have any of several sorts of directives in mind: prudential, legal, political, or moral. He may be talking about what education ought to do to promote its own interest; to obey the laws of the land; to satisfy the principles binding upon it as a part of a democracy, oligarchy, or some other type of body politic; or to satisfy the principles and rules applying to it as an object of moral interest. Directives of these various sorts may oppose one another; and when they do, the moral directives have supremacy over the others. To say that a prudentially, legally, or politically correct act is immoral is to condemn it; to say that a morally right act is imprudent, illegal, or contrary to political principles is not to condemn it but to express a regret or to raise a puzzlement about the relationship between one's moral beliefs and one's respect for prudence, law, or political society. Accordingly, proposals about America's academic institutions may be justified or challenged, even if they are prudentially sound and in keeping with the nation's laws and political principles, on the ground that they are morally proper or improper. In sum, by neglecting to examine what education morally ought to do in a democratic commonwealth, the post–World War II discussions about the nation's academic institutions have failed to consider what the main mission of those institutions morally should be in the kind of political society that the United States is.

That these criticisms and proposals have not analyzed education's moral role in the democratic state does not mean that none of them has said anything about education, democracy, or morality. Some plainly have talked about education; others, about democracy; and still others, about morality. Indeed, some have dwelt upon education's political role in democratic society. It is one thing, however, to talk about one or more of these topics and quite another to examine the issue at hand. A person cannot address the question without speaking on all the topics, but he can discuss one or more of them without taking up the issue. Thus, an argument on education's political role in a democracy does not ask about education's moral role in the society; and an argument about the presence or absence of moral instruction in America's academic institutions does not pose the question either. If inquiries into America's scholastic institutions had been concerned with the moral role of education in a democratic state, they would have been in an advantageous situation. Each would have been able to avoid possible conflicts between whatever positions it had on what the educational and noneducational operations of the institutions should be; on what the institutions should do to serve the nation as a democracy and to serve it as a social organization guided by economic interest or some other nonpolitical principle; and on what the institutions are prudentially, legally, or politically bound to do and what they are morally obligated to do. Moreover, because in examining the question the inquiries would have focused on the chief mission of the institutions, American society as a democracy, and the supreme standards of directives, each would have had a viewpoint with which to identify and discuss other issues pertaining to the institutions.

II

AN INVESTIGATION of education's moral duty in the democratic state has to be conducted within a theoretical framework. There must be a source of principles with which to discuss the issue, and a theoretical framework contains concepts and statements that may function as such principles. Claims concerning the question have to be justified, and they may be supported by principles of the framework. Not just any theoretical framework can work as an adequate source of principles for an inquiry into the issue. The concepts and statements of a theory might be vague, ambiguous, and confused. Its statements might be self-contradictory or might contradict each other. It might involve inferences that violate the canons of deduction or induction. It might not take into account all aspects of the given question. What is to be sought, then, is a framework whose concepts and statements are clear, unambiguous, and in order; whose statements are noncontradictory; whose inferences are logically correct; and whose concepts and statements relate to all aspects of education's moral obligation in democratic society. The framework necessarily will be complex. To pertain to all aspects of the question, it will have to speak to the topics of morality, democracy, and education; and to do this, it will have to involve a theory of morality, a theory of democracy, and a theory of education.

As evidence of why an inquiry into education's moral role in democratic society should rest upon adequate theories of education, democracy, and morality, the views of two commentators pertaining to the political function of the nation's educational institutions will be examined. The views belong to James B. Conant, a distinguished and highly influential educator of the 1950s and 1960s, and the late Morris Janowitz, an eminent sociologist since the 1960s. Conant's position will be treated as a case of what happens when recommendations for the nation's academic institutions do not rest upon an adequate theory of democracy, and Janowitz's will be presented as a case of what happens when such proposals do not rest upon an adequate theory of morality. While the view of neither person rests upon an adequate theory of education, it will not be scrutinized with respect to this deficiency. If the reader becomes convinced through an analysis of the two positions that any view of education's moral function in a democracy needs to be grounded on an adequate theory of democracy and of morality, he or she should become convinced also that it ought to be based upon an adequate theory of education.

Conant regards the United States as a "modern democracy."[1] In clarifying education's political role in a modern democracy, he starts by quoting some passages from Thomas Jefferson that make two points about education in democracy: a "general diffusion of learning" will enable the citizens of a democracy to maintain their liberty; the complete education of people of "worth and genius" will provide a democratic state with leaders.[2] For Conant these two points suggest the "double duties" of the schools of a modern democracy.[3] He asks how these objectives may be best achieved in the twentieth century.[4]

In elaborating an answer to his question, Conant stresses two features of the United States as a political society. Although the nation is a modern democracy, it embodies "basic tenets,"[5] developed through history,[6] which distinguish it from other particular modern democracies and constitute it as an "American democracy." As examples of these tenets Conant mentions religious tolerance, mutual respect between vocational groups, belief in the rights of the individual, private ownership and the profit motive, federal union, the Anglo-Saxon tradition of the common law, and due process of law.[7] The equality appropriate to the United States as a democracy in the twentieth century does not mean what it did in de Tocqueville's time; it has come to signify ". . . not parity of status for all adults but equality of opportunity for the young."[8] This equality implies "a relatively fluid social structure" and "mutual respect between different groups."[9] Consequently, Conant proposes that what should be taught generally in the nation's schools—along with history, economics, language, natural science, arts, and mathematics—are the basic tenets of American democracy. He proposes also that the complete education of persons of worth and genius can be best obtained in schools providing equal social opportunity, schools ". . . where the youth of very different backgrounds and outlooks share a common experience, where the extracurricular activities and at least a common core of studies including English cut across vocational interests and cover a wide range of scholastic aptitudes."[10]

During the course of his argument Conant fails to clarify the terms *modern democracy* and *American democracy*. He does associate liberty, equality, and national unity with modern democracy; and he does cite examples of the basic tenets of American democracy. In neither case, however, is he very helpful. First, he does not make obvious the meanings of *liberty* and *equality*. Even after extensively quoting Jefferson on the importance of education for liberty, he neither delineates Jefferson's concept of liberty nor indicates that he accepts it. And in saying that equality, or "equal social opportunity for youth," implies a "relatively fluid social structure" and "mutual respect between different groups," he employs ambiguities in trying to explicate the term. There is more than one possible meaning of *a fluid social structure* and of *mutual respect between different groups*. Conant does not indicate which meanings he is using. Second, the relations of liberty, equality, and national unity to modern democracy and the relations of the fundamental tenets of American democracy to American democracy are hardly perspicuous. Equality and national unity are intimated to be conditions of liberty, but are these three the only qualities of modern democracy? And what are the fundamental tenets of American democracy besides those indicated by examples? Is liberty a means of modern democracy's end, or is it the end? What does it mean for a tenet to be basic to American democracy? Is it basic as a means to American democracy's end? Or is it basic as the end? These questions do not receive answers.

One consequence of his obfuscation is that Conant does not succeed in making plain the political role of the schools in a modern democracy. According to him, the role is suggested by the fact that such a state needs a citizenry capable of maintaining its liberty and that such a state also needs leaders, viz., people of genius and virtue. Nobody will deny that liberty is an ingredient of democracy, but some will doubt that it is the only essential ingredient. Jefferson, for example, holds it to be but one; he contends that life and happiness are also essential. At times, especially when discussing equality and national unity in a modern democratic state, Conant seems to think that liberty implies many matters ordinarily conceived as essential to democracy but different from liberty; but he never makes definite what they are. Thus, it may be wondered if the schools of a modern democracy ought to prepare citizens to maintain their liberty and not prepare them to do anything else. To have made evident that liberty is the essence of modern democracy, Conant would have had to explain the nature of modern democracy and of liberty. Also, nobody will deny that a democratic state needs leaders of genius and virtue, but in fact all states need such people. Hence, it is not enough for Conant to say just that the schools of a modern democracy should completely educate persons of genius and virtue. To perceive what education will effect the genius and virtue desirable in the leaders of a modern democratic state, one must have an understanding of that genius and virtue. This understanding Conant has not made possible. To have made it so, he would have had to proffer the terms and propositions which spell out the tasks of leaders in a modern democracy.

Another consequence of Conant's vagueness is that his specific recommendations on how the schools of the United States are to achieve their proper objectives are not very useful. He contends that, if the nation's citizens are to be capable of maintaining their liberty, they must be taught the basic tenets of American democracy along with a large variety of standard subject matters. As far as it goes, the contention seems acceptable; but it does not travel far. Since Conant has not explained what he means by liberty, he does not indicate what significance the standard subject matters and the fundamental tenets have for it and, thus, how these subject matters and tenets might most effectively be taught to preserve it. Moreover, since he does not indicate what, besides his examples, are the basic tenets of American democracy, he does not reveal what other tenets are to be taught. To have made possible a determination of all the tenets, Conant would have had to present the nature of American democracy. He holds that if the youth of the United States who have genius and virtue are to be furnished a complete education, *all* students must attend schools that promote equal social opportunity. Since, however, he has not made plain which genius and which virtue are desirable for the United States, he does not enable one to determine which opportunities should be provided to develop what genius and what virtue. To have shown the genius and virtue appropriate to the United States, he would have had to suggest the function of a leader in an American democracy.

For Janowitz, citizenship is "bound up with political freedom"; it depends upon political institutions and values that make possible and encourage the sharing of power by a state's members.[11] To rule permanently is to be not a citizen but a ruler of a body politic; to be ruled permanently is to be not a citizen but a subject of such a society.[12] Involving political freedom, citizenship has a special kinship to democracy; there are, however, differences between citizenship in a democracy and in a nondemocratic society. In a democracy citizens permanently share in the exercise of power; they share in the civic life of ruling and being ruled in turn. In a nondemocratic commonwealth they do not permanently share in the exercise of power.[13] There is more to citizenship, however, than just the sharing of power. There are the rights that each citizen has with respect to the sharing of power, and there are the duties that each has in relation to its sharing.[14] In addition citizenship involves civic consciousness, which is the allegiance of the individual citizen to his state. Civic consciousness "refers to positive and meaningful attachments a person develops to the nation-state. . . . It involves elements of reason and self-criticism as well as personal commitment."[15] In a democracy civic consciousness embodies certain values: equality of opportunity, individual freedom, "transcendental" social forms, a sense of collective obligation, and collective problem solving that is motivated by a sense of moral responsibility for the collective well-being.[16] The political role of education in the democratic state, then, necessarily includes civic education.

In the United States or any other Western democracy, Janowitz holds, *civic education* means "exposing students to central and political traditions of the nation, teaching essential knowledge about the organization and operation of modern governmental institutions, and fashioning the identification and moral sentiments required for performance as effective citizens."[17] Since the Second World War, he further declares, the quality of civic education has seriously declined in this nation. This decline is evidenced in the classroom by the decreasing emphasis on civic consciousness and the increasing emphasis on individual rights. It was rendered "to a considerable extent by 'intellectuals' and teachers more concerned with immediate political issues than with an education format for understanding the long-term trends in the American 'experience'."[18] What American educational institutions ought to do, therefore, is to restore civic consciousness to its proper place in civic education. Janowitz maintains that because the nation's classroom instruction presently makes economic goals paramount, it is incapable of teaching the meaning of political obligations associated with citizenry.[19] He proposes that a different sort of institution be used for instilling civic consciousness in the nation's youth. What he recommends is an institution of national service including both military and civilian components.[20] In the military component, service would be voluntary and for a term of two years. Personnel would be assigned not to specialized programs but to "run-of-the-mill" combat missions that could be learned in a few weeks. Aside from subsistence allocations and minimum cash payments, compensation would come from financial aid for education. In the civilian component, service would be voluntary also but for a term of only one year. Priority at the present time would be given to conservation work and to meeting the needs of neglected elderly people. Compensation would be similar to that given for military service.

There is no doubt that Janowitz is concerned mainly with the political and not the moral role of education in the democratic state. He is chiefly interested not in what education ought to do in the United States according to a set of moral beliefs but in what it should do in order to help the nation fulfill its ideals as a democracy. Thus, in Janowitz's discussion there are many explicit references to political society in general and to democracy specifically but precious few to morality. It would be a mistake, however, to think that Janowitz has no concern with education's moral duty in a democratic commonwealth. Underlying his argument are certain moral values and a commitment to a philosophical moral tradition, and these reinforce his position on education's political duty in the democratic state. Some of the moral values are specified when he declares that collective problem solving, voluntarism, and a sense of moral responsibility for the collective well-being are values that men and women should hold.[21] The philosophical moral tradition is described briefly when he explains what it means for him to be a sociological realist. Sociological realists are schooled in philosophical pragmatism; they have a long tradition of investigating efforts to achieve "a higher morality" in regulating societal institutions. "The political and social construction of the social entity called the 'citizen' has clearly been one such profound historic effort."[22] Insofar as Janowitz views education in a democracy as politically bound to promote citizenship, which he regards as a part of the higher morality in regulating societal institutions, he advocates a position on education's political role in democratic society that is supported by moral ideas that he has.

Despite his avowal of a moral orientation, Janowitz does very little by way of explaining the approach. He does clarify the concept of *citizenship* rather well, but he leaves the terms in which he specifies some of his other moral values somewhat vague. *Collective welfare, voluntarism, freedom,* and *value* itself are just a few of these terms. Moreover, he does nothing to justify some of the statements he makes as elements of his moral theory. When he claims, for instance, that collective problem solving (among other matters) is a value that all should hold, he does nothing to defend the statement; and when he maintains that citizenship is one of the higher moral values in regulating social institutions, he provides no morally relevant reason for the statement. So, even though Janowitz's view of education's political role in the democratic state is undergirded by a moral theory, it is not upheld by the theory very well. To the extent that the theory has vague concepts, it gives no guidance as to which objects are covered by the concepts and, therefore, which features of education and democracy are morally worthy. Thus, it does not indicate which features of the United States constitute a morally valuable object called "the collective welfare"; all that it actually does in this respect is to say that America's collective welfare, whatever it is, is morally estimable. Moreover, to the degree that the theory does not defend its statements, it cannot serve as an instrument for protecting claims about what education morally should be in the United States. Having failed, for example, to justify citizenship on moral grounds, the theory cannot explain why educational institutions in the nation morally should make the learning of citizenship one of their major aims. None of this means that the nation does not contain features that constitute a morally desirable collective welfare or that education in America morally ought not to treat the learning of citizenship as a cardinal goal. But it does mean that these and other points in Janowitz's proposal for what education should be in the United States have to be founded on an adequate moral theory.

III

GRANTED THAT DISCUSSIONS of American education should employ a theoretically sound view of its moral role in democratic society and that post–World War II commentators on the topic have not used such a perspective, there are good reasons for setting forth a properly grounded statement of the role. Providing such a statement now will not help anyone to rewrite the discussions of American education of the past four decades, but it will furnish a tool with which to reexamine those discussions. Moreover, it will supply an instrument with which future investigations of the nation's educational operations may be guided. Still further, it can stimulate additional inquiry into the role and thereby rouse public argument on the matter.

Conceiving education's moral role in democratic society on a theoretical basis is traditional. It dates back at least to the eighteenth century, when Thomas Jefferson and others concerned themselves with education in the United States; and it became one of the favorite approaches used in the first half of this century by serious observers of American schools, the most notable being John Dewey. It might be thought, therefore, that an acceptable statement of the role can be had through a search of extant statements. Supporting this approach is the dictum that there is no need to reinvent the wheel. Seeking a new acceptable statement runs the risk of not finding it; and even if the undertaking is successful, it will end simply by duplicating what is already at hand.

Despite the cogency of this point, however, there are stronger and opposing points to be made. For one thing, it is not evident that any of the extant views of education's moral role in the democratic commonwealth has an adequate theoretical foundation. During this century the theoretical frameworks of a variety of those views have been subjected to the scrutiny of scholars; and while they often have been judged to be admirable intellectual constructions, none of them has been found to be without some serious difficulty. Jefferson's philosophical principles, for instance, are bedeviled by vagueness and inconsistency; and Dewey's political theory is too narrow in its conception of the state (see Chapter 3, Part III of this book). For another thing, new theoretical approaches to education's moral duty in democracy are needed from time to time. They are likely to give insights and raise issues that extant approaches have not furnished and posed. These insights and issues, in turn, serve as reference points for reexamining the extant orientations and thereby for learning more about the latter's strengths and weaknesses. Thus, even if a theoretical framework has been regarded for a long time as adequate, it might be found, upon scrutiny within the light of a new theory, to have shortcomings.

A difficulty confronting the construction of a theoretical framework for a view of education's moral role in the democratic commonwealth is that the several theories constituting the framework need not be coherent with one another, or share principles with one another. If they do not have common principles, they cannot support jointly a meaningful formulation of the role, which they must do. A way to overcome this obstacle is to derive the fundamental concepts and statements of each constitutive theory from the same source. A difficulty facing any perspective on education's moral duty in democratic society is the necessarily high level of generality. Because the perspective must concern any moral responsibility of any education in any democracy, it must consequently be very general; and if it remains quite general, it will not speak to any specific aspect of education's moral role in such society. This obstacle may be circumvented by examining diverse specific facets of the role from the standpoint of the perspective. While this strategy will not necessarily cover every specific facet of the role, it can include a diversity large enough to suggest how others might be investigated.

Construction of the theoretical foundation for a statement of education's moral obligation in the democratic state may begin with an analysis of the concept of *action*. In the following chapter, examination of that concept will lead to a scrutiny of voluntary action that will produce a set of fundamental principles appropriate for a theoretical foundation. The moral theory of this work is influenced explicitly and strongly by the thought of Alan Gewirth, who has provided a profound, systematic, and thorough discussion of the moral significance of voluntary action. The democratic theory of this work, determined mainly through analyses of the concept of the state and of democracy, may be described as one of traditional liberalism. The educational theory of this work, shaped principally through a consideration of the concept of education, bears a family resemblance to theories developed by analytical philosophers of recent decades. After formulating, on the basis of these theories, a view of education's moral role in democratic society, our inquiry will use that view to discuss specific questions concerning the role. The topics of those questions are curriculum, equality, moral education, and education decision making. Along the way there will be occasions to discuss ideas of some philosophers, social scientists, and educators, both ancient and modern. Comparing and contrasting their ideas with those of this work will help clarify the latter.

Action and Morality

I

MORALITY, POLITICAL SOCIETY, AND EDUCATION involve action as a pervasive element. The central concern of morality is the action of one person toward another; the members of a political society interact with each other as do teachers and students. To be a moral person is to be prepared to act in specified ways; to be a citizen or an official of a state is to be the subject of certain acts; and to be a teacher or a student is to perform given acts. A point of moral rules and executive and judicial decisions is to order the conduct of people and of a state's members while the point of pedagogical precepts and decisions is to order the behavior of teachers and students. The fundamental principles of morality are a basis of directives; the ideals of a political society serve as guides of action by both rulers and ruled; and the content of education consists partly of skills and dispositions of action. The prevalance of action in morality, political society, and education helps to explain why they are often called "practical matters."

In view of the important place occupied by action in morality, political society, and education, the concept of action should be regarded as a source of principles for discussing the moral role of education in a democratic state. The principles to be discovered in the concept are partly factual and partly moral.

II

ACTION MAY BE ANALYZED in the terms of doing something.[1] At least, when we hear action expressions, such as *action, act, activity, behavior, conduct,* and

15

deed, we tend to interpret them as referring to doings of things, such as speaking, running, thinking, working, studying and eating.[2]

A doing of something has a subject, which is sometimes called an "agent." In addition, a doing of something might be significantly related to objects, i.e., related to objects by virtue of its qualifying them. Objects get qualified by doings of things sometimes as conditions, obstacles, facilities, tools, materials, and goal-objects. The subject of a doing of something, whatever objects are relevant to the doing, and the interactions among the subject and the objects constitute the doing's context. As commonly acknowledged, a doing of something terminates; and it may, thereby, be spoken of as having an "outcome," "result," or "effect." The outcome of a doing of something may be either or both the context of the doing upon its cessation ("The fighting ended in a confused state") or some element of the context upon the doing's termination ("The conflict ended with many casualties"). Accordingly, a complete description of a doing of something must include references not only to the doing's subject and objects but also to its outcome.

Actions may be construed as performed or had. An action is performed if its subject is not compelled to do what he is doing. This means that the agent is forced by neither external nor internal forces, whether they are physical or psychological. An action is had if its subject is compelled to do what it is doing. Accordingly, subjects of performed actions are capable of not doing what they are doing whereas those of had actions are incapable of not doing what they are doing. While agents of performed actions desire to do what they are doing, they do not act because their desire to act makes them act. If they did, they would be acting under coercion. People who act because some desire of theirs makes them act have their actions. Insofar as an action is performed, it is free. Even if an action is constrained, it is free as long as it is performed; for its agent, who is capable of not doing what he or she is doing, does not have to act within the given constraints. The agent of a performed action also is free, but being the agent of a performed action is only one sense of a free person.[3] Another sense is a person without constraints; still another sense is a person with freedom of choice, which is not necessarily presupposed by performed action. The performance of an action implies that the action's agent chooses, at most, to do a particular thing rather than not to do it. Hence, if performance of an action logically presupposed free choice, it would mean that free choice would be a Hobson's choice, which it definitely is not. Free choice requires that an agent may choose among several alternative actions and not just between doing a particular thing and not doing it.

Performed actions are voluntary when their agents freely choose the actions and are informed of what they are doing.[4] The latter means that they know who they are, what they are doing, whatever purposes they might have, who are the recipients of what they are doing, and the immediate outcomes of their doings. Accordingly, an involuntary action might have a subject who is informed of what he or she is doing but who does not freely choose to do what he or she is doing; or the action might be freely chosen by its agent but be involuntary in that the agent is not informed of all aspects of what he or she is doing. Because of their freedom and knowledge, agents acting voluntarily may be described as in control of what they are doing whereas subjects acting involuntarily, because of their lack of freedom or knowledge, may be described as not in control of what they are doing. Thus, hyperactive students who behave well because of drugs they have been given by psychiatrists act involuntarily because they are compelled to do what they are doing. The loving father who pays ransom to the kidnappers of a daughter acts involuntarily because he is forced to do what he is doing. And the hunter who mistakes another for a deer and kills him acts involuntarily in that he is not informed of what he is doing. It follows that the agent of a voluntary action must be one who is capable of choosing actions freely and acting wittingly. Human beings, divinities, and corporations commonly are allowed to be agents of voluntary actions; lower animals rarely are acknowledged to be such.

While some voluntary actions are ordinarily described without any reference to standards or rules, others may be described with reference to them. Hence, a voluntary action might be spoken of as "mere bodily movements" or as "good dancing," as "merely running" or as "racing poorly," as "pressing his lips against hers" or as "kissing her properly." Although many voluntary actions are deliberate, that is, determined as a result of careful thought, not all of them appear to be. Some strolling is deliberately performed, but much of it is not.[5]

A mental matter important for actions is intention, which is an agent's acting with respect to his or her action's end. An intended end, as commonly understood, is a conceived state of affairs. If it is only conceived, it might be referred to simply as "an intention," "an ideal," "an objective," "a goal," or "a purpose"; but if it is actual as well as conceived, it might be spoken of as (among other things) "an actualized intention" or "a realized objective." An intended end, of course, is not just any conceived state of affairs; more specifically, it is a state of affairs conceived by an agent who desires (in the sense of "wants," not "longs for") to realize it and, moreover, desires to realize it through his given action. It surely would be odd to be told that Washington intended to defeat Cornwallis but desired neither to defeat him at all nor to defeat him through the engagement at Yorktown. Even though an intention logically presupposes a desire, a desire to bring about a conceived state of affairs does not entail an intention to do so. Despite a desire to realize a conceived state of affairs, we might, because of insufficient desire, uncontrollable circumstances, or whatever, determine no course of action or make no effort to realize the state of affairs.

Any voluntary action is intentional. For an agent to act freely and knowingly is for him to want to do what he is doing and to know what he is doing. So, because the agents of voluntary actions freely and consciously choose to act, they plainly act so as to fulfill desired states of affairs even if the ends are nothing more than their performance of the given actions. Obviously, the subject of any involuntary action might act without intention. A chemical action is always involuntary and never with intention, and human beings sometimes do not know what the ends of their actions are. Nevertheless, the agent of an involuntary act might act intentionally. Hence, the father who ransoms his daughter acts involuntarily but intentionally. It follows, then, that if something is done intentionally, it may be done voluntarily or involuntarily. If it is done without intention, it is done involuntarily.

That agents act intentionally does not mean that their intentions must be occurrent. They may be dispositional. As a matter of fact, people often do act from habits rather than from explicitly held intentions. But to say that the intention involved in an action is dispositional is not to say that it is not present. It is to say only that the agent is acting without concentrating upon his intended end.[6]

III

THE PRECEDING DISCUSSION has specified various features of doing something: subject, object, context, performing, having, desire, knowledge, voluntariness, result, rule, mental, intention, occurrence, disposition, and others. Doing something, subject, object, and context are generic characteristics of action; they pertain to any action of any kind. The other features are specific characteristics. While some of them belong to actions of one type, others belong to actions of another variety. Performance and knowledge, for instance, are traits of voluntary actions whereas having is a trait of involuntary actions. Accordingly, in seeking to clarify education's moral role in the democratic state, we are likely to find some principles of action more useful than others. The generic principles surely will be helpful; but as they are significant of any action of any kind, they will not yield insights into actions especially related to morality, political society, and education. By contrast, the principles of intentional action show promise of providing an understanding of actions especially associated with morality, political society, and education, which typically, if not distinctively, embody intentional actions.

Whether generic or specific, the features of action that have been mentioned are purely factual. Each of them is a fact of action, either in general or of a definite type; none of them poses any value, duty, right, or other normative matter. It may be asked, then, whether or not action has any normative features. A clue to an answer may be found by a brief consideration of the principles of subject and object. As already intimated, the subject of an action may be rational or nonrational; and the object of an action also may be the one or the other. The action of a nonrational subject towards any object, whether rational or nonrational, never contains norms; but the action of a rational subject upon an object, whether rational or nonrational, might embody norms.[7] When rational subjects act toward purely physical objects, they might treat them as just means to ends; but if they do, they are committed to the norms embedded in the means-end relationship, e.g., efficiency. Also, when a rational subject acts toward a rational object, the latter might interact with the former; and if there is an interaction, the subject and the object constitute a social relationship and, thus, are bound by the norms of such a relationship. Since the time of Immanuel Kant it has been generally recognized that the parties to any social relationship must respect each other as persons, which implies that the subject of a social action must never treat a rational object purely as a means. What has been said here about norms of action is rather vague and impressionistic, but it does suggest that we should search seriously for norms of action that might be important in understanding education's moral role in the democratic state.

It seems appropriate to look, at least initially, for norms of moral action. As commonly conceived, moral principles are superior to all other principles of action; this means that people should not follow a principle of any other kind that opposes a principle of morality that they accept.[8] Accordingly, if any norms of moral action were identified, they could function as constraints upon political and educational actions. A promising way to locate some moral principles is to examine the argument of Alan Gewirth on the normative structure of voluntary action. His work provides a formulation of what he regards as the paramount moral principle and of another that is nearly as important. Moreover, the work is one of the most careful and best known of recent inquiries dealing with the normative structure of voluntary action. Even though Gewirth's argument is flawed in several places, it is largely correct; also, the weaknesses in the argument may be corrected without revising Gewirth's moral theory radically.

Gewirth begins his discussion of the normative structure of voluntary action by talking, from the perspective of the agent of a voluntary action, about the structure in general. Gewirth views a moral action as an interpersonal, voluntary action.[9] Voluntary action has two generic features: the agent's acting unforcedly and wittingly and the agent's acting for "some end or purpose that constitutes his reason for acting."[10] The former trait Gewirth calls alternately "voluntariness" and "freedom" whereas the latter he dubs alternately "purposiveness" and "intentionality."[11] In having a purpose, an agent necessarily desires it; and in wanting the purpose, he or she conceptually has a favorable interest in it and thereby values, with respect to relevant criteria, the purpose by logical necessity.[12] The agent's valuation of the goal means that he or she implicitly judges it to be good. The term *good* has "the common illocutionary force of expressing a favorable, positive evaluation of the objects of purposes to which it is attributed."[13] Hence, to want an objective is logically to be committed to saying, in view of criteria, that the object is good. The criteria by which an agent of voluntary action implicitly judges his or her objectives to be good "need not be moral or even hedonic; they run the full range of the purposes for which the agent acts, from the momentarily gratifying and the narrowly prudential to more extensive and long-range social goals."[14]

But, Gewirth insists, agents of voluntary actions evaluate more than their purposes at hand. Because they regard their actions as means to things they regard as good, they must prize also the actions, including the actions' voluntariness and purposiveness; and this means that they, in order to be consistent, must appreciate the voluntariness and purposiveness of all their voluntary actions.[15] In effect, the purposiveness of an agent's voluntary actions encompasses, from the standpoint of the agent, three kinds of goods: the basic aspects of the agent's well-being that are the proximate necessary conditions of the performance of any and all his actions, the present level of his or her purpose fulfillment, and the raising of the level of his or her purpose fulfillment.[16] Finally, because the agents of voluntary actions take as good the generic features of their respective voluntary actions, they logically must maintain that they have rights to these features. After all, what could be a more urgent object of an agent's rights claim than the necessary conditions for his or her engaging in voluntary action in general and particularly in successful voluntary action? Because the agent views the generic features of his or her voluntary actions as necessary for the possibility of his or her agency, is it not logical that the agent hold that all other persons refrain from interfering with these conditions and, on occasion, help him or her secure these conditons?[17]

Upon proceeding to analyze the moral structure of voluntary action,

Gewirth examines such action from the viewpoint of its recipients as well as from that of its agents. The recipients of a moral agent's voluntary action are themselves prospective agents of voluntary actions and, as such, also have rights to voluntariness and purposiveness. Hence, the agent ought to refrain from interfering with their voluntariness just as they should refrain from interfering with his or hers; and the agent ought to refrain from interfering with and, when appropriate, to help secure their purposiveness just as they should refrain from interfering with the agent's and, at times, help secure the agent's purposiveness.[18] In view of these points, Gewirth comes to the following conclusion:

> It follows from these considerations that every agent must acknowledge certain generic obligations. Negatively, he ought to refrain from coercing and from harming his recipients; positively, he ought to assist them to have freedom and well-being whenever they cannot otherwise have these necessary goods and he can help them at no comparable cost to himself. The general principle of these obligations and rights may be expressed as the following precept addressed to every agent: *Act in accord with the generic rights of your recipients as well as of yourself.*[19]

This precept, which Gewirth labels the "Principle of Generic Consistency" (PGC), is for him the supreme principle of morality.

A doubt about Gewirth's analysis of the normative structure of voluntary action arises when he makes his first claim about the general normative structure of voluntary action. The doubt concerns Gewirth's justification of his claim that the agent of any voluntary action regards his or her purpose as good.

According to Gewirth, any voluntary agent wants to do what it is his or her purpose to do; and his or her desire to attain the goal consists in a pro-attitude toward the goal. Wanting to realize the end means that the agent focuses attention on the purpose of the given action rather than other possible objects of attention, that he or she tends to move toward the attainment of the goal rather than other possible objects, and that he or she has a favorable interest in, or favorable mind-set toward, attaining the goal. This favoring need not be vehement or inclinational, but it does comprise an intending to attain the objective "such that interference with its attainment would cause at least momentary annoyance or dissatisfaction."[20] After giving this account of what he means by the connection between purpose and wants, Gewirth contends that the connection is important for the agent's valuation of his or her aim: "For from this connection stems the fact that the agent necessarily regards his purposes as good and hence makes an implicit value judgment about them. . . ."[21] The putative fact that agents view their goals as worthy stems from their having objectives: the agents desire to attain the goals and, therefore, value them. The realization of any purpose, it will be remembered, is the object of a want, which desire entails a favorable interest in and, thus, a valuation of the purpose's fulfillment. By virtue of this valuation, the agent of concern looks upon the fulfillment as good. Gewirth does not mean that goodness is identifiable with a positive interest; but he does insist that such interest is the "primary, although by no means the only, basis of judging something to be good."[22] At any rate, because all agents necessarily desire to achieve the objectives of their actions, they necessarily have positive interests in and, at least implicitly, prize the objectives of their actions. In sum, an agent esteems his or her purpose because he or she desires to realize it.

This argument certainly looks promising; at least, by its own terms it does demonstrate that the agent's desire to accomplish a purpose entails that the agent values that purpose. The question, then, is whether or not the argument should be accepted on its own terms. More specifically, the question is whether or not Gewirth's conception of desire by an agent of voluntary action should be accepted. Gewirth, as we have seen, itemizes several conceptual criteria of a voluntary agent's desire: attention, tendency, and favorable interest. It seems quite in keeping with normal discourse, which Gewirth professes to use as a source of conceptual meaning,[23] to take attention and tendency as conceptual criteria of desire; for it surely would be odd to say that Mary wants to learn algebra but never gives any heed to it or never directs any of her efforts toward learning it. It is doubtful, however, that ordinary talk insists that a desire logically includes a pro-attitude toward its object.

For one thing, it is wrong to maintain, as Gewirth does, that the negative feeling engendered by interference with an agent's intention to achieve a given goal necessarily signifies that the agent approves the goal. Gewirth apparently presumes that the only possible cause of the negative feeling associated with such an interference is the agent's being detained from reaching something in which he or she is positively interested. This, however, is not the only possible cause of annoyance or dissatisfaction brought on by interference with an agent's intention to reach a given end. Agents acting with regard to ends may be described, Gewirth has indicated, as moving themselves toward the ends. Thus, they may be spoken of as "set" or "keyed" to attain the ends or as "bent upon" or "headed toward" their attainment. And when any agent's tendency toward an end is interrupted, the agent may be referred to—without any reference, implicit or explicit, to his or her failure to reach something he or she approves—as feeling disturbed because of the interference.

For another thing, any voluntary agent's desire may be described without referring to any favorable mind-set. To describe A as wanting X is to say among other things that A does not now have X; that A pays heed to X; that A directs some effort toward obtaining X; and that A, given the opportunity and an absence of overriding conflict, will obtain X. But it is not to say that A necessarily favors X. A, of course, *might* favor X. However, A does not have to be referred to as having a positive interest in X in order to be described as desiring X. Indeed, normal discourse allows us to talk about a desire that involves no favorable interest on the part of its subject. Such a desire might be a caprice, or a desire formed or had capriciously. According to the *Oxford English Dictionary*, the primary meaning of *caprice* is "A sudden change or turn of the mind without apparent or adequate motive; a desire or opinion arbitrarily or fantastically formed; a freak, whim, mere fancy." Also according to the same work, the meaning of *capriciously* is "In a capricious manner; according to caprice; arbitrarily." While desires formed fantastically are pertinent to some contexts, the ones relevant to the problem discussed here are those had arbitrarily. A desire is not held arbitrarily when its subject has a reason for wanting its object; it is held arbitrarily when its subject does not have a reason for wanting its object. Thus, if Tommy does not now have a book, pays heed to books, makes an effort to obtain a book, will obtain a book when it is feasible to do so, but has no reason for obtaining a book, he desires the book arbitrarily, or capriciously. We all, or at least most of us, have encountered persons, in ourselves or others, who seem to want something without reason. A person suspected of having a capricious desire is typically, but not exclusively, one whose concerned desire appears suddenly, endures briefly, and runs counter to his or her established life. The husband who never before has been interested in extramarital sex, but who all of a sudden and for a short time wants to engage in it, is one who well might be considered as possibly having a desire without reason. The same may be said of the successful career woman who suddenly and briefly desires to give up her career and become devoted totally to being a housewife and mother. Even though we might not ever be convinced that given possibly capricious desires are without reason, we, as the *Oxford English Dictionary* testifies, find nothing silly in thinking that they might be capricious.

Dictionaries, of course, are fallible. Hence, rather than taking a dictionary as the indisputable authority on the normal conception of desire, one should ask whether or not desire by a subject who has no reason for having it really makes sense. Suppose that Betty says she wants a saucer of mud but, upon demand, can furnish, directly or indirectly, no reason for wanting it, not even "Just to have it."[24] Would not we think that Betty has misspoken, that

she does not really desire the saucer of mud? As G. E. M. Anscombe has remarked, "To say, 'I *merely* want this' without any characterization is to de-
prive the word of sense . . ."[25] What may count as a subject's reason for desiring X is the subject's stating in some way that he or she approves of X in
some respect. Because, therefore, normal discourse conceives desire as involving a reason for the desire, the contention that the notion of an arbitrary desire
makes sense is patently wrong, dictionaries notwithstanding. Accordingly,
one cannot describe a desire by a voluntary agent fully unless one refers to a
reason by the agent for the desire (e.g., a favorable mind-set toward the
desire's object.)

Even though this argument might be greatly appealing, it rests upon a serious confusion. It confuses the sense of desire with the sensibility of desire; in
other words, it mistakes the meaning of desire for the rationality of desire. It is
one thing to have a desire; it is quite another to have a reason for the desire.
Betty may not be sensible in wanting a saucer of mud; but if she does not have a
saucer of mud, gives attention to a saucer of mud, directs some energy toward
obtaining one, and obtains it when she feasibly can, she certainly desires a saucer
of mud.

In showing that Gewirth does not soundly support his claim that voluntary agents necessarily prize their goals, the preceding discussion has great significance for his moral theory. It implies that all the principles resting, directly
and indirectly, upon the claim have a weak foundation.

As far as can be told, Gewirth places only one principle directly upon the
claim. It holds that voluntary agents necessarily value their respective actions.
That Gewirth puts this principle immediately upon the claim can be seen from
the fact that he supports the former by appealing directly to the latter: agents
must appreciate their actions because they perform them in order to attain
things that they necessarily regard as good—their goals.[26] According to the
analysis argued here, agents do not necessarily view their aims as worthwhile
and, thus, do not perform their actions in order to obtain something that they
necessarily esteem. Hence, an agent cannot properly be said to prize his or her
action from necessity on the ground that he or she necessarily values its end. It is
acknowledged that agents do necessarily prize their actions as means for fulfilling their purposes, but this is not to say that they have to regard their purposes
as valuable. It has been intimated that voluntary action, whether its end is appreciated by its agent or not, is deliberative: its agent looks upon the action as
preferable to alternative actions for attaining his or her end. It follows that the
agent has to allow that the action is valuable for achieving his or her objective. In
granting this, however, the agent need not make any concession about the

worth of the objective. The standards employed in choosing an action might make sense only if they are used for choosing one meant to attain a valued end. Efficiency, for instance, might make sense as a standard only because it will enable agents to gain ends that they value as quickly as is feasible. Even so, the standards used might make sense in choosing an action meant to achieve a capricious goal. Being desired arbitrarily, a capricious objective does not have to be attained immediately or within the confines of prudence, morality, aesthetics, or any other normative area; but it is to be achieved during the duration of the involved desire. In choosing an action, therefore, an agent with a capricious objective might employ no standard other than effectiveness; that is, the agent might consider no aspect of an entertained action other than whether or not it is likely to realize his or her purpose. If the agent does entertain several actions that seem equally effective, he or she can select among them arbitrarily, e.g., by a coin toss. In any event, if the agent chooses an action simply for its effectiveness, he or she values it as a means in that he or she prefers it to actions that are not effective or are less effective than the chosen one in fulfilling the given aim. The agent, of course, does not prefer it to actions that are as effective as the chosen one but are rejected arbitrarily.

The principle that agents view all of their other actions as worthy follows from the contention that they appreciate their present actions. After all, if agents appreciate actions of theirs because they see them as means to things they esteem, the agents must value all other actions of theirs that they perceive as means to things they prize. Because the claim about the agent's esteem of all his or her other actions derives from the one about the agent's valuation of his or her present action, it derives indirectly from Gewirth's original contention. The claim that agents deem as worthy the generic features of their respective given actions follows from the claim that they esteem their actions and, thus, indirectly from Gewirth's initial claim. Because the contention that agents value the generic features of all their other respective actions comes directly from the assertion that they prize the generic features of their present respective actions, it comes indirectly from Gewirth's starting contention. The principle of generic rights, or that each and every voluntary agent has a right to the generic features of his or her actions, is supported even more indirectly by Gewirth's initial claim; for this principle is upheld immediately by those principles concerning any agent's valuing the generic features of his or her actions, given and otherwise. And, of course, the PGC, which purports to follow from the principle of generic rights, rests still even more indirectly upon the claim. Despite the fact that the support received by each of these contentions from Gewirth's original claim is indirect and despite the fact that the indirectness of that support varies in degree from claim to claim, each of the contentions rests upon the same flawed foundation. Each is as unsound as the other.

IV

EVEN IF IT HAS BEEN SHOWN that Gewirth does not properly support his claim that any agent necessarily views his or her goal as good, it has not been proved that the claim is false or otherwise unacceptable. It is conceivable that the claim can be defended well by arguments not yet examined.[27] Nevertheless, rather than inspecting additional arguments in favor of the claim, one may attempt to dispose of it by presenting what are believed to be compelling reasons for accepting the opposing contention that an agent may or may not value his or her goal. The reasons should look familiar, for they derive from our criticism of Gewirth's theory. After providing those reasons, we should consider a modification of Gewirth's moral theory: the replacement of his claim about voluntary agents' valuing their goals by the newly propounded claim.

The first reason in support of the opposing claim is that the concept of a capricious purpose runs counter to the proposition that all agents logically must value their purposes. Implying that an agent might hold a goal without appreciating it, the concept signifies that not all agents have to esteem their goals. The second reason was alluded to in our examination of the concept of desire. In a challenge to Gewirth's view that a desire is marked among other things by a favorable interest on the part of its subject, it was argued that any desire may be described sufficiently to depict it as a desire without its subject being referred to as having a favorable interest. A similar point may be made about the description of an agent's purpose. To say that X is the purpose of a voluntary action is to allow (1) that X is the end of the action, which is to say that the realization of X is that for which the action is headed. It is to grant also, as previously suggested, (2) that the agent of the action desires and intends to bring about X. It is to concede still further, as already intimated, (3) that the agent has chosen the action through deliberation as a means for attaining X. And it is to allow even still further, as indicated above, (4) that the agent has made the purpose the end of his or her action unforcedly and wittingly. By following these criteria, it is submitted, one may describe an object sufficiently to identify it as the purpose of a voluntary action; but in following them, one does not grant that the agent does or does not prize his or her goal. Criterion 1 clearly implies nothing about the agent's valuation of his or her objective. Criterion 2 is noncommittal about the matter because, as earlier explained, neither the concept of desire nor that of intention requires a voluntary agent to esteem or not to esteem his or her aim. Criterion 3 is noncommittal for the reason that, as already pointed out, while deliberation implies that a voluntary agent values his or her action, it does not entail that the agent values his or her purpose. And criterion 4 is noncommittal because, as previously mentioned, agents may make objects their purposes voluntarily without having to prize or contemn the purposes. Given, then, that we may describe the purpose of a voluntary agent without implying thereby that the agent does or does not appreciate the purpose, we have good reason for maintaining that the agent logically may or may not value the purpose.

That the agents of voluntary action logically may or may not prize their aims does not mean, it should be remembered, that they are not necessarily rational, or sensible. Just as any agent with a valued purpose may justify his or her action by appealing to the purpose and a desire to fulfill it, any agent who does not prize his or her objective may justify his or her action by appealing to the objective and a desire to reach it. Moreover, just as agents with appreciated goals may justify their actions further by appealing to the deliberation whereby they have chosen the actions, agents not valuing their aims may justify their actions further by appealing to the deliberation whereby they have chosen the action. Nevertheless, there is a respect in which some agents might not be rational. Agents with esteemed ends, it has been mentioned, may justify their actions still further by appealing to the worth of their ends; but agents who do not esteem their aims, it also has been noted, cannot justify their actions in this way. In truth, they cannot justify their actions by appealing to any aspect of their ends other than their wanting and intending to attain them. All other aspects are insignificant as justifying factors for them. Accordingly, an agent with a prized purpose is rational in the respect that the agent may justify his or her action by appealing to the worth of that purpose; and an agent who does not esteem his or her aim is not rational in the respect that the agent may not justify his or her action by appealing to any value of that purpose. So, an agent with a valued objective and an agent without an appreciated objective are equally rational insofar as they both can justify their actions in similar respects; but the former is more rational than the latter in that the former can justify his or her action by appealing to his or her valuation of the objective, and the latter cannot justify his or her action in this respect.

Upon granting that agents may or may not appreciate their goals, one must acknowledge that evaluativeness is not a generic feature of voluntary action. Nevertheless, because it is a distinguishing trait of what is, from the standpoint of morality, the most important type of voluntary action; and because voluntariness (uncoerciveness and knowledge) and purposiveness (intention and deliberativeness) are generic features; they all may be referred to as the chief characteristics of voluntary action. In any event, one now will do well to consider what difference the proposition that agents may or may not value their purposes makes for Gewirth's moral theory if that proposition, instead of Gewirth's claim that the agent appreciates his goal, is taken as the theory's initial principle. Some principles Gewirth has based upon the claim have to undergo modification in meaning if not in wording, and several principles for which there are no counterparts among Gewirth's principles have to be injected into the theory.

The principle that agents necessarily prize their actions does not require change in either wording or meaning. To be sure, it can no longer rest upon Gewirth's claim about the appreciation of aims; but it can stand upon the proposition that agents may or may not value their aims. According to Gewirth, an agent esteems his or her action because the agent perceives it as a means for obtaining something he or she regards as good; but according to the position being entertained here, the agent values his or her action for either of two reasons. If the agent's aim is not prized, his or her action is prized simply because he or she sees it as more effective than other actions for achieving the aim; but if the agent's goal is appreciated, his or her action is valued because it is preferable to other actions for attaining something deemed worthy. Moreover, because the principle that agents have to value all their other actions derives from the one that they must prize their present actions, it too may rest upon the proposition that agents may or may not esteem their purposes and, thus, does not require alteration in word or meaning. The principles that an agent necessarily esteems the generic features of his or her present action and that the agent must esteem the generic features of all his or her other actions, which follow from their principles about the agent's valuation of his or her actions, do not need any change in wording; but they do require an alteration in meaning. The generic features of voluntary action, it will be remembered, are voluntariness and purposiveness. While the present inquiry agrees with Gewirth that deliberativeness is a part of the purposiveness of any action of any agent, it denies that this is the case with evaluativeness. Deliberativeness pertains to the capability that any agent has for choosing an action through deliberation; evaluativeness pertains to the standards, judgmental skills, factual knowledge, and other elements constituting the capability that an agent who prizes a goal has for valuing goals. So, rather than being necessarily integral to the purposiveness of any and all voluntary actions performed by an agent, evaluativeness is necessarily ingredient to the purposiveness of only those voluntary actions whose agents deem their aims as worthy. In saying, therefore, that agents necessarily appreciate the generic features of their present actions and those of all their other actions, one allows that they must value deliberativeness as a feature of each and every action of theirs; this is not to allow that they have to favor evaluativeness, which might be absent from their present actions, as such a feature. Of course, even if an agent does not value the aim of his or her given action and, thus, does not deem as good evaluativeness as a feature of the action, the agent can appreciate evaluativeness as a feature of prospective actions whose goals he or she might value.

The principles that agents necessarily assert a right to the generic features of their present action and that they assert a right to the generic features of all their other actions also have to be modified in meaning. By contrast with Gewirth, when it is stated here that agents must assert a right to the generic features of any and all their actions, it is not intended that they have to assert a right to evaluativeness as one of these features. If an agent regards as worthy the aims of his or her given action, the agent must appreciate evaluativeness as a feature of that action and, hence, has to assert a right to evaluativeness as such a feature; and upon conceiving himself or herself as an agent of prospective actions whose ends he or she might esteem, the agent has to assert a right to evaluativeness as a feature of such prospective actions. Yet, if an agent does not value the end of his or her present action, the agent cannot prize evaluativeness as a feature of that action and, insofar, has no ground on which to assert a right to it as such a feature; and upon conceiving himself or herself as an agent of prospective actions whose ends he or she might not value, the agent lacks a basis on which to assert a right to evaluativeness as a feature of such actions.

At this point, several principles with no counterparts in Gewirth's presentation of his theory must be introduced. Because it is contended here that agents may or may not prize their goals, it is denied that any agents have to be able to appeal to a valuation of their objectives as a reason for their actions; but it is conceded that an agent who appreciates his or her purpose and, hence, can give the valuation of it as a reason for his or her action is, in this respect, more rational than an agent who does not value his or her purpose and, therefore, cannot appeal to an esteem of it as a reason for his or her action. Besides this principle of degrees of rational agency, there is the principle of degrees of claim; this principle holds that a rational agent asserts a claim to an action to the extent that he or she has rational grounds for performing the act. This means that if an agent has reason for all aspects of his or her action, the agent has rights to all the aspects; if not, the agent lacks a right to any feature for which he or she has no reason and thereby diminishes his or her claim to any feature for which there is a reason. Moreover, the tentativeness of an agent's reason for his or her action determines the strength of a claim to the action. The basis for the principle of degrees of claim is the more general one that a rational agent establishes a right to an action by having a reason for it. It is arguable that this larger principle lurks behind Gewirth's defense of his principle of generic rights, and it also is arguable that the principle of degrees of claim lurks behind his defense of the Principle of Proportionality (discussed further in Part V of this chapter). In any event the conjunction of the principle of degrees of claim with that of degrees of rational agency leads to the principle of superior and inferior rights, which states that, all other things being equal, agents prizing their goals have claims to the generic features of their actions that are greater than those of agents who do not prize their goals. The former agents, according to the principle of degrees of rational agency, are more rational than the latter; and because the former are more rational than the latter, the former, according to the principle of degrees of claim, have rights to the generic features of their actions that are superior to those had by the latter. Thus, all other things being equal, the agent who esteems his or her purpose has claims to the voluntariness and deliberativeness of his or her action that are stronger than those of the agent who has his or her purpose by caprice. This holds whether the two agents are the same person acting with an esteemed purpose at one time and with a capricious purpose at another or whether the two agents are different persons.

The PGC can be revised with reference to the principles that have been inferred, directly and indirectly, from the proposition that agents may or may not esteem their aims. Gewirth's PGC, it may be recalled, simply says: "*Act in accord with the genric rights of your recipients as well as of yourself.*"[28] The revised version of the PGC may be couched in the same terms, but it must be seen as having a meaning somewhat different from that intended by Gewirth. Because the agent of a voluntary action takes himself or herself to be a prospective, as well as an occurrent, agent of voluntary actions, the agent also, in order to be consistent, must take the recipients of his or her current action as prospective, if not occurrent, agents of voluntary actions. And because the agent lays claim to the generic features of his or her voluntary actions to the extent that he or she has reasons for the actions, the agent further, in order to be consistent, must allow that the *recipients* of his or her voluntary actions have rights to the generic features of *their* respective voluntary actions to the degree that they have reasons for their actions. This allows that an agent with a valued purpose not only has relatively superior rights to his or her action's generic features but also has a right to the evaluativeness of the action, which from our standpoint, it will be remembered, should not be regarded as a part of the generic features of voluntary action. It also implies that an agent, who sees his or her recipients as having certain duties toward himself or herself, also sees that he or she has definite duties toward the recipients. For instance, the agent ought to refrain from harming them and assist them occasionally in securing the conditions of their well-being; and, all other things being equal, the agent is obligated, when rendering assistance, to give priority to those recipients who as agents appreciate their aims. So, while the PGC formula may be used to express these various points, it must be understood to emphasize the place given by them to the relative superiority and inferiority of generic rights. That is, it should be seen to say: act in accord with the generic rights of your recipients as well as of yourself and, in so doing, consider the relative superiority and inferiority of these rights. This version of the PGC will be dubbed the "Revised Principle of Generic Consistency" (RPGC).

V

WHILE THE PRINCIPLE OF GENERIC CONSISTENCY is central to Gewirth's conception of the moral structure of voluntary action, it certainly is not the whole of his conception. A moral principle developed by him as a guide in the application of the PGC is his Principle of Proportionality (PP): "When some quality Q justifies having certain rights R, and the possession of Q varies in the respect that is relevant to Q's justifying the having of R, the degree to which R is had is proportional to or varies with the degree to which Q is had."[29] This principle, which is remindful of Aristotle's dictum that equals should be treated as equals and unequals as unequals, is not derived by Gewirth from his claim that any agent esteems his goal. It is derived, rather, from another contention, namely, that there are "degrees of approach to full-fledged agency."[30] At any rate, it is shown by Gewirth to be especially helpful in applying the PGC to cases involving the generic rights of human fetuses, children, the mentally deficient, and lower animals. It seems quite important for any inquiry into education's role in a political society. Such an inquiry must say something about the education of children and the mentally deficient in a political society, and it might have to say something about shaping people's attitudes toward human fetuses and lower animals. For this reason, this discussion of the normative structure of voluntary actions should not end until it determines a principle corresponding to the PP.

As a matter of fact, the PP neatly fits in, as it stands, with the view of the normative structure of voluntary actions that has been advanced here. Why it does is rather obvious: its wording is so general that it accommodates varying conceptions of given subject matters. Thus, it uses the term *some quality Q,* which may apply to a quality that Gewirth has in mind or a different one that we have in mind. Moreover, it utilizes the term *certain rights R,* which may refer to rights that Gewirth intends or different ones of which we are thinking. Yet, even though the principle may be employed by us as Gewirth states it, it should not be expected to enable the present position always to lead to conclusions identical to Gewirth's.

A reason why not is also the reason why the principle may be used by us without any change in wording, namely, objects to which the principle's major terms refer according to our view of the normative structure of voluntary action are somewhat different from those to which the terms refer according to Gewirth's view. According to both Gewirth and ourselves, a quality to which the term *some quality Q* may refer is deliberativeness. As far as Gewirth is concerned, deliberativeness logically implies evaluativeness and vice versa; but for us deliberativeness does not logically imply evaluativeness even though the latter does logically imply the former. Thus, from Gewirth's standpoint one cannot claim greater or lesser rights to deliberativeness unless one takes the quality to be coupled with evaluativeness whereas from our position one can claim greater or lesser rights to deliberativeness without connecting it with evaluativeness.

There is another reason why the Principle of Proportionality will not always lead to conclusions identical to those to which it leads Gewirth: we maintain, and Gewirth does not, that the agents of voluntary actions who evaluate their purposes hold in higher esteem their generic rights insofar as they pertain to voluntary actions with valued goals than they do their generic rights insofar as they pertain to voluntary actions without prized objectives. According to this contention, the agent who values his or her purpose must regard as more valuable the qualities by virtue of which the agent possesses his or her generic rights as they bear on voluntary actions with prized aims than the qualities by virtue of which the agent has his or her generic rights as they concern voluntary actions without such aims. For instance, the agent must have a greater appreciation of his or her ability to choose an action in view of a goal he or she judges to be worthwhile than of his or her ability to select an action with respect to a purpose on whose worth he or she has no opinion. In following the Principle of Proportionality, therefore, agents must take into account the distinction between qualities required for the possession of generic rights related to one sort of voluntary action and those necessary for the possession of generic rights related to the other sort. Hence, even if the agents hold that their respective qualities required for having generic rights pertinent to voluntary actions with valued purposes are not as developed as the qualities by virtue of which recipients possess generic rights relevant to voluntary actions without prized objectives, they should claim their generic rights pertinent to voluntary actions with valued aims are greater than the recipients' generic rights bearing on voluntary actions without esteemed purposes. Gewirth, of course, would not come to this conclusion by following the Principle of Proportionality. Because he looks upon any agent of any voluntary action as perceiving his or her purpose as good, he does not distinguish between an agent's generic rights relating to voluntary actions with esteemed goals and his or her generic rights pertaining to such actions without valued purposes. Consequently, he does not distinguish between the qualities an agent must have to possess the former generic rights and the qualities required for him or her to have the latter rights.

That the Principle of Proportionality will not permit conclusions always identical to those that it lets Gewirth make becomes plainer through a consideration of an argument in which he establishes a point very important to his moral theory. The point is that "superior agents" should be accorded "greater rights to freedom and well-being: more power to choose and control their own and other persons' participation in transactions and more means of fulfilling their purposes."[31] To support his conclusion, Gewirth employs the PP as his major premise and uses as his minor premise the observation that some human beings, by being better qualified as agents of a voluntary action, are superior to others as such agents.[32] While our position does not compel any change in the PP, it does call for some alteration in Gewirth's minor premise. In referring to agents of voluntary actions, the premise intends for Gewirth that all such agents regard as good their respective purposes. The premise, however, cannot mean this for us. It must be revised to read: some human beings, by being better qualified as agents of voluntary actions who do not value their individual goals or as agents of such actions who do esteem their aims, are superior to others as agents of the one sort or another. In keeping with these changes in the minor premise, we logically must alter Gewirth's conclusion to read: agents of voluntary actions who prize their aims and who are superior to other agents of the sort have greater rights to the generic features and the evaluativeness of their actions; agents who do not esteem their objectives and who are superior to other such agents have greater rights to the generic features of their actions; but agents who value their goals have greater rights to the generic features of their actions than do agents who do not value their purposes even though the former agents might not be superior to the latter ones in deliberating about their respective actions. The last part of this conclusion reflects the contention that any agent who prizes his or her purpose should claim that his or her generic rights relating to voluntary actions with valued aims are greater than any recipient's generic rights bearing on voluntary actions without esteemed objectives. Accordingly, we accept the wording of the PP but not exactly what Gewirth intends by the wording. To prevent confusion, the principle with our interpretation will be called the "Revised Principle of Proportionality" (RPP).

But whether the Principle of Proportionality is called "Revised" or not, it might fall prey to misinterpretation. Specifically, it might be taken to mean that talents and only talents count when one assesses the claims of different agents to actions requiring capabilities; it might be regarded as a principle of unconstrained meritocracy. The reason why the principle should not be viewed as intending this is that it allows that matters other than talents may be considered when one evaluates the claims of agents to actions requiring certain capabilities. As stated by Gewirth, it will be remembered, the PP speaks of "some quality Q" that "justifies having certain rights R"; and while some quality Q might be a talent, it might be something else, too. It might be, for instance, a moral handicap or some character trait, such as courage, that is in the public interest. Therefore, the talents required by given actions should be taken as the sole determinants in competing moral claims to the actions only when no other qualities are required by the actions; and they should be regarded as overriding only when all other qualities required by the actions have been determined to be less important than the talents. Extreme meritocracy, accordingly, is not entailed by applications of either the PP or the RPP.

VI

THIS EXAMINATION of the concept of action has produced both factual and normative principles. The factual principles, which were located largely by linguistic analysis, are features of all action or features of different types of action. Examples of the former are subject, object, doing something, and context. Examples of the latter are free choice and knowledge, which characterize voluntary action; and having, which is a trait of nonvoluntary action. The normative principles, which were identified mainly through a critique of Gewirth's theory of the normative structure of voluntary action, primarily are specific characteristics of voluntary action with valued objectives and secondarily are generic features of all voluntary actions. Instances of the former are the worthiness of the evaluation of purposes, which is a specific feature of voluntary actions with esteemed aims, and the right to evaluate objectives. Examples of the latter are the worthiness of voluntariness and deliberativeness, which characterize voluntary actions without prized ends as well as those with valued ends. When voluntary actions have recipients, they assume the quality of being moral; and when they are moral, they are subject mainly to the RPGC. Another moral principle to which they might be subject is identical in wording (but not in meaning) to Gewirth's Principle of Proportionality.

As previously indicated, the factual principles are likely to prove useful in an investigation of education's moral role in a democratic state. The principles significant of action in general, because of their universality, probably will be somewhat important for an understanding of the multifarious actions embodied in any political society and in any aspect of education. The principles closely relevant to intentional actions, because of their specificity, should be especially important for a comprehension of the intentional actions involved in any political society and in any facet of education. It should be evident too that the normative principles are likely to be helpful in our inquiry. While the evaluative and deontic commitments of nonmoral actions might have significance for political society and education, the evaluative and deontic commitments of moral actions appear to be quite appropriate to an understanding of political society and education. Actions in which the citizens and governments of political society engage typically have recipients and, thus, a moral quality; and the actions in which the parties of education, namely teachers and students, engage typically have recipients and, therefore, a moral quality, also. Furthermore, because moral commitments override, by their very conception, any commitments opposed to them, the moral commitments of action pose a framework within which all political and educational commitments, moral or nonmoral, must be constructed. This means that our principles corresponding to Gewirth's Principle of Generic Consistency and to his Principle of Proportionality must serve as principles of whatever we conclude about education's moral role in a democratic state.

The norms of action identified through inspection of Gewirth's inquiry might not be the only ones useful in comprehending education's moral role in a democratic state. There might be norms of political and of educational action; and if such norms do exist, they should be quite helpful in comprehending the role. Any discussion of the norms of political and educational action, however, must wait until later.

The State

AN UNDERSTANDING of education's moral role in a democratic state includes a grasp of what the democratic state is, and that depends upon a comprehension of what a state is. In developing this comprehension, we are concerned with a state not in the sense of a government but in the sense of a body politic, political society, or commonwealth. But in calling a state a "body politic," we do not say much. Dictionaries are quite vague about what a body politic is; and political philosophers disagree, sometimes widely, in their conceptions of it. This is not to suggest that a political society cannot be comprehended, but it is to indicate that it can be grasped only with some difficulty.

REGARDLESS OF THEIR DISAGREEMENTS on what a commonwealth is, all political theorists concur that its members are rational in some sense and may be corporate agents, such as business corporations, as well as noncorporate ones, such as human beings.[1] Not just any rational agent, of course, may count as a member of a state. People keeping to themselves might be rational agents, but they are not members of a state: they do not make up a social group, which is a generally recognized mark of a body politic's members. To say that agents are "social" is to say they are interactive with each other, dispositionally if not occurrently.[2] Whether or not agents interact is simply a matter of fact. Interaction alone is neither good nor bad; it is of itself not something to which the members of a social group are or are not committed. As indicated in our discussion of action, however, a social pattern of action by rational agents is not understandable by reference to factual principles only; it can be comprehended fully only if reference is made to a normative principle, to wit, personhood. Thus, not only must the rational agents constituting a social group be seen as interacting with each other; they also must be conceived as being obligated to treat each other as persons, who are, in an important sense of the term, self-determining, or voluntary, agents.

Although a social group might be the membership of a state, it might not be. Unlike the members of some social groups, the members of a state are supposed to interact with each other according to a set of rules; that is, they have rights and duties in their interactiveness that are delimited by the rules of concern. More to the point, a state is a society, which includes, among other things, "a number of individuals bound together by . . . normative rules. They behave predictably in relation to one another because of this normative system. These rules define the rights and duties which they have towards one another, the ends which they may pursue, and the ways in which it is legitimate to pursue them."[3] While the rules of a society are central to it, they do not have to be articulated and instituted. They may be nothing more than reflections of the desires, aversions, habits, and customs of the society's members. Regardless, a society's rules rest upon reasons. Because a society's rules are rules of rights and duties, the reasons supporting them might well embody principles for justifying rules of rights and duties. Moreover, because a society's rules are supposed to regulate its members' behavior with respect to whatever intended ends the society has, a justification of the society's rules well might employ its aims as well as the rules' principles. The principles upholding a society's rules might or might not mirror the cultural norms of the society's members. They might constitute a set with impeccable logical order; or they might be tantamount to a set with inconsistency, ambiguity, and other logical problems. The principles supporting imposed rules frequently do not reflect the cultural norms of those members upon whom the rules are imposed. That the members of a society might not be aware of the principles justifying their society's rules helps to explain why they occasionally may be described as having lost sight of their society's principles. And the historical instances of political society whose laws are justifiable by appeals to both equality and liberty provide evidence that the principles supporting a society's rules might be inconsistent or ambiguous. Principles defending a society's rules are principles of that society *because* they defend rules of that society. As shall be noted soon, however, they need not be the only principles of the society.

Besides having members and rules, a society has some intended end. Athletic societies, religious societies, literary societies, political societies—all have conceived ends with respect to which they act. The intended ends of a society may be general and enduring or specific and momentary. Instances of the former sort are a society's ideals; examples of the latter are the goals of a society's policies, programs, and plans. That an intended end belongs to a society does not imply that it belongs to each of the society's members. It would be odd if no member of a society were positively interested in its intentions, but it would not be strange if one or more of its members were not positively interested in them. A good member makes his society's ends his own, but not all members of a society need be good ones. Moreover, that a society has an end does not mean that its members will cooperate with each other so as to fulfill it. Good members are cooperative, but not all members must be good ones. Accordingly, the proposal by some social theorists to define a society in the terms of cooperativeness with respect to a common intention is wrongheaded.[4] Even though the members of a society are rational agents, they do not, simply because they are rational, have to cooperate with each other in view of a common intention. It is one thing to be rational; it is quite another to be eminently rational. Even though a society's rules necessarily rest upon reasons, its ends do not have to have justification; they might be whimsical. Even so, the intended ends of societies frequently are backed by reasons, reasons that embody principles for justifying intentions of societies. Like the principles supporting a society's rules, those that undergird the intentions might or might not reflect its member's cultural norms; they might or might not be consciously held by its members; and they might lack logical integrity. Like the principles that defend a society's rules, those supporting a society's intentions are principles of the society. The justification of a society's ideals and basic rules classically is provided by its founders, although it might be given by subsequent persons. Thus, the ideals and constitution of the United States were justified by that country's founders; whereas those of mediaeval European states were justified, by philosophers, long after their founding. In any event, because a society's rules and intended ends are its major distinguishing components, the principles justifying a society's rules and intended ends are its chief principles. Unlike those of other sorts of societies, the intended ends of a commonwealth characteristically include ideals. The chief principles of a political society must consequently be capable of upholding general and enduring ends.

A society, as intimated above, may be informal or formal. It is *informal* insofar as its rules are not articulated or instituted. To the extent that its rules are not articulated or instituted, rights and duties are not codified;

positions are assigned by circumstance or tradition; the ideals of the society might be only dimly perceived; and procedures for resolving disputes and conflicts are not fixed. A society is *formal* in as much as its rules are articulated and instituted. The articulation and institution of its rules codify rights and duties, establish procedures for assigning roles, specify any intentions, and fix procedures for resolving disputes and conflicts. Without question a state is a formal, not an informal, society. The feature most generally associated with any state is government, which conceptually incorporates the articulation and institution of laws. By virtue of its government's laws, a state has established procedures for appointments to offices and for the settlement of disputes and conflicts and may have explicit declarations of intentions. Yet, while a body politic is a formal society, it does not necessarily exclude informal social elements. As a matter of fact, the familial and neighborhood groups found in actual states typically have been informal societies. The reason why a state including informal subsocieties is not qualified by their presence as informal is, roughly speaking, that the state is a whole and they are merely parts of the whole.

Human agents occupy space, and it is common for formal associations to have territorial limits. The North American Soccer League had a territory; General Motors has one; the Greek Orthodox Church has one; and so forth. Historically, land area is one of the most famous traits of the body politic. States have fought each other because of boundary disputes. Exiled national groups have longed and plotted to return to their homelands. Immigrants seeking a better life in another state often wish to return to the "old sod." Indeed, there is a theory that the history of states can be best understood by reference to their individual geographies. While territory may be characteristic of different sorts of formal groups, it is not distinctive of a body politic; but the way in which a state relates to its domain is significant. Even though the North American Soccer League (NASL) operated within North America, it certainly did not comprise all within the area. By contrast, Canada embodies everything within its boundaries including those operations of the NASL within its territory, and the United States includes everything within its domain including those operations of the NASL within its territory. The inclusion by a body politic of all within its boundaries is sometimes labeled "territorial inclusiveness."[5] That a commonwealth embodies whatever is within its boundaries means that whatever is within its boundaries belongs to it and belongs, in all its aspects, to it as an element of it. Thus, nothing within the domain of a political society is beyond the pale of that society's authority.[6] It is usually allowed that everything, in all its aspects, within the boundaries of a body politic is subject to that society's authority; but it also is commonly granted that a state might not exercise its authority over everything within its domain. (Thus, it is only relatively recently that states have exercised authority over their air space.) Territorial inclusiveness, however, is not sufficiently distinctive of states. A body of adventurers might stake out an area to which no other association lays claim and make all within the area its own. Yet, the group, even if it has a formal structure, does not become a state merely by assuming territorial inclusiveness.

As mentioned earlier, states are universally conceived as having governments.[7] It is admitted that any formal society may have a government—a body whose designated function is to articulate and institute the society's less fundamental rules, to enforce all the society's rules, and to resolve disputes and conflicts concerning the rules.[8] Yet, government is not a feature that a state simply *may* have; like territorial inclusiveness, it is a necessary trait of a state. With respect to its authorized power, state government is distinctive: it is supreme to any other government within the state's domain. Within a state there may be other societies with governments (e.g., athletic clubs, business corporations, and churches) and there may be governing bodies that are, in effect, subdivisions of the state's government. Regardless of the number and power of the other governments within a state, however, the state's government is supreme. It may override any of them; but they, severally or collectively, may never override it. Thus, a state's legislation often negates the rules of other governing bodies within the state, and its courts frequently overturn the judicial decisions of other governing bodies within its domain. John C. Calhoun's doctrine of interposition, accordingly, which allows the governments of the various so-called "states" making up the United States to interpose themselves between their respective subjects and the government of the United States, is applicable only if these are governments of true states. Moreover, because the putative government of present-day Lebanon cannot control many terrorist groups within the area, it fails to be a government; consequently, contemporary Lebanon fails to be a state. The supremacy of a body politic's government over other governing bodies is remindful of the sovereignty of the state, but it is not identifiable with that sovereignty. Among other reasons, a state's government is subordinate to whatever fundamental laws the state has.[9]

Also characteristic of a body politic is that its government is independent of any government outside the state's territorial limits. Just as a state's government may consent to follow proposals and requests from internal governing bodies, it also may consent to accept proposals and requests from external ones.

But just as it may not be coerced by domestic governments, it may not be coerced by external ones. A commonwealth's government may be supreme to external governments, or it may be equal to them. If, however, it becomes subject to one or more external governing bodies, as contemporary Lebanon is occasionally subject to Syria and Israel, it thereby fails to characterize the society that it serves as a state. Implicit in this statement is the point that statehood is a quality that adheres to societies in degrees. It makes sense to refer to one society as a full-fledged state and another as an incomplete one. For instance, a society might be recognizable as a state even if its government is sometimes coerced by foreign governments; furthermore, it might be identifiable as a state even if its government is occasionally not supreme to all other internal governments. If, however, a society's government is forced regularly to do the bidding of external or internal governments, it is not to be regarded as a state. Thus, a society whose government is controlled by the governing board of a bank or a labor union may be viewed as a state by a Marxist; but for us it is no state at all or, at best, is a corrupt state.

The authorized power of state government is plainly awesome. By virtue of its internal supremacy, it may exert an influence over the members of a commonwealth that no other governing body within the commonwealth's domain may exercise. To help maintain its external independence, it may compel the sacrifice of lives of its members, which no other government within the commonwealth may do. And to help maintain its supremacy, it, along with any subdivisions that it might have, has the authority to control the use of force and the levying of taxes. As a matter of fact, the exertions frequently made by individuals, factions, business interests, labor unions, and others to gain control of governments is strong testimony to the enormous power that state governments are commonly recognized as having. Why, then, does a body politic have a government with such power? An explanation is to be found, at least partly, in the intended ends of a state. While a state is like other associations in that it has ideals, it differs from them in what some of its ideals are. Any state has the special intentions of protecting its members from physical violence and theft, protecting them from foreign domination, and providing a way to settle disputes and conflicts among its members.[10] It is the received wisdom of political theorists and statesmen that the attainment of these and other special intentions of a commonwealth requires a government with the supremacy and independence characteristic of a state government.[11]

The fact that a state has special intentions does not mean that these must be its only intentions. States are rational agents of a sort. Like a human being, a state may have purposes and, through its government, voluntarily seek to fulfill them; furthermore, the actions chosen by a state for attaining its goals might have, and necessarily do have, recipients. Insofar as a state has principles by which it justifies its intentions, it is an agent that values its ends; and insofar as it does not have such principles, it is an agent that might not prize its aims (Chapter 2, Part IV). The major difference between a state and a human being as rational agents is that the former is a corporate rational agent while the latter is not. A corporate rational agent necessarily contains other rational agents as members whereas a noncorporate one need not. Thus, a business corporation necessarily has rational agents for its directors, employees, and owners; and while an informal recreational club, which is not a corporate body, has rational agents as members, a human being does not. The rational agents ingredient to a corporate rational agent may be other corporate as well as noncorporate rational agents. A political society, for instance, might embody business corporations as well as human beings. However, the existence of a corporate rational agent is logically independent of the existence of the individuals who are its member rational agents. It is this last characteristic that distinguishes corporate rational agents, which are societies of a sort, from noncorporate societies: while the existence of a corporate society does not necessarily depend upon that of the individual rational agents ingredient to it, the existence of a noncorporate society might depend upon that of its individual member rational agents. The decisions of a corporate rational agent, of course, are made for it by one or more of its member rational agents; those of noncorporate rational agents may be made, as in the case of human beings, for the agents by themselves.

As rational agents, states are the bearers of rights and duties. Some of these are the rights and obligations peculiar to states, which are usually discussed in disquisitions on the laws of nations. Others are the rights and duties of simple political interest. Still others, however, are rights and obligations of morality. States do have moral rights relative to their respective goals and courses of action, and they do have moral duties relative to the recipients of their courses of action. According to our moral theory, for instance, any state has a right to the generic features of voluntary action and possibly to the evaluativeness of voluntary actions; this implies, among other things, that it has a moral right to determine its actions without outside interference. Moreover, any state has a moral duty to respect the rights of its recipients to the generic features of voluntary action and the evaluativeness of voluntary actions; this means, in part, that a state must respect the moral rights of its members and of foreign moral agents. Plainly, therefore, the moral obligations of a state function as constraints upon the means it may employ to achieve its ends as well as upon what ends it may set for itself. While, according to our moral theory, any state is morally bound to protect its members from physical violence and theft, to protect them from foreign domination, and to help settle their disputes and conflicts, the state might also be morally obligated to have additional objectives. The members of any state have moral rights to the conditions necessary to voluntariness and deliberativeness—for instance, health, education, and life. While the members of a state look to it for the protection of their lives, they might rely upon other associations for their health and education. They might, for instance, look to a guild of physicians for their health and a church for their education. On the other hand, they might have no association other than the state to care for their health and education. If the state is the only association that can care for its members' health and education, it is morally bound to do so, at least within the limits of its abilities. In sum, any commonwealth morally has to provide its members with security and a way to settle their disputes and conflicts. But a body politic might have the moral duty of providing other conditions necessary for voluntariness and deliberativeness.[12] Consequently, the goals of a state might be as severely limited as those advocated by Robert Nozick,[13] as extensive as those proposed by Plato,[14] or as moderately limited as those proposed by John Dewey.[15]

In saying that a state has rights and duties according to our moral theory, we intend that the Revised Principle of Generic Consistency applies directly to the rules of that society just as it applies directly to the rules of any other rational agent qua moral agent. As Alan Gewirth has explained,[16] many morally relevant situations are multilateral, comprising very complex interactions among numerous persons. These interactions may involve conflicts of freedom or well-being among many persons. Social rules, which prescribe ways of acting within roles and set rewards for compliance with the prescriptions and sanctions for violations of them, are means of regulating such conflicts as well as other aspects of the interactions. The person who occupies a social position, therefore, is directly subject not to the RPGC but to the social rules governing that position. Even though social rules apply directly to the occupants of social positions, these rules in turn are directly subject to the RPGC, which, being the supreme principle of morality, applies directly to all other rules of morally relevant conduct. Insofar as the members of a political society are occupants of positions, they are subject directly to the rules governing their positions and only indirectly to the RPGC. Thus, legislators are directly under the rules governing their positions; soldiers are directly under the regulations of military positions; and voters are directly subject to the rules governing their positions. Of course, when the members of a state interact with each other as moral agents but not as occupants of positions, they are directly under the RPGC.

III

THE PRECEDING ANALYSIS of the concept of a commonwealth seems to comprise the essentials of what a state normally is understood to be: a formal society with territorial inclusiveness, with a supreme and independent government, and with the intention of providing security for its members and a way to settle their disputes and conflicts. In the course of examining the concept, however, several points that require more attention have been made. Two of these points are ambiguous, and the other is vague.

Because it was stated that a commonwealth is subject to definite moral restraints and to certain moral duties of purpose, it might be thought that a body politic is a distinctive moral association. More specifically, it might be thought that the state is an association that originates because of, according to some moral theory, the moral needs of its members to be secure and to live in harmony with each other, and operates within moral limits to satisfy these moral needs of its members. Although this interpretation of meaning is compatible with what was stated, it certainly is not the meaning that was intended. First, it was not meant that the commonwealth necessarily has its genesis in moral need. To be sure, a state might come into existence because of its members' moral needs; but it does not have to. A state could arise from conquest, religious conviction, matrimony, or by virtue of any of several other nonmoral causes. Second, the purposes of a political society do not have to be perceived by its governmental officials from the standpoint of moral duty. Security for and harmony among subjects might be regarded from the standpoint of exploitation; as the Neo-Marxists have maintained, insecurity and conflict might be seen by rulers as detriments to productivity by their subjects. Third, a state's government does not necessarily stay within moral limits in its efforts to attain the state's objectives. Moral limits can always be exceeded, and history is replete with immoral acts by state governments.

It must be stressed that our conception of the state is independent of our conception of the moral structure of action. That is, our view of the moral structure of action in no way delimits the defining characteristics of political society. If our idea of the commonwealth were dependent upon our or any other view of the moral structure of action, it plainly would fly in the face of common understanding, according to which a state is independent of any theory of morality. This is not to say, of course, that common understanding holds that a state is impervious to moral judgment; and it surely is not to say that our position views a state as impervious to judgment by the moral principles that we have formulated.

Because it has been stressed that the minimal ideals of a political society are to furnish its members' security and a way to settle their disputes and conflicts, it might be thought that a state's government, being its agency for attaining its ideals, is necessarily representative. A state's members are interested in living in security and in harmony among themselves. So, because a state's government has the task of necessarily looking after some of the interests of its members, it might be taken as essentially representative of its members to some extent. There surely is nothing new in the idea that a body politic's government is necessarily representative. Dewey, for instance, wrote, "By our hypothesis all governments are representative in that they purport to stand for the interests which a public has in the behavior of individuals and groups."[17] Nevertheless, there are difficulties in the contention that any state's government is representative. It means that there never have been unrepresentative governments, which makes one wonder how there could be taxation without representation. It also means that states did not come into existence until representative governments did, which was relatively recently. Thus, Dewey had to concede, "It may be said that not until recently have publics been conscious that they were publics, so that it is absurd to speak of their organizing themselves to protect and secure their interests. Hence states are a recent development."[18] These difficulties, however, should not be charged to our conception of the state; at least, it ought not to be construed as purporting that governments are necessarily representative.

There is no question that security and harmony are interests of a state's members, but there is doubt that a government is representative just because it looks after these interests of its subjects. To call a government representative is to allow that it intentionally, not incidentally, cares for its subjects' interests, which means that it perceives their interests as their interests. As the history of feudalism and colonialism testifies, however, governments might protect the security and help settle the disputes and conflicts of their subjects only by way of looking after the interests of officials or segments of subjects. Moreover, as we have already indicated, states might have goals other than those of the security and harmony of their members; and there is no reason to assume that the additional goals will be interests of their members. So, just as our view of political society allows the state to come in various moral shades, it also regards state government as occupying a wide spectrum of representativeness—ranging from none at all, to somewhat, to complete.

Finally, we should clarify our contention that the members of a commonwealth are rational agents. The statement that the members of a commonwealth are rational agents surely does not signify that each and every member is, as an empirical matter, a rational agent, occurrent, prospective, or retrospective. If the statement had this meaning, it could not account for the fact that the incurably insane, who are neither occurrently nor prospectively rational, are usually members of some states and that the senile, who are at best only retrospectively rational, are members of some political societies.

For the same reason, the statement certainly does not purport that a member of a commonwealth is necessarily rational. Moreover, the statement definitely does not intend that the member of a body politic is typically a rational agent. If the statement had this for a meaning, it would be nothing more than an empirical claim; whereas, far from being an empirical claim, it is a conceptual claim. Still further, the statement emphatically does not mean that the members of a state collectively act rationally. The history of the national state furnishes ample evidence that citizenries might tend to act irrationally as often as they act rationally. Lastly, the statement does not purport that a member of a political society who is occurrently a rational agent is purely a rational agent. It is common experience that occurrent rational agents often struggle with impulses, compulsions, and other irrational forces and occasionally lapse from rational agency. What our statement does mean is that any member of a political society is a kind of being that may be understood by reference to the principles of rational agency (e.g., voluntariness, deliberativeness, and evaluativeness). He or she may be an occurrent, prospective, or retrospective rational agent; or as with the member suffering Down's syndrome, he or she may be simply a deviation from rational agency. Human beings are not the only beings that may be comprehended with respect to rational agency; being rational does not entail being human.[19] Whether the members of a commonwealth are human or not, however, they do not necessarily have the same rights. Any member of any state, as earlier indicated (this chapter, Part II), has rights to security and to a way for settling their disputes and conflicts; but beyond these rights a member might have special qualifications and consequent special rights. Thus, in an oligarchy those with property have rights that the propertyless do not have; and in virtually all states youth, the incurably insane, and criminals do not possess all the rights that other members might have.

IV

TWO QUALITIES GENERALLY RECOGNIZED as central to political society are authority and justice. State officials are supposed to have authority, and by virtue of their authority they are supposed to be obeyed. The laws of a commonwealth are to be just, and justice is to be rendered when they are broken. Each member of a commonwealth is to receive a just share of the society's goods and services, and justice is to be rendered whenever a member suffers injury. These qualities will be considered now as they apply to our conception of the state.

Through its rules a body politic explicitly authorizes certain persons, known as officials, to exercise power on its behalf. They might be, for example, monarchs, bureaucrats, judges, sheriffs, legislators, or voters. Because the power of political officials is granted by the laws of the society that they serve, it is legitimate power as far as that society is concerned. While there is general agreement that the laws of a commonwealth are what establish its governmental authorities, there are profound disputes over the source of the legitimacy of the commonwealth's laws—contentions that reflect some of the classical ideas of political philosophy. God, reason, nature, the people, and ownership of the means of production are only some of the outstanding candidates that philosophers have put forward as this source. According to our own conception of political society, the source is none of those just mentioned. It is, rather, the state itself. The approximate reason why the state is the source is that it is the source of legitimacy of all its rules in that its intended ends and their supporting principles (if any) justify its laws.

A state, of course, cannot found itself; it must be the creature of other rational agents. Because of this fact, it might be thought that a commonwealth has a source of legitimacy in its founding, and, therefore, is not itself the source of legitimacy of its rules or, hence, its officials' powers. That is, it might be thought that the powers of a political society's officials are ultimately authorized by the founders of the society. The creation of a state need not involve any authority pertinent to the event. There is some doubt that Chiang Kai-shek had authority to create the Republic of China and that he lent the state any authority. Moreover, while some founders of bodies politic might well bear authority to establish their respective societies, they do not thereby give the societies any authority. It is one thing to have authority to found a political society; it is quite another to lend authority to it. In bearing authority to create a political society, a person is granted permission by others to establish the society on their behalf; or a person is recognized by others as having the personal qualities that qualify him or her to create the society on their behalf. Thus, Thomas Jefferson, when he was appointed by the Continental Congress to help draft a declaration of independence, was given permission by the Congress to help found the United States. And Fidel Castro was accepted by the people of Cuba as the founder of their state because he was recognized by them as having the personal characteristics to establish the society on their behalf.

Yet, even if it is the case that the powers of a commonwealth's officials do not derive their authority ultimately from the founders of the society, might it not be that the officials receive their original authority from the society's sanctioner (i.e., the persons who have solemnly approved the society)? After all, the official powers of a state that has been blessed by God or some godlike person certainly would be especially authoritative. Despite the prima facie attractiveness of this proposal, it too is liable to two objections. First, because a state might not be sanctioned, the proposal cannot account for the ultimate authority of every political society. That a state need not be blessed should be apparent to all. Second, it is highly doubtful that the sanctioner of a state, even if it has one, is the ultimate source of the society's authority. Because the sanctioner of a body politic is a rational agent, he or she sanctions the society only if he or she has grounds for so doing. The features of a body politic that might serve as the reasons for its being blessed are its purposes and whatever principles justify them; any other feature that serves as a reason for blessing the society (e.g., laws, success, and wealth) is contingent in that its qualification for that function logically presupposes the society's goals and, thus, any principles justifying them. So, just as the ends of a state authorize (or justify) its laws and, thus, its officials' powers, they authorize (or justify) the sanctioning of the state. Far from a state's sanction being the source of authority for the society's objectives, the reverse is the case: the society's aims are the sources of the authority for its own sanction. The point of the sanction of a state, then, is not that it bestows authority upon the society but that it seriously calls attention to what the blesser sees as the worthiness of the society, especially the worthiness of its objectives and the principles underlying them.

Knowing that the source of authority for a commonwealth's rules and governmental powers consists of the society's ends and their supporting principles helps to resolve the question of political obligation—that is, why citizens are obliged to obey the laws and yield to the power of their respective states. The members of a political society who accept its goals have an obligation to obey its laws and acquiesce to the exercise of its powers to the extent that the laws and the exercise of the powers help fulfill the goals. Because they accept the ends of the society, they assent to the authority of its rules and powers; and if they disobey its rules and resist the exercise of its powers, they act contrary to that whose justification they accept and, thus, act irrationally. Being rational agents, however, they are bound to act rationally. Citizens, of course, might agree to the ends of their state for any or all of various reasons—prudential and moral being some familiar kinds. If they accept them because of prudential reasons, they are prudentially as well as politically obligated to be subject to the laws and powers.

Hence, when the rules and powers run counter to the society's ideals, they have prudential or moral reasons for refusing to obey the rules and refusing to accede to the exercise of the powers.

As often happens, citizens might accept the intentions of a state for reasons of one kind but still cling to beliefs providing reasons of another type that oppose their consenting to those intentions. Accordingly, they might have reasons both for obeying the society's laws and yielding to its powers, and for disobeying its laws and opposing its powers. Citizens actually might find some of a state's goals agreeable to their moral beliefs and some of them contrary to their moral beliefs. Hence, they might have supreme reasons both for obeying some laws and acquiescing to the exercise of some governmental powers, and for disobeying other laws and opposing the exercising of other governmental powers. According to our moral theory, then, insofar as the member of a state is an occurrent or a prospective agent of voluntary actions, he or she is bound to obey the society's laws and follow its officials' orders only to the extent that they conform to our revisions of Gewirth's Principle of Generic Consistency and his Principle of Proportionality.

V

IN THEORETICAL TREATMENTS of the state, the kinds of justice most widely discussed are retributive, distributive, and corrective. Retributive justice is the fair punishment of the violators of laws, and states usually are expected to punish fairly those who break their respective laws. Distributive justice is the fair allocation of a society's goods and services; and bodies politic are supposed to distribute their wealth, honors, offices, and other goods as well as their services according to some principle of fairness. Corrective justice is reparation granted to a party, individual or collective, because that party has suffered a wrong by another party; and any political society is expected to try to prevent its members from violating each other's rights and to help determine what reparations are due to whom. That our view of the state allows for these types of justice is easily apparent.

Room for retributive justice comes mainly through a recognition that certain rules of political society, known as criminal laws, are of a special sort. Like many other legal rules, criminal laws set forth imperatives; but unlike many other legal rules, they may include coercive sanctions, which typically call for the punishment of violators of the imperatives.[20] The punishment of criminals may be administered for diverse reasons (e.g., prevention of crime, rehabilitation of offenders, engrossment of revenues, and payment of a "debt" to society).[21] Regardless of the reason for which it is administered, however, the punishment of a criminal is a major condition of retributive justice.[22] The other major condition is fairness. Different societies may have different standards of what counts as fairness in punishment, but each of them must have some such standard for punishment. Many of them have employed fittingness and responsibility as standards. A given punishment must fit the involved crime, and the perpetrator of the crime must be responsible for his deed.

There are stock political justifications of retributive justice. One of them is that such justice helps to support the intentions and principles of the state. Another is that such justice simply reflects the fact that criminal law calls for the punishment of its violators for no reason other than that they are its violators. From the standpoint of the moral structure of action, the moral justification of retributive justice is instrumental: such justice is morally justified to the extent that it supports the Revised Principle of Generic Consistency, or, more specifically, insofar as it protects the rights of a state's members to the generic features of voluntary action and to the evaluativeness of voluntary actions where the members value their respective purposes.[23] To the extent, therefore, that retributive justice in a given political society is morally justifiable, the criminal laws of the society must reinforce this moral precept. But the precept does more than justify retributive justice; it also serves as a principle for determining the fairness of punishment. It calls for fittingness in that it requires the severity of a punishment to be proportional to the concerned criminal deed's severity of threat to the moral rights of the given commonwealth's members, and it calls for responsibility in that it requires punishment to be administered only to subjects of voluntary actions.

Our idea of the state definitely provides a place for distributive justice in any political society. First, the idea allows that every body politic has a distributive function. That every political society has the intentions that it does intimates that every such society has an allocative function; for to attain the goals of a state, by their very nature, is to distribute wealth, service, offices, or other matters of the state among its members. To provide security, for instance, is to allocate it to somebody. Moreover, that a commonwealth has a government means that it has offices and, therefore, distributes them.

Second, the view we are propounding provides for standards of fairness of distribution. More specifically, it allows that there are several sorts of such standards. One type is legal standards. A function of a political society's laws is to determine which matters shall be allocated with regard to the society's purposes and who is to receive what share of these matters. Insofar as the society's laws have this function, they are the society's standards of legal fairness of distribution. Thus, if the wealth, service, offices, and honors of a society are or are not allocated according to its laws, they may be described as distributed in a legally fair or unfair way. The ideals of a state form another kind of standard. Because the ideals of a state establish reference points for the allocation of its wealth, services, and so forth, they may serve as standards for evaluating the fairness, and especially the political fairness, of the allocation. If the distribution of matters follows a commonwealth's laws but opposes its ideals, the ideals, according to which the laws are to dictate the distribution of matters, become a measure by which to say that the society's laws do not fairly distribute the matters from a political standpoint.

A further sort of political standard consists of the principles a body politic might have. The principles of a political society, it will be recalled, are whatever principles underlie its intentions and laws. If principles support its intentions, they may serve as standards for assessing the distributive fairness of the intentions; and if principles undergird its laws, they may function as standards for evaluating the distributive fairness of the laws. Because those who establish the intentions and laws of a political society are fallible, they are liable to formulate some intentions and issue some laws that are inconsistent with any given principles; they are also liable to omit some intentions and laws consistent with any given principles. Whenever the principles behind a state's intentions conflict with any of the latter or call for intentions that the society does not have, the principles may serve as standards by which to evaluate the society's intentions as reference points for the fair distribution of wealth, service, and so forth. Suppose, for instance, a Lockean political theory is the basis of a commonwealth's intentions and laws. Suppose also that well-being is not a goal in the society as it is in the theory, and that the society's constitution conflicts with the theory's dictum on the separation of powers. The theory, then, may be employed as a standard for criticizing the society's ideals for not making well-being a reference point in the distribution of wealth, service, etc., and as a standard for criticizing the society's basic law encouraging conflicts of interest in the distribution of such matters.

Finally, the moral principles we earlier formulated constitute a group of standards of distributive fairness. It might be, and often is the case, that wealth, services, and so forth, are distributed according to the laws, ideals, and principles of a body politic but still are not allocated fairly from a moral standpoint. For instance, such a possibility would occur in a political society whose principles shape the ideals and laws of the society and the ideals and laws determine the distribution of matters in the society. Insofar as the society's principles pose, through the ideals and laws they shape, a distribution that is compatible or incompatible with what some moral principle poses, the principles of the society may be judged as to their distributive fairness by the moral principle. It is not enough, then, to subject allocations in a commonwealth to legal and political standards of fairness; they must be subjected to moral standards too. Certainly, our versions of Gewirth's Principle of Generic Consistency and his Principle of Proportionality are appropriate as moral standards for judging distributive fairness. The former principle provides that wealth, services, and so forth must be allocated in view of the rights of a state's members to the generic features of voluntary action and to the evaluativeness of voluntary actions where the members esteem their respective objectives.[24] The latter principle provides that allocations in a society have to be proportionate to the degree that the society's members individually possess the qualities required to exercise the rights just mentioned.[25] Thus, it would be morally unfair for a state to let children and the feebleminded vote; and it would be morally unfair for a state to furnish educational opportunities to members not qualified for the opportunities. Because moral principles are superior to all others, any state with standards of distributive fairness opposed to the moral precepts propounded here should revise its standards to agree with the precepts.

Plainly, corrective justice too is accommodated by the present conception of political society. Because an essential goal of any body politic is to help its members resolve their disputes and conflicts, which center around the members' various rights and duties, any such society is committed to corrective justice (i.e., to helping determine which rights of which members have been violated by whom and what reparations are due the injured members). Given this commitment by a commonwealth, the laws of the society are bound, in part, to specify the rights of its members and to indicate appropriate reparations for violations of their rights. In truth, the laws of some actual states are well known for setting forth the rights of their respective members although they usually are less known for the reparations they pose.

Two major issues in the philosophy of law are whether or not the members of a state have rights not articulated by the laws of a society, and whether or not the members of a state should have something as a right merely because the laws of the society declare it as a right. From the standpoint of our idea of the commonwealth, a resolution of each issue may be had by reference to the fact that a political society has intentions and might have principles, as well as by reference to the point that any body politic is subject to our reformulation of Gewirth's Principle of Generic Consistency. The ideals of a political society, the principles that it might have, or both the ideals and the principles may be used as criteria to determine if the society's laws grant all the rights that politically should be accorded to the society's members. This is because the ideals are supposed to be fulfilled partly by the society's laws and because the principles are meant to justify the society's purposes or laws if not both. For the same reasons, the ideals and the principles may be employed as measures to determine if the society's laws give rights to the society's members that politically should not be given them. The RPGC, of course, may be used to determine if the society's laws grant all the rights that morally should be given to the society's members or grant any rights that morally should not be given to them.

The Democratic State

I

THE IDEA OF A DEMOCRATIC BODY POLITIC, having been a subject of inquiry since ancient times, has become a subject of widely varying views. Theorists have disagreed over whether a democratic state is marked by one or by more than one feature; and while those leaning toward the former position have disparate opinions on what the distinctive trait is, those inclined toward the latter position take disparate stances on what the several distinctive characteristics are. Moreover, because the idea of democracy has gained general approval, the term *democratic* often has been used to describe social matters that people favor even though such matters are not apparently integral to the democratic body politic. One hears, for instance, of democratic education, democratic families, democratic art, and democratic economies. So, in order to demarcate the quality or qualities that make a commonwealth democratic, we must take into account divergent views of the subject and be cognizant of what is and is not relevant to the democratic state.

II

IT IS GENERALLY ACKNOWLEDGED that democracy involves self-government, sometimes called "the rule of the people." Aristotle held that a political society is a democracy "when those who are free are in the majority and have sovereignty over the government."[1] Thomas Aquinas described democracy as the rule of the populace.[2] Thomas Jefferson viewed it as the rule of the public will.[3] Joseph A.

Schumpeter wrote that "the democratic method is that institutional arrangement for arriving at political decisions in which individuals acquire the power to decide by means of a competitive struggle for the peoples' vote."[4] Robert A. Dahl stated that "democratic theory is concerned with processes by which ordinary citizens exert a relatively high degree of control over leaders."[5] And Charles Frankel argued that "democracy is a system in which men acquire the right to govern through a system of free and open competition for votes, and in which they make their decisions while under the pressure of outside groups whose right to put them under pressure they must protect."[6] To be sure, not every conception of democracy regards self-government as integral to a democratic commonwealth. Marxist-Leninist theories, for instance, are notorious for claiming that a veritable democracy has, not self-government (which, according to such theories, is merely a device whereby the capitalist class exercises control over state government) but government by the communist party (which, again according to such theories, is the vanguard of the proletariat class). Regardless of any theories denying the significance of self-government for democracy, self-government is part and parcel of the standard concept of the democratic state. Hence, it has been said: "In any normal sense of the word democracy, a form of government which provides no opportunity for the legitimate expression of popular preferences and which confines the right of significant political action to a small minority of the population is the reverse of democratic."[7]

By its nature, self-government is instrumental; it exists not for its own sake but for that of something else. Being an institution of a state, self-government is supposed to promote a political good—namely, the interests of that state. These interests are defined largely by the state's major principles, its intentions, its laws, and its existential conditions. When self-government serves the interests of a body politic, it is politically good; when it harms the interests of a body politic, it is politically bad. The interests of a political society, as already explained, may or may not be morally good; that is, they may or may not support the chief characteristics of the actions of the society's members, which consist of evaluativeness as well as voluntariness and purposiveness. If self-government, therefore, promotes a state interest that is morally good, it is morally good; if it promotes one that is morally bad, it is morally bad. So, even if self-government is natural to rational agents, as some have claimed,[8] it is not good, politically or morally, for that reason.

The instrumental value of the institution of self-government should not be confused with the moral rectitude of its rules. Because social rules (Chapter 3, Part II) are directly subject to the Revised Principle of Generic Consistency, the rules of self-government, in our thinking, are morally right or wrong insofar as they follow the RPGC, not insofar as self-government promotes something morally worthwhile. Because the moral correctness of the rules of self-government may be determined differently from the way that the instrumental value of government is determined, the rules of self-government might be morally correct even though the instrumental worth of the institution might be perceived from the standpoint of nonmoral standards (for instance, those of the state's interest). Whether or not the rules of self-government are necessarily morally correct and whether or not the rules might be morally correct (incorrect) when the institution is morally bad (good) will be discussed later (this chapter, Part V).

Because of the conditions of its value to a state, self-government is not necessarily worthwhile for every state. A point frequently made about self-government is that it is workable in a commonwealth only if the society's members are informed of its interests and are inclined to exercise their civic duties. Thus, citizens will not elect the persons whom a commonwealth needs as leaders if the citizens are not aware of the qualities of leadership required by the society, and they will not even bother to vote if they do not feel that they should. A point that is equally important but not as often made is that self-government is workable in a body politic only to the extent that the society's citizens perceive its interests as compatible, if not identifiable, with the major characteristics of their actions and, by logical necessity, with the major features of the actions of all other members of the society, who are rational agents. Because rational agents favor the chief characteristics of their actions (Chapter 2, Part IV), the members of a political society, when exercising self-government, rationally will support the society's interests only if they regard them as more or less compatible with these characteristics of their actions.[9] It is not surprising, accordingly, that states whose interests are opposed to the voluntariness, purposiveness, and evaluativeness of the majorities of their various members typically do not practice self-government; nor is it surprising that states whose interests are identifiable with these qualities of their various members often do practice self-government. Of course, a state whose interests are compatible with the main characteristics of the actions of its members might not practice self-government. It might be a monarchy, an aristocracy, or a communist state. One reason traditionally offered to justify such political societies is that a monarch, aristocrats, or rulers from a communist party can discern the compatibility of a state's interests with the major characteristics of the actions of its members better than the members themselves can discern it.[10]

That self-government is a necessary condition of democracy does not imply, of course, that it is a sufficient condition too. Whether or not it is depends partly upon its meaning and partly upon historical circumstances. Self-government, all hands agree, means that the members of a political society exercise some control over the society's decisions. Control over decisions is to be exerted by the members' participation in the making of the state's decisions or by their electing officials to represent them in the making of the decisions.[11] But which members of a body politic are to have the right to exert control has differed from one era to another. In ancient Athens and antebellum America, the members regarded as having this right were free males. Neither slaves nor free females were recognized as having it. Nowadays, however, no society with a policy of involuntary servitude is recognized as having self-government; and females are respected as having the right to vote and hold office. So, while Periclean Athens and antebellum America usually are admitted to have had self-government, no present-day society satisfying a description of either of them would be said to have self-government. In short, the concept of self-government has changed in modern times. Whereas self-government used to mean the enjoyment of the right to vote and hold office by the free males of a commonwealth (as long as the free males, unlike those of ancient Sparta, constituted a large segment of the society's total population), it now is the general enjoyment of the right to vote and hold office. The general enjoyment of this right means, among other things, that the right is to be denied to no member of a given society except on relevant grounds (e.g., citizenship, mental competency, and minimum age). According to its current conception, it is submitted, self-government is a sufficient, as well as a necessary, condition of democracy.[12] Any society today that meets a description of self-government in its contemporary sense is allowed to be democratic, and any society in previous times that fits such a description is allowed to have been democratic. We will define a democratic state, then, as one that contains the general enjoyment of the right to vote and hold office.

This view of the democratic state is neither unique nor strange. Thus, F. A. Hayek stated, "Strictly speaking it [the word *democracy*] refers to a method or procedure for determining governmental decisions."[13] Yet, while the view is familiar, it surely is not the only one on the matter. Those views differing from ours do not deny that democracy embodies self-government in its current sense. What they maintain, rather, is that democracy contains more than self-government. Some of these insist that it embraces several institutions in addition to that of self-government, and others claim that it involves certain principles as well as self-government. For a specimen statement of the former views, this passage by T. D. Weldon will do: "In modern terminology the foundations of democracy are representative government, universal suffrage, social equality, and, of course, the Rule of Law."[14] For a specimen statement of the latter views, this passage by S. I. Benn and R. S. Peters will do:

> We have taken 'democracy' to mean not merely a set of political institutions like universal suffrage, parliamentary government, and decisions by majority procedures, but also a set of principles which such institutions tend to realize. These are (to repeat Bentham's words): *'responsibility of the governors . . . the liberty of the press . . . the liberty of public associations . . .'* These are intimately connected . . . with the . . . principles of impartiality and respect for persons as sources of claims and arguments, . . . which underline all the central political ideas, like justice, liberty, and equality.[15]

While we do not claim that our conception of democracy is the only acceptable one, we must note that none of the conceptions constituting these two sorts is acceptable.

The various views of the first conception suffer from an inclusion of institutions that are highly doubtful as marks of a democratic commonwealth. Of the four institutions listed by Weldon, only one, universal suffrage, is essentially characteristic of democratic societies. Representative government fails because self-government may assume the form of direct participation. Social equality fails because a commonwealth with a hierarchical class system would pass for a democracy if it had self-government. The United States and Great Britain, for instance, have hierarchical class systems; but they are, in normal thinking, democracies. The rule of law fails because it is characteristic of forms of political society other than democracy. In truth, a tyranny appears to be the only kind of state that does not insist that all its decisions and actions should conform to its laws.

The different versions of the second conception of democracy are marred by several difficulties. They attribute principles to the democratic state that do not belong to it, they fail to attribute some principles to the democratic state that do pertain to it, and they involve a logical confusion. When Benn and Peters assert that self-government "tends to realize" the principles of gubernatorial responsibility, the liberty of the press, and the liberty of public association, they appear to be making an empirical generalization about self-government; but because they explicitly say they are stating the meaning of *democracy,* they do not intend to be making an empirical statement about self-government. When they declare that self-government "tends to realize" the named principles, they presumably intend only that the concept of self-government implies these principles. To be sure, self-government does entail that the rulers of a body politic, in Bentham's phrasing,[16] must give reasons to the society's members for "every act of power" exerted over them; and it does imply the liberty of the press, or, more broadly, the security by which every member of a political society may make known his or her complaints about the government of the society. It is conceded further that self-government entails public association of a sort; but it is not granted that it implies what Benn and Peters, following Bentham, intend by public association: the security by which malcontents may plan and practice "every mode of opposition short of actual revolt." Such a broad construal of public association would permit harassment, the destruction of property, bodily injury, and the violation of any other right that is short of "actual revolt." And self-government, a part of whose worth is that it purports to protect the rights of the members of any society that it serves, does not allow the unjustifiable violation of the rights of any of the members of any state that it serves. It does not allow the unjustifiable violation of the rights of the minority any more than it permits the unjustifiable violation of the rights of the majority.[17]

Besides claiming that the concept of democracy implies a principle that it does not, Benn and Peters fail to note some principles the concept does entail. They do not mention that it implies the principle of civic duties, which embodies the various obligations of the members of a political society with self-government. Nor do they specify that the concept entails the principle of public interest, which historically has been given various formulations. (In the terms of our theory of action it is the compatibility of the interests of a state with the chief characteristics of the actions of the several members of the state.) That these are principles of a democratic society is obvious from an appeal to the popular understanding of what such a society is, but it is apparent also from an examination of the patterns of interaction in a self-governed commonwealth. To show that these patterns are subject to the principle of civil duties, one needs to refer to only a pair of such obligations. There cannot be officers of such a society unless its members participate in elections and are willing to serve as officers; hence, its members are obligated to participate in elections and to be willing to serve in office. Being prescribed by the laws of the body politic that it serves, self-government is a factor shaping the interests of any such society. So, in caring for state interests, the officers of a democracy must look after the government of the society, which means among other things that they must help keep the government workable. To do this, they have to explain that state's interests to its members. Only thereby will the officers help assure that the members will have a fully informed perception of this compatibility of the state's interests with the main traits of the members' actions. To recognize that the interactions of a self-governed society are subject to the principle of public interest, one only has to remember that the perception of the compatibility of the state's interests with the chief characteristics of its members' actions logically presupposes the concept of the public interest, which is the compatibility of such interests with such characteristics.[18]

That Benn and Peters, as well as others, have not given an accurate and full list of the principles entailed by the concept of a self-governed state does not mean, of course, that a conception of democracy as being self-governed political society subject to all the principles entailed by self-government cannot be had. But even if such a conception were meticulously and unerringly elaborated, it would not be essentially different from the one we are advocating. The reason why it would not be should be manifest: to say that a democratic state is a political society with self-government is to say that it is such a society subject to all the principles entailed by self-government. Thus, any effort to conceive the democratic state as being a state that is self-governed and, in addition, is subject to the principles implied by self-government, is confused in that it tries to treat as logically separable from self-government principles that are not logically separable from it.

III

GRANTED THAT A DEMOCRATIC STATE is distinguished by a certain form of decision making, we must consider whether or not that form says anything about the substance of such a state, that is, about the content of its intentions and its decisions. If it is concluded that self-government reveals nothing about the substance of any political society that it serves, it must be conceded that democracy is purely procedural and that, therefore, any state ideal or decision is democratic regardless of its content as long as it has been fashioned through self-government. If it is concluded otherwise, it must be admitted that democracy is not purely procedural and that, consequently, a state ideal or decision might not be democratic even if it has been shaped through self-government. The former position has received backing from some philosophers. When Hayek stated that the word *democracy* refers strictly to a "method or procedure for determining governmental decisions," he also added that it does not refer to "some substantial good or aim of government (such as a sort of material equality)."[19] The latter position gains credence from common speech. Such expressions as "democratic ideal" and "democratic policy" are used; and when they are, they more often than not are employed to refer not to any procedure by which the intention or policy has been established but to the content of the intention or policy. At a first glance, therefore, a resolution of the issue is not apparent.

Perhaps a helpful approach to answering the question is to determine whether or not the concept of self-government presupposes anything about the ideals and decisions of a democratic commonwealth. Obviously, the concept contains some presuppositions, two of which are familiar. The first is that the members of any society served by self-government generally are competent to elect officials and hold office. It simply would not make sense for a state to have self-government if it were not assumed that the members of the society generally were competent to practice self-government. Some political theorists have maintained that human experience supports this assumption,[20] but whether or not experience supports it is irrelevant to the point that the assumption is presupposed by the concept of self-government. The second familiar presupposition of the concept is that every member of a democratic society (with such exceptions as children, the mentally incompetent, corporations, and resident aliens) has a sufficient claim to the right to elect officials and hold office. It would be irrational to grant all members (with noted exceptions) the right of self-government if it were believed that one or more of them did not have a good enough claim to that right. Even the proponents of democracy who have recognized that some members might have greater talents for citizenship and statesmanship than others, have not allowed that those with greater talents have a sufficient claim to the right of self-government while those members with lesser talents (with the noted exceptions) do not have such a claim.[21]

That the concept of self-government does contain the two presuppositions just mentioned does not clearly indicate that the concept presupposes anything especially significant of the ideals and decisions of a democratic commonwealth. After all, the two presuppositions of concern say nothing explicit about the content of ideals or decisions. Nevertheless, the concept of self-government logically presupposes an assumption that bears upon the content of the ideals and decisions of a democratic society.

The assumption was expressed earlier in the form of a common observation about the workability of self-government: self-government will work only to the extent that the members of any state served by it perceive the state's interests as compatible with the major characteristics of the members' actions. Because the government of any state is to serve the interests of that society (interests that are definable in the terms of the society's basic principles, ideals, laws, and existential conditions), the self-government of a democracy works only to the degree that it serves the given society's interests. If self-government is to serve a state's interests, the members of the state must elect officials who will serve its interests; and when the members themselves hold office, they must act so as to serve its interests. This condition presupposes that the members are informed of the society's interests and that they are willing to participate in elections and to hold office; but it also presupposes that the members identify the state's interests with the chief characteristics of the members' actions or, at least, see its interests as compatible with these characteristics.

Given that the members of a democratic commonwealth have to perceive society's interests as compatible with the major characteristics of the members' actions, what significance does this hold for the content of the ideals and decisions of the commonwealth? At a highly general level, the claim means that a democracy's ideals, which help to define the state's interests, must be such that they can be perceived by its members as compatible with these characteristics. The claim also implies at a highly general level that the state's decisions must be such that they, in supporting its interests, reflect these characteristics. At a level of some specificity, the claim entails that any democratic commonwealth has security and order as ideals and makes decisions to realize these ideals. This entailment, it is recognized, follows from the point that a democracy is a state; for the very concept of a state implies (Chapter 3, Part II) that any such society has security and order for ideals and a government that decides how to attain these and any other ideals of the society. A democratic commonwealth, however, does not have just any security and order as intentions. Because something can be an ideal of a democracy only if it can be regarded by the society's members as compatible with their voluntariness, purposiveness, and evaluativeness, the security and order suitable as ideals of a democracy must be such that they are perceivable by the society's members as compatible with these qualities. To get a clearer understanding of the security and order suitable as ideals of a democracy, a person will do well to consider a certain element of the chief characteristics of a rational agent's actions.

According to our discussion of the normative structure of voluntary action, the constitutive elements of voluntariness are liberty and knowledge. Of these factors, the one that looks more familiar as a political ideal is liberty. To tell whether or not the liberty of rational agents depends upon political society, we will consider some conditions necessary for such liberty; and to do that, we will focus on the conditions required for only one aspect of that liberty, namely free action, which has been defined (Chapter 2, Part II) as an action with an agent capable of not doing what he or she is doing. One sort of condition of free action is biological: agents of a free act must not suffer biological factors that would compel them to do what they are doing. Another type is psychological: agents cannot suffer any habit, attitude, or other psychological element that would make them do what they are doing. Still another kind is physical: agents cannot be subject to any physical force that would coerce them to do what they are doing. The last sort to be mentioned is economic: the agents cannot suffer economic circumstances that would drive them to do what they are doing. Of these classes of conditions, one, the physical, surely depends upon the state for its existence.

While a state must aim at security and order, it does not have to seek a security and order that establish conditions conducive to free action by its subjects. No political society ever strived harder for security and order than did ancient Sparta, but no subjects of any other body politic were ever less free than were those of ancient Sparta. Nevertheless, that a state might pursue a security and an order that contribute to free action by its subjects is undeniable. In World War I, for instance, the Allied powers fought the Central powers "to make the world safe for democracy." And a point of John Stuart Mill's *On Liberty* and all other libertarian theories is that civil order is to promote, not hinder, the freedom of a society's subjects.[22] The dependence of at least some of the physical conditions of free acts upon the state is equally unquestionable. To appreciate this claim, a person does not have to take a Hobbesian view of human nature; he has only to consider some points about agency, rationality, and state government. It is understood that any rational agent faces the possibility of being coerced by another agent into action, but it also is recognized that certain measures can be taken that will help reduce the possibility. Indeed, it seems evident that certain measures must be taken if the possibility is to be reduced. (1) Rules must be articulated that will proscribe all acts that unjustifiably and inherently impose actions upon other rational agents (e.g., assault, kidnapping, rape, and enslavement). (2) A power must be established to enforce these rules. And (3) a power must be established to judge the applications of these rules. Only by the articulation of proscriptive rules can one have any assurance that rational agents will know that certain acts are forbidden; and if acts unjustifiably and inherently forcing rational agents into action are not proscribed, then there is no point to proscribing acts that might or might not force rational agents into action, unjustifiably or not. The proscriptive rules of concern are more likely to be obeyed if they are accompanied by enforcement powers than if they are not. Without being subject to the scrutiny of a judgmental power, the enforcement of these rules might involve more infringements upon the liberty of innocent agents than it otherwise would; and it might cause agents to distrust the enforcement power and, thus, to recur to physical violence in order to protect their liberty, which in effect would aggravate the violations of liberty.

The institution of the measures just mentioned can be accomplished only with the aid of a state. A rule-making body is required for the implementation of measure 1. Implementation by such a body is the only imaginable alternative to implementation by individual rational agents, who may or may not articulate the proscriptions and may or may not agree upon what the proscriptions should be. The articulation of proscriptions is pertinent to the business of rule-making bodies. Moreover, not only would such a body carry some guarantee that the proscriptions of concern would be articulated, but it also would provide necessarily a uniformity of view on what specific acts are to be proscribed. The proscriptions, however, cannot be articulated by just any rule-making body. To establish a physical condition of free action, they have to be obligatory for rational agents regardless of any other rules to which such agents are subject. In other words, they have to override any opposing rule applying to any agent to which a rule-making body makes them applicable. For the proscriptions to have such superiority is for them to have legal sovereignty. They can have legal sovereignty only if they are laws of a political society, and they can be such laws only if they are articulated by the legislature of a state.

It follows that the implementation of measures 2 and 3 depends upon political society. The enforcement of a state's laws has to be under the state's police powers; if it were not, it would undermine the supremacy of the society's government. Because, therefore, the enforcement called for in measure 2 is the enforcement of state laws, it must rely upon a state's police powers. Similarly, because the application of a commonwealth's laws has to be judged by the society's judicial powers, the judgment of the application of the proscriptions recommended in measure 1 depends upon a state's judicial authorities. Our reasons as to why the physical conditions needed for free action must rely upon the state are reminiscent of Locke's explanation of why human beings have to leave the state of nature and enter the state of society: they must in order to have access to the legislative, police, and judicial powers necessary for the enjoyment of their natural rights.[23] At any rate, because the attainment of the physical conditions conducive to free action is important for democracy and can be had only with the help of a body politic, it is an ideal especially pertinent to a democratic state.

While it is interesting to learn that a democratic society's ideals and decisions concerning security and order have a special content, it would be further interesting to discover whether or not a democratic society necessarily has any special ideals and decisions other than those pertaining to security and order. It will help resolve this issue if we switch our focus from free action to another sense of the liberty of rational agents: the absence of constraints. Freedom from constraints does not necessarily lead to freedom of action, for the absence of some constraints might inhibit the performance of actions. Nevertheless, it is recognized commonly that freedom from some constraints is required for the performance of action. The constraints that inhibit freedom of action may be classified broadly as positive and negative. A positive constraint is some condition whose presence hinders the occurrence of a voluntary action, whereas a negative constraint is the absence of some condition that is required for the occurrence of voluntary actions. Familiar positive constraints are handcuffs, chains, prisons, strait jackets, and other physical restraints. Well-known negative constraints are bodily impairment, ignorance, and poverty. It is our thesis that at least some negative constraints logically pose contents of intentions and decisions for democracy that lie beyond those of security and order.

Territorial inclusiveness (Chapter 3, Part II) means that a state comprises wholly and as a constitutive element everything within its domain. If, accordingly, a rational agent is within the boundaries of a commonwealth, he or she belongs, in all his or her aspects, to that society as an element; and because everything within the territory of a state is subject, in all its aspects, to the state's authority, any rational agent within a state's boundary is subject in all aspects to its authority. An element of a body politic who is a rational agent is the normal meaning of a member of a state. When, therefore, persons are members of a democratic society, they are members of that society in all their aspects and are subject, in all their aspects, to its authority. No trait of their actions, then—be it liberty, knowledge, deliberativeness, or evaluativeness—lies outside the sphere of the society; none is beyond the society's authority. It follows that the prevention and removal of negative constraints of the members of a democratic commonwealth fall within the domain of the society and are subject to the authority of the society. Because rational agents favor the major characteristics of their actions, the members of a democratic society tend to regard as desirable the prevention and removal of negative constraints relevant to themselves; and because the members of such a state recognize that the prevention and removal of these constraints are subject to the state's authority, they look upon the state as ultimately responsible for seeing to it that these constraints are prevented and removed. A democratic state, consequently, if it is to have members who will participate in self-government, must have the ideals of preventing and removing the negative constraints of its members and decide upon arrangements that will realize these ideals.

The society must give the responsibility and support for making and implementing the policies and programs on the prevention and removal of negative constraints to those institutions that show the best prospects of being successful in achieving that end (within the framework of the society's basic principles, ideals, and laws); otherwise, the state's members will perceive its decisions on distributing the responsibility and support as incompatible with their freedom. Because an institution's prospect of success in a task is an empirical matter, the question of which institutions are most likely to be successful in preventing and removing negative constraints has to be answered by reference to empirical findings. None of this is to say that every instance of a democratic state's decision that is incompatible with its members' liberty will cause its members to quit participating in self-government, but it is to say that any such decision will tend to weaken their desire to participate and that a pattern of decisions of the sort is likely to diminish, if not extinguish, their participation.

Before concluding this discussion of the ideals and decisions of democracy, we should emphasize that the prevention and removal of negative constraints has extensive significance for the chief characteristics of the voluntary actions of a commonwealth's members. Knowledge and deliberativeness are conditions required for the occurrence of any voluntary action; evaluativeness is a condition required for any voluntary action whose goal is valued by its agent. It follows, then, that ignorance, the lack of deliberativeness, and the lack of evaluativeness are negative constraints. So, in seeking to prevent and remove negative constraints, a democracy—in order to have ideals and make decisions that are compatible with the actions of the rational agents who are its members—has to intend and attempt to prevent and remove any ignorance, lack of deliberativeness, and lack of evaluativeness pertaining to its members' voluntary actions, both present and future. The prevention and removal of ignorance, the lack of deliberativeness, and the lack of evaluativeness plainly involve the freedom of inquiry and freedom of expression; but their prevention and removal further involve education or something resembling it. It appears, then, that the prevention and removal of negative constraints has much importance for education's moral role in a democratic state.

IV

THE FOREGOING DISCUSSION DEALT with the issue of whether or not self-government, the mark of democratic society, has substantive implications for the intentions and decisions of a democracy. We now want to take up the question of whether or not self-government is important for the content of the major principles of a democracy, namely, whichever ones it might use in defining its intentions and laws. It will be contended that self-government does pose specifiable principles to which a democratic body politic may appeal in an effort to ground its intentions and laws.

Although a body politic must have intentions and laws (Chapter 3, Part II) but need not have chief principles, the democratic state necessarily does have major principles. Self-government, we have argued, will work in a state only if the state's interests are perceived by its members as compatible with the major features of their actions; and interests of a political society are delimited by whatever main principles it holds and by its intentions, laws, and existential conditions. Because self-government is the essential mark of democracy, it is in the interest of a democratic commonwealth that its interests be seen by its members as compatible with the central traits of their voluntary actions. Accordingly, if a political society is to be democratic, it logically must ground its interests, including its intentions and laws, ultimately upon the principle of public interest, or the compatibility of a state's interests with the central traits of its members' voluntary actions. Because a democratic state has to rest its intentions and laws upon the public interest, which conceptually includes the principles of voluntary action, it ultimately must base its intentions and laws upon the principles of voluntary action.

The notion of self-government's workability implies another central principle for a democratic commonwealth. That a government is workable means, roughly, that it is capable of succeeding in its tasks. If, therefore, self-government is to be workable, it must be perceived by the given democracy's members as capable of succeeding in looking after the society's interests. This purports that the intentions and laws of a democracy must be such that they support interests that, in the eyes of the society's members, can be cared for successfully by its government. To paraphrase Aristotle, democratic politics is the art of the possible. Whether or not the democratic state logically must have other basic principles need not be determined here. It should be noted, however, that because a democracy does have basic principles, which are employed in setting its intentions, it necessarily esteems its intentions. Hence, a democratic commonwealth is an agent of actions marked by evaluativeness.

A problematic element in the fundamental principles of the democratic state is that of perception by the society's members. Perceptions are fallible, of course; even those of rational agents might be incorrect. When, therefore, members of a democracy perceive the state's interests as being in the public interest, they might be mistaken.[24] To help minimize mistakes in their perception of the public interest, the members of a democratic body politic must have access to information on the society's interests, on the major features of the members' actions, and the relationship between the interests and the features. Self-government, consequently, accords to the members of any democracy a right to free communication on matters of public interest. This point seems especially relevant to a discussion of education's moral role in the democratic state.

V

SO FAR, THREE STEPS HAVE BEEN TAKEN to clarify the special characteristics of democracy. The essential mark of democracy has been presented; some of the contents of the intentions and decisions of a democratic state have been indicated; and several ideas that might serve as central principles for a democratic commonwealth have been specified. One further step will be a discussion of democracy's moral significance.

Let us begin by considering whether or not self-government has moral worth. It has been mentioned that the government of any body politic is supposed to serve the society's interests and that it is morally estimable insofar as the interests it promotes are morally desirable. It also has been explained that a state interest has moral worth if and only if it favors the main traits of the voluntary actions of a political society's members, or (what comes to the same thing) if and only if it is in the public interest. That the public interest contains moral value is plain: it includes the major features of voluntary action, and they are moral goods. So, if a state's interests are in the public interest, they are compatible with moral goods; that is, they are identifiable with, support, or at least permit the existence of such goods. If they are identifiable with these goods, they have moral value by virtue of their being moral goods. If they support or permit the existence of these goods, they have moral worth by virtue of their instrumentality. The public interest has moral desirability, therefore, because it is identifiable with moral goods or favors their existence. Thus, because the interests of the democratic commonwealth conceptually are in the public interest, they are morally valuable by logical necessity; and insofar as self-government serves state interests in the public interest, it also is morally desirable by logical necessity. Of course, the interests of an actual democratic society, which might be flawed as a democracy, need not be in the public interest: even if they are perceived by a majority to be in the public interest, they still might be opposed in fact to the public interest. It follows that the moral worth that the government of an actual democracy has by serving the society's interests is empirically contingent.

Another morally estimable quality of self-government is that it, as a rational agent, values its purpose. The government of any political society is supreme and independent (Chapter 3, Part II). It is supreme to any other government within the state and independent of any government outside the state. It seems safe to say, then, that the actions of a commonwealth's government characteristically are free—they are things the government is capable of not doing. It also seems defensible to regard them as witting. The officials of any state government are rational agents, and they are bound to be fully informed of what they do on behalf of the society. Hence, monarchs and presidents alike have advisors. Officials, of course, are not omniscient; but when they act in ignorance, they fail as officials. The voluntary actions of any body politic certainly involve purposiveness and deliberativeness, for the actions of any state have goals and are the outcomes of deliberations by officials. Whether or not the voluntary actions of any kind of state contain evaluativeness is not readily clear, but that those of the democratic state involve it is clear. Because self-government serves the interests of a given democracy—which interests ultimately rest upon the principles of the public interest, voluntary action, and governmental success—it selects its goals with respect to those interests and ultimately those principles. Accordingly, its actions are evaluative. Other moral goods of self-government are the capacities and dispositions that it has as an agent that prizes its aim. Because the democratic state characteristically regards its ends as worthwhile, it has to have the capacities and dispositions that enable it to evaluate and pursue them regularly; and these are moral goods (Chapter 2, Part II).[25]

But whether or not self-government necessarily has moral worth is separate from the question of whether or not it necessarily has moral rectitude. While the moral desirability of a democracy's government depends upon its serving state interests with moral worth or upon its possessing some quality of moral value, its moral correctness is contingent upon its rules' agreeing with the RPGC. In attempting to determine whether or not self-government is morally correct by conceptual necessity, one must recognize that such government consists of numerous rules and that, therefore, it would be very difficult to consider the possible moral rectitude of each and every rule of such government. We shall examine three of them: the rule of participation, the rule of inquiry, and the rule of popular will.

The rule of participation says that each and every member of a democratic society (with the exception of members lacking relevant characteristics, namely, age, mental competence, and residence) has the duty to vote on officeholders and under certain circumstances to be a candidate for office. This duty implies that every member (with the noted exceptions) has the right to vote and under certain circumstances to seek office. Accordingly, the rule conforms with the requirements of the RPGC in an obvious but important respect: by making governmental participation a matter of duty and right, the rule makes such participation voluntary; in so doing, it conforms with the RPGC's insistence that rational agents have rights to major features of voluntary action.

The rule of inquiry states that the members of a democratic commonwealth are bound to seek information and understanding on matters of public interest. While our discussion of the moral value of self-government mentioned that such government gives the members of a democracy a political right to free communication on all matters of public interest, it did not declare that such government also politically obligates them to seek information and understanding on these matters. To enhance the likelihood of their having true perceptions of the public interest, the members of a given democracy must have information about and understanding of the public interest.[26] This means not only that they have a political claim to such information and understanding but also that they have a political obligation to do anything that is required for the proper functioning of the society. As a member of a political society, it is commonly allowed, a person has a political obligation to do anything that is required for the proper functioning of the society and that he is especially able to do.[27] Hence, because the pursuit of information and understanding regarding the public interest is vital to the proper working of a democracy and insofar as the members of a democracy are rational, and, thus, especially qualified to engage in the pursuit of this information and understanding, they are each politically bound to seek the information and understanding. Having the political duty to do this, they also have the political right to whatever is involved in fulfilling the duty, including free communication on all matters of public interest. Hence, the political right of free communication on all matters of public interest may be derived from the political duty to seek information and understanding of all matters of public interest. That the obligation to pursue information and understanding on matters of public interest is consonant with the RPGC is indubitable. By seeking the information and understanding, members of a democracy will be in a position to help make the interests of their state compatible with the voluntariness, deliberativeness, and evaluativeness of their actions and, thus, will respect each other's rights to these matters.[28]

The rule of popular will says that the decision of the officers of a democratic body politic should reflect the will of a majority or, at least, a plurality of the members. In saying that the decisions of the officers of a democratic government should reflect the popular will, the rule certainly does not mean that the decision always will reflect this will; for it recognizes that elected officials will betray their constituents' trust from time to time. Nevertheless, it further recognizes that voting can impress the popular will upon officials—not only voting in elections but also voting to remove officials from office and voting in referenda. Thus, the rule of popular will entails limits to terms of office, the recall of officeholders, and referenda. Finally, the rule of popular will does not intend that a majority or plurality may effect, through voting, decisions that violate the political rights of the minority. A majority or plurality can bring about such decisions, of course; but because the members of a majority or plurality and those of a minority have the same political rights, the former members have to respect the political rights of the latter.

However, to understand how the rule of popular will agrees with the RPGC, it is necessary to take into account more than the meaning of the rule. The attitudes of the voter and the officeholder in a democracy also must be considered. It has been emphasized that the members of a democracy will not, as rational agents, participate in its government unless they perceive the society's interests as being compatible with the major features of their voluntary actions. Thus, when members of a democratic state run for office, they will have some perception of the state's interests as being compatible with the chief characteristics of the voluntary actions of the society's members. And when members of a democracy vote for candidates, they will vote for those who they believe see the state's interests as they perceive them and who will serve the state according to their perception of its interests. In following the rule of popular will, therefore, a democracy's government is inclined to act from respect for the rights of the society's members to the chief characteristics of voluntary action. Insofar, the rule is consistent with the RPGC.

VI

ANOTHER ASPECT OF THE MORAL SIGNIFICANCE of the democratic state is the moral rectitude and worth of the distributive institutions of a democracy.[29]

That the distributive institutions of a democratic commonwealth contain morally right rules is apparent. In making distributions, a political society acts according to its intentions and laws and, consequently, according to any central principles it might have. The intentions of a democracy, it has been explained (this chapter, Part III), include the provision of a security and order compatible with the chief characteristics of the voluntary actions of the society's members and, among other possibilities, the removal of negative constraints upon its members' freedom of action. So, when a democratic state allocates wealth, services, positions, and so forth according to its intentions and laws and any central principles it might have, it must distribute them so as to furnish to all members security and order compatible with the main traits of their voluntary actions and to remove negative constraints of freedom of action suffered by its members.[30]

Along with the distribution of security and order go war and punishment; and while war and punishment have the function of protecting members of a society, they do not function to protect those against whom they are waged and administered. When, therefore, a democracy wages war, it does so to protect the major features of the voluntary actions of its own members, not those of its enemies; and when it inflicts punishment, it does so to protect the main traits of the voluntary actions of its innocent members, not those of culprits. There are, nevertheless, strictures upon the wars waged and the punishment administered by a democratic commonwealth. Because the members of such a society regard the deprivation of any major feature of voluntary action as bad, they must regard as bad the deprivations, albeit necessary, imposed by warfare upon their enemies and by the punishment of criminals. Hence, a democratic state, in order to have the backing of its members, must wage war against and inflict punishment upon only those who threaten the chief characteristics of its members and must impose upon enemies and criminals no greater deprivations than are required to secure these characteristics. In view of these limitations, a democracy's distributive institutions, governmental or not, are bound by a certain rule for the maintenance of security and order: goods, services, positions, and so forth are to be distributed so that they will protect, as far as is necessary and no farther, the members of the state from those and only those who threaten the main traits of their voluntary actions. Because this rule directs the allocation of resources for security and order with respect to the intentions of a democracy, the rule is politically fair; and insofar as it agrees with whatever laws the society has for fulfilling these intentions, it is legally fair. It also is morally fair and correct, for it agrees with the RPGC on several counts. It aims to protect the rights of a democracy's members to voluntary action. By permitting war and punishment to be waged against and inflicted upon only those who do threaten the rights of a democracy's members to voluntary action, it respects the rights of the innocent to voluntary action. Finally, it respects the rights of enemies and criminals to voluntary actions wherever those rights pose no threats to the rights of the society's members to voluntary actions.

A negative constraint upon a person's freedom, it will be remembered, is the absence of a condition required for the occurrence of voluntary action. Plainly, a democratic state, even though it must seek to remedy negative constraints among its members, cannot remedy just any negative constraint; for it cannot remove or alleviate any which is irremediable in principle or at least in practice. It follows that a democracy rationally can intend to remedy only negative constraints that it takes to be practically remediable although it rationally can intend to develop means for removing or alleviating constraints that it regards as remediable in principle but not in current practice. It further follows that the members of a democratic commonwealth should not expect the state to try to remove or alleviate any negative constraints that they recognize as irremediable in practice.

By eliminating negative constraints of its members' freedom, a democracy helps to assure that the members will have equal opportunity in acting voluntarily but not that they will have equal results in voluntary actions. Unequal results may occur among members for various reasons. Two of the chief reasons are that different members might have unequal talents and that some members might have favorable circumstances in which to act while others might not have such circumstances. The remedying of negative constraints cannot include the elimination of deficiencies in talent that cannot be remedied in practice, nor can it guarantee the sameness of circumstances in which members act even when they are equal in talent. Indeed, a policy to make certain an equality of results among the voluntary actions of the members of a society, democratic or not, is logically absurd; for it takes the control of the actions away from the members and, thus, renders the actions involuntary. Accordingly, disadvantage in a democratic commonwealth is to be understood in terms of the inequality of opportunity for voluntary action, not the inequality of results of voluntary action. An inequality of results might be indicative of a disadvantaged condition in a democracy, but it is neither equivalent to nor identical to the latter.

While the disadvantaged in a democratic state all suffer negative constraints, they need not suffer the same ones or suffer the same number. In short, some members may be more or less disadvantaged than others. A person with severe intellectual deficiencies is much more disadvantaged than a person with a moderate physical deficiency. When, therefore, a democratic society distributes resources, services, positions, and so forth with respect to negative constraints but cannot remedy every constraint of each of its members, it must determine which constraints of which members it will seek to remedy. To do this, it must consider, in order of political priority, *(a)* which constraints are remediable in practice, *(b)* which of the affected individuals are vital to the workings of the state, *(c)* which of the members are disadvantaged because of any of the state's policies, past or present, and *(d)* the degrees of disadvantage among its members. Why it must consider *a* has been explained already. It must consider *b* for the reason that it needs any individual crucial to its operations. It must consider *c* because any democratic state, being responsible for its policies and having to have policies compatible with the major features of its members' voluntary actions, is politically, but not necessarily legally, liable to compensate especially those of its members who have been adversely affected by any of its policies incompatible with the main traits of their voluntary actions. And it must consider *d* because, all other things being equal, it is logically committed, given its interest in its members as agents of voluntary action, to helping the more disadvantaged in preference to the less disadvantaged.

In sum, then, the key rule binding a democracy's distributive institutions, governmental or not, with respect to negative constraints is this: wealth, services, offices, and so forth are to be allocated, in face of certain priorities, so as to remove or alleviate all negative constraints affecting each and every member. The priorities of concern have been suggested, if not specified, already: pressing requirements of security and order, the essential importance of some individuals to the society, the political obligation of the state to those placed in a position of disadvantage because of state policies, and a democracy's commitments to the preferential treatment of the more disadvantaged. Given the reference to security and order, it should be clear that the rule governing distributions for remedying negative constraints can be applied, from the standpoint of a democratic society as a political entity, only with regard to the application of the rule governing distributions for security and order. It also should be evident that the latter rule can be applied, from a political standpoint, only with reference to the application of the former. That applications of the two rules need coordination and integration should not be surprising, for this feature of their applications shows up in popular discussions of contemporary politics as the "guns-versus-butter" issue and as the "law-and-order-versus-welfare" issue. At any rate, the rule governing a democracy's distributive institutions with respect to negative constraints is consistent with the RPGC. It aims to overcome deficiencies that prevent members of a democracy from exercising their rights to voluntary action. And in the priorities that it establishes for distributing resources inadequate to remedy all given negative constraints, the rule allows, as does the RPGC, that security and order are essential to voluntary action; that some individuals occasionally are vital to the maintenance and protection of a group's rights to voluntary actions; that a democratic state, like any other agent of voluntary action, is obligated to remedy the negative constraints that it has imposed upon persons; and that the more disadvantaged are to be treated, all other things being equal, in preference to the less disadvantaged.

Those familiar with the work of John Rawls will recognize that his difference principle bears some significance for the rule we have claimed to control a democracy's distributive institutions for remedying negative constraints. According to Rawls, the difference principle holds that "the higher expectations of those better situated are morally just if and only if they work as part of a scheme which improves the expectations of the least advantaged members of society."[31] In reference to distributive institutions, then, the principle entails, among other things, that the distribution of resources for remedying the negative constraints afflicting the better-off is morally just only if it also works to remedy the negative constraints afflicting the worse-off. This entailment is satisfied by our rule. In giving special treatment to those essential to the workings of the state, the rule recognizes that this treatment is to improve not only the prospects for the essential members but also for all other members, including the most disadvantaged. And in giving priority to the more disadvantaged, the rule implies that the less disadvantaged may be helped only if aiding them improves the prospects of the more disadvantaged. None of this is to say, of course, that Rawls would agree with the argument that has been set forth to justify the rule concerning distributions for remedying negative constraints. His difference principle rests upon his view of "rational persons concerned to advance their interests"[32] whereas our rule rests upon an analysis of democracy and ultimately an analysis of action.

If it is evident now that at least some of the rules of a democratic state's distributive institutions are morally correct, it also should be manifest now that at least some of the wealth, services, offices, awards, and other distributive matters of a democracy are morally valuable. The presence of security and order and the absence or reduction of negative constraints contribute to something of moral value—the moral well-being of persons. Hence, the resources distributed by a democratic commonwealth with a view to providing security and order and to remedying negative constraints clearly have instrumental moral worth. But if the resources distributed by a democracy to furnish security and order and remedy negative constraints have moral worth, then something else of such a society has moral value too: the institutions, functional or organizational, that distribute these resources are obviously instrumental in their allocation; and being means to something of moral worth, however instrumental, these institutions themselves have moral value.

In sum, a democratic state has a positive moral significance with respect to its distributive institutions. These institutions involve at least some rules of moral rectitude; and they, including the resources that they allocate, have moral worth. In furnishing a moral justification of democracy, therefore, we need not appeal just to the moral correctness of self-government; we may appeal also to the moral rectitude and value of a democracy's distributive institutions, including the resources allocated by them. Besides having moral significance for a democratic state, the distributive institutions of such a society have importance for educations' moral role in the society. Knowledge, skills, and dispositions are resources associated with education that may be distributed to provide security and order and to remedy negative constraints; and schools and colleges are some of the major institutions for allocating these resources. Clearly, then, an examination of education's moral role in a democratic commonwealth must consider the distributive function of education in such a society.

VII

IN CLOSING OUR DISCUSSION of the democratic state, we need to make some additional comments on the relationship between that kind of state and morality. When analyzing the concept of political society, we maintained that any body politic is a moral agent in that it is an agent of interpersonal voluntary actions; and we explained that a member of political society is a moral agent in the same respect. Nevertheless, it was insisted that our conception of political society was independent of our own theory of morality. A person does not have to accept our analysis of the logical implications of moral agency in order to accept our view of the state. When examining the concept of democracy, however, it was argued that such a society not only is a moral agent but is committed to certain values advanced by our moral theory—namely, the major characteristics of voluntary action—that serve as principles undergirding its ideals and laws and, thus, its interests. It appears, therefore, that a person must accept our moral theory in order to accept our idea of the democratic state.

This impression, however, is premature. If a person had to accept our analysis of the logical implications of moral agency in order to accept our view of the democratic state, it would be because we determined what a democracy is by analyzing the logical implication of moral agency. We did not do that, of course. There was no claim that a democratic commonwealth respects the major characteristics of its members' voluntary actions *because it is a moral agent* and, consequently, logically has to respect those features of other moral agents' actions that it prizes in its own actions. Instead, there was a claim that such a society respects the major characteristics of its members' voluntary actions *because its government will not work unless it does so.* So, far from democracy's respect for the central features of voluntary action being explained in the terms of the logical implications of moral agency, it has been explained in the terms of the workability of self-government, which kind of government we took as the essence of democracy. It may be said, then, that the moral correctness ascribed to the democratic state is an accompanying, but not an essential, feature of the society.

It may be wondered whether or not other sorts of states logically have to respect the main traits of their members' voluntary actions. The members of any body politic are moral agents, and the government of any body politic is supposed to be workable. Why, therefore, does not any type of political society have to respect the voluntariness, purposiveness, and evaluativeness of its members' voluntary actions in order to have a workable government? Our answer concerns the point that different sorts of government require different conditions in order to be workable. Self-government requires the participation of a society's members; other governments do not. Self-government, then, will not work unless the given society's members particpate; and they, being rational agents, will not participate if they perceive that the interests served by the government run counter to the major characteristics of their voluntary actions. By contrast, a government that does not require the participation of a given society's members may work even if the society does not respect the central features of its members' voluntary actions. This does not mean that a commonwealth must have self-government in order to respect the main traits of its members' voluntary actions. There is nothing contradictory in the notion of a state that has a dictatorial government and looks after the major features of its members' voluntary actions. While this allows that states other than democracy may contain moral value, it does not mean that nondemocratic states of moral worth are necessarily as morally worthy as democratic society is. Assuming that self-government encourages a greater exercise of voluntary action by a society's members than does any other form of government, one suspects that democracy contains greater moral value than does any other kind of commonwealth.

Education

I

THE TERM *education* REFERS to a cluster of concepts; that is, it has different senses that are logically connected with each other. Accordingly, clarification of *education* must locate the term's different senses and identify the logical relations among them. This task is complicated by the fact that the terminology used to discuss education has shifted in meaning over the centuries and currently tends to be ambiguous and sometimes hopelessly vague in meaning—a point that can be appreciated from a look at a dictionary's definitions of *education, learning, teaching, knowledge,* and their cognates. In analyzing education, therefore, it is important to sort out past meanings from current ones, distinguish the meanings that are relevant from those that are not, and be alert to any meanings that are beyond the pale of full clarification. Finally, even though philosophers and other theorists have furnished an abundance of theories of education, they collectively have failed to furnish a cohesive view of the matter. Some of their theories largely disagree with each other. The theories also differ on which aspects of education are emphasized or ignored, and some are purely descriptive while others are normative as well as descriptive. Consequently, there is no received theory to follow in explaining education.

Our attempt to examine education will be guided by the principles of action we have been using. Not only are we committed to these principles, but it seems impossible to discuss education without appealing to some principles of action.

II

A STANDARD NOTION is that education is a practice. People speak of the "practice" of law and medicine, and they talk about the "practice" of education. Because the practice of anything consists of activities, the practice of something specific differs from that of something else specific in that the activities constituting the former practice differ from those making up the latter. The activities ingredient to the practice of education are learning activities, that is, activities that help bring about learning. To say that Anne Sullivan educated Helen Keller is to allow that the former did something that resulted in the latter's learning something. To speak of the education of Henry Adams is to imply that he learned something of a certain sort. And to refer to traveling, reading, discussions, and other activities as educational is to grant that they contribute to learning of some type. That the practice of education consists of learning activities does not mean that every learning activity is a part of the practice. An act of propaganda, for instance, might be a learning activity but well might not be an educational activity.

To learn something is to gain it, which means, of course, that one cannot learn it before possessing it and that there is a standard whereby its being gained is determined.[1] Simply acquiring an object is not sufficient for learning it, however; retention of the object is necessary, too. How long the object has to be retained is a contingent matter. For a child, something may be described as learned when it is retained for only a brief period, whereas for an adult the same thing may be described as learned only if it is held for a longer period of time. Also, some matters, such as the rules of a foreign language, may be said to be learned if they are retained for the most part; whereas others, such as the facts of one's identity, are said to be learned only if they are retained in their entirety. Whether or not an object of gain and retention is an object of learning is somewhat dependent upon how it is acquired. If it is acquired directly because of a natural process, a medical intervention, or a physical transfer, it is not an object of learning; but if it is gained directly by virtue of a conversation, conditioning, or intimidation, it is an object of learning. The sorts of objects of gain and retention that may be objects of learning seem many and diverse, and the ways of acquiring that qualify matters of gain and retention as objects of learning seem equally numerous and varied. Moreover, it might be that some objects of gain and retention can be regarded equally well as learned or as not learned, and that some ways of acquiring matters can be viewed equally well as qualifying or as not qualifying objects as learned.

Regardless of the object learned and the way it is learned, learning takes place as the direct result of some action on the part of the learner. The action may be physical or mental, overt or covert, conscious or unconscious, or deliberate or not. Hence, a purely passive student logically cannot learn anything. This point was recognized by E. L. Thorndike when he defined learning as the establishment of a bond between a stimulus and the learner's response to it, and it was acknowledged by John Dewey when he insisted that learning takes place through student activities. A person, of course, may learn as a result of some action by a second party; but if he does so, he learns, strictly speaking, from that action indirectly, not directly. Some action by the learner intervenes between the learning and the action by the second party. Thus, successful teaching—which is the paradigm of an activity that indirectly causes learning—leads to action by the student that effects learning; and learning something just by picking it up from one's environment implies an interaction between the subject of the learning and the environment. While teaching, studying, and other notable learning activities are intended to help bring about learning, learning activities need not be intended to help bring learning about. Thus, traveling might lead to learning even when it is not meant to do so. Similarly, the activities involved in the practice of education may lead to educational learning intentionally or unintentionally.

While it is tempting to define *education* as a practice, it is important to recognize that there is another sense of the term. The terms *law* and *medicine* refer to more than practices; they also refer to intellectual disciplines, or fields of study. Hence, there is a sense of education as an intellectual discipline as well as one of it as a practice.[2] This is the meaning people typically have in mind when speaking of a "university's department of education" or "university's college of education" or when describing a student as "majoring in education." As a field of study education has several aspects, the most notable being pedagogy, research, and recommendation. The pedagogical aspect prepares persons for positions in the practice or the study of education—for such roles as teacher, researcher, and administrator. The research facet seeks, through empirical and nonempirical means, facts and theories about the practice of education, the study of education, and education in its other senses. It involves, for example, history of education, educational psychology, sociology of education, and philosophy of education. The recommendation aspect proposes policies, programs, and plans by which the practice and the discipline of education and education in its other senses are to be conducted. Such proposals have been shaped by a variety of agents, ranging from philosophers, professional educators, and professional consultants to clergymen, legislators, and judges. The pedagogical component passes on established facts, theories, and proposals concerning education in its several senses; the research component provides new facts and theories respecting education in its various senses; and the recommendation component furnishes new proposals regarding education in its different senses. Plainly, the discipline of education does not seek and pass on facts, theories, and proposals just for the sake of doing so; rather, it seeks and passes them on mainly for the sake of the practice of education.

Education also has the sense of being a profession.[3] What distinguishes professions from other sorts of occupations need not be addressed here; it is sufficient to note that occupations in the practice and in the discipline of education may be professions. It is ordinary to refer to teaching and academic administration as "professions," and it is proper to refer to jobs in educational research and in education consulting as "professions." In addition, members of the various educational occupations frequently belong to associations called "professional organizations." Finally, it is standard to speak of all professional occupations in the practice and in the discipline of education as constituting the "profession of education." Yet another meaning of education portrays education as a consumer market. Through much of history the practice and the discipline of education typically have been consumers of goods. They most notably have had to use buildings, texts, and writing materials and to board and house students and faculty. Until this century, however, they were only a small part of any society's consumer economy. During the present era the consumption of goods by the practice and the discipline of education has increased enormously. It has come to involve vast outlays for the purchase of land and for the construction, furnishing, and maintenance of thousands of buildings. It has come to involve the purchase of millions of copies of books as well as the purchase of food to feed millions of students. And it has come to involve the acquisition of innumerable pieces of very expensive research and instructional equipment. The result of this surge in consumption is that the practice and the discipline of education are tantamount to a major consumer sector. Hence, in recent decades business executives and salesmen often have referred to their dealings with this newly significant sector as "the education business."[4]

While these are all genuinely different senses of education, they are not all logically independent of each other. Education as a practice is comprehensible without any reference to education in any of the other senses. Philosophers, statesmen, and others discussed education as a practice long before education in any of the other senses had been conceived. Because education as a discipline contains some educational practice as a component and functions to serve the practice of education, it cannot be understood without reference to education as a practice. Moreover, it should be evident that neither education as a profession nor education as a consumer is comprehensible without reference to the practice, as well as the discipline, of education. From these observations it follows that education as a practice is logically primary among the various senses of the terms. Education as a discipline is logically secondary, whereas the remaining senses are tertiary.

The account of the meanings of education just given is not complete. Thus, some scholars and critics conceive education to be the certifier of workers for industry, the custodian of society's youth, and the vehicle for social mobility. It is doubtful, however, that the other senses of education are conceptually independent of all the ones already discussed. For example, education as a certifier, a custodian, or a vehicle presupposes education as a practice.

III

BECAUSE EDUCATON AS A PRACTICE is the independent and primary sense of the term, it will be investigated further. As already explained, some objects of learning might not be educational; that is, they might not be matters that, upon being learned, qualify a person as educated, partially or wholly, or contribute to his or her becoming educated, partially or wholly. Thus, expectoration is not likely to be an educational object of learning. To help determine which objects of learning are educational, one will do well to refer to several extant conceptions of what it means to be educated. Many social scientists hold that people are educated insofar as they have acquired the cultures of the societies of which they severally are members.[5] Some philosophers argue that a person is educated to the degree that he or she has learned the major elements of the theoretical disciplines and understands the world according to these disciplines.[6] A few religious groups claim that human beings are educated to the degree that they, by studying the intellectual disciplines, acquire false beliefs and evil characters.[7] Some professional people maintain that one is educated insofar as one becomes an expert with a sound understanding and appreciation of human life.[8] Some academics insist that a person is educated to the extent that he or she is versed in the standard works of the arts and sciences.[9] And some social critics hold that people are educated in that they have developed according to their interests as perceived by themselves.[10] Despite differences among these and other extant conceptions of an educated person, they all share a certain feature: to be educated is, at least in part, to possess beliefs, intellectual skills, emotions, or other matters that are describable, from the standpoint of some theory of the mental, as "mental." This is obviously the case with those conceptions referring to the intellectual disciplines and to understanding; it is also the case with those appealing to interest, which comprises desire and belief as well as other mentals. It is not quite as evident in the view that an educated person is a member of a society who has acquired its culture. Social scientists, nevertheless, usually interpret culture to include beliefs, emotions, appreciations, and other mentals. Apparently, then, mentals are regarded generally as objects of learning that may fall within the domain of education.

This conclusion, however, does not mean that just any sort of mental matter might be a kind of educational object of learning. Sensations are mentals that may be naturally had; and when they are, they are not objects of learning, educational or otherwise. Moreover, the conclusion does not intend that mentals are the only matters that may be spoken of as educational learning objects. As a matter of fact, nonmental matters usually have been regarded as such objects. Habits of bodily exercise have been treated by Plato and others as educational; and different physical skills of dance, music, and art have been viewed by educators since at least the classical renaissance as educational.

One type of learning object that may count as educational is knowledge. From people on the street to the philosopher it is agreed that anybody not knowing anything should not be called "educated," and it is recognized that to refer to a person as "educated" is to be liable to describe some knowledge that the person has. None of this is to say that knowing something is simply an accompaniment to or a symptom of being educated. What the commonplace means, rather, is that knowing something is conceptually connected with being educated. In brief, some knowledge must logically be an object of learning for any person who is educated. Beginning in ancient times and continuing into the present, educational theorists often have differed on which knowledge might count as an educational learning object. Some have held that educational knowledge essentially is universally true and applicable to abstract matters, whereas others have contended that it must be true for particular circumstances and applicable to concrete matters.[11] Some have maintained that educational knowledge must be useful, whereas others have contended that it need not be.[12] In some cases the reason for the differences among the answers has related to differences in theories of knowledge, but in other cases it has arisen from disagreements among special conceptions of education. That the question can be given an answer that concords with all those that already exist is highly doubtful, but that it can be resolved without appeal to special theories is clear.

According to the ordinary view of the matter, knowledge of something is belief in a true proposition with justification.[13] A proposition, it may be said, is a statement that is either true or false. The justification involved in the knowledge of a proposition has both a subjective and an objective aspect. The subjective side is that the knower assents to the proposition because he or she has, or is aware of, evidence that shows the truth of the proposition; the objective facet is that the knower assents to the proposition because he or she is prepared to defend his or her belief in the proposition publicly. The former is subjective in that the knower's belief, being caused by this evidence, is private; and the latter is objective in that the knower's belief, being caused by his or her ability to defend the belief publicly, is subject to public scrutiny. That a person simply happens to believe a true proposition—even a multitude of true propositions—is not an adequate ground for regarding him or her as educated to any degree. The same may be said about people who can do no better than to recite set defenses of their beliefs. A true belief might belong to a child or dolt; but if it does, it does not qualify him or her as educated to any degree. The parroting of proofs, demonstrations, and other arguments favoring beliefs is usually taken not as a mark of being educated but rather as a sign of being uneducated. Hence, the proponents of education in the "basics" sometimes confuse memorized "facts" with knowledge.

Yet, whenever a person provides an informed defense of a true proposition that he or she believes, thereby showing that he or she holds the belief because of adequate evidence that he or she has, the person might be spoken of as educated to some extent. Thus, when students explain why beliefs of theirs are true, the students frequently are regarded, because of their explanations, as being educated or on their way to being educated. This is so whether the beliefs are true for all times and places or for particular times and places, whether they pertain to abstract or concrete matters, and whether they are useful or not. What counts to a large extent in recognizing people, because of something they know, as educated or becoming educated is that they understand why the true beliefs they have are true. The universality of a belief's truth and the abstractions of a belief's subject matter may be of interest to epistemology, but they are irrelevant to the normal concept of the practice of education. The usefulness of a belief certainly has interest for prudential considerations, but it is immaterial to the standard concept of education as a practice.

While it is true that an educated man or woman necessarily knows something, it also is the case that a man or woman who knows something might not be educated. The reason why concerns the fact that any proposition is meaningful for other matters.

Knowledge of a proposition entails comprehension of its meaning, but comprehension of its meaning does not necessarily require an understanding of its significance for other matters. Hence, one may comprehend what it means for squares to be rectilinear without understanding what the rectilinearity of squares signifies about the relation of squares to other rectangles. If knowledge of a proposition excludes an awareness of the proposition's importance for other matters, the knowledge can be described properly as "isolated" or "fragmentary"; if it contains a comprehension of the proposition's significance for other matters, it may be referred to as involving "a grasp of connections." A grasp of connections may be narrow or broad; a science student might relate the meaning of a textbook statement to only closely related matters or to more distantly related ones, such as those in a manual for constructing a model rocket. While a broad understanding might bear upon the connections between only one statement's meaning and some distantly related matter, it might cover more; might cover matters to the extent that it is comprehensive. More specifically, a comprehensive understanding is a grasp of what all the propositions and other statements a person comprehends mean for one another, for his or her other mentals, and for the objects of his or her experience.

It commonly is agreed that fragmentary knowledge and knowledge with a narrow understanding are educational deficiencies, and it ordinarily is allowed that knowledge with a comprehensive understanding is educational to some degree. Indeed, it normally is held that a person with knowledge is not educated unless he or she has a comprehensive understanding. The point has been made as follows by R. S. Peters, who dubs a comprehensive understanding "a cognitive perspective":

> For a man might be a very highly trained scientist; yet we might refuse to call him an educated man . . . What then is lacking which might make us withhold the description of being "educated" from such a man? It is surely a lack of what might be called "cognitive perspective". The man could have a very limited conception of what he is doing. He could work away at science without seeing its connection with much else, its place in a coherent pattern of life. For him it is an activity which is cognitively adrift.[14]

A cognitive perspective, it should be explained, is knowledge of a sort. If a person claims to grasp a set of relations, he or she necessarily allows that the relations are such and such, which is to say that the person believes the relations to be such and such. But if a person cannot justify a belief, subjectively and objectively, he or she does not comprehend the relations; and if the relations are other than believed, with or without justification, he or she does not grasp them. Accordingly, a comprehensive understanding is a person's justified true belief, or knowledge, about what the propositions he or she comprehends mean for one another, for his or her other mentals, and for the objects of his or her experience.

Yet, that a comprehensive understanding is knowledge does not mean that having it necessarily makes anyone educated. As already indicated, the statements with meanings that are subject to a cognitive perspective may or may not be propositions. Nonpropositional statements, being neither true nor false, cannot be justified as true or false; but they may be justified as sound. So, even though they are not matters of knowledge, they are matters of justification. It is conceivable that none of the propositions and other statements with meanings that are subject to a comprehensive understanding is justifiable by the person with the cognitive perspective. Each of them might be a matter of inadequately supported belief on the person's part; each might be nothing more than a matter of entertainment by the person; or they all might be a combination of inadequately supported belief and of entertainment. In any case the person with the cognitive perspective would not be educated. It was mentioned previously that those who believe propositions, if they can defend them as true, show signs of being educated. The obverse may be noted about those who cannot justify statements they believe: they show signs of not being educated. The reason, quite simply, is that it is characteristic of being educated to be able to defend whatever one believes, a point reflected by the fact that universities are famous for encouraging their faculty and students to challenge one another's beliefs. If, therefore, people have a cognitive perspective of propositions and other statements that they cannot justify, they have a cognitive perspective that does not make them educated. The function of entertaining a proposition or a statement of any other kind is to see whether or not it is believable. Hence, it is conceivable that somebody (a cynical sophomore, perhaps) with a cognitive perspective involving only propositions and other statements that are simply entertained is following a Cartesian procedure of suspending belief in any statement until it has been found believable for adequate reasons and is using his or her cognitive perspective in the assessment of the statements. Such a person likely would be regarded as educated to some extent. Even so, it also is conceivable that somebody with such a cognitive perspective examines the statements presented to him or her just for the sake of examining them and employs the cognitive perspective, if he or she does use it, only as a means for perpetuating the entertainment of the statements. Such a person would be viewed as overlooking the function of the entertainment of statements and, for that reason, would be looked upon as educationally deficient. Accordingly, a comprehensive understanding of statements that a person entertains only for the sake of entertaining them does nothing to make that person educated. It hardly needs mentioning that a cognitive perspective of statements that are partly matters of unjustifiable belief and partly matters of pointless entertainment does not engender education. Combining educational deficiencies does not eliminate them.

It should not be thought, however, that a person is fully educated just because he or she has a cognitive perspective of statements justifiably believed or entertained with a view of establishing their credibility. The statements involved in the perspective, even though covering a broad range, might be small in number; and they might be so related to each other that they lack any depth. That anyone with a skimpy and superficial repertoire of beliefs or prospective beliefs is educated at all is highly doubtful. A paucity in beliefs or prospective beliefs is taken usually as indicating an educational lack, and superficiality in beliefs or prospective beliefs is regarded commonly as a pitfall to be avoided by any educational program.

What, then, should be said about a cognitive perspective of statements believed justifiably or inspected for credibility that are both numerous and profound? Is that the sort of cognitive perspective sufficient for being educated? While some such comprehensive understanding is needed, not just any kind of comprehensive understanding will do. Belief statements may differ from one another in several major aspects. They may have different subject matters; that is, they may be about different matters. Their justifications might require diverse methods. For instance, the justifications of statements in mathematics and psychology use respectively deductive and inductive methods, whereas the justifications of statements in philosophy, morals, and aesthetics depend upon various methods of argumentation. Finally, the justifications of belief statements might contain different reasons. For example, the reasons justifying the laws of motion are sharply different from those justifying Tolstoy's judgment that *Uncle Tom's Cabin* is a good novel. In order to be deemed educated, people are not expected to believe justifiably or entertain seriously statements that concern all particular subject matters and whose justifications involve all possible methods and all possible reasons. But they are expected to believe justifiably or examine seriously statements that concern all subject-matter areas that there are and whose justifications involve all the methods and all the principal reasons that there are. It is this point that lies behind the long-standing and generally held observation that science and technology specialists typically are uneducated insofar as they usually have little familiarity with the liberal arts, and liberal arts specialists typically are uneducated in that they tend to have little familiarity with science and technology.[15] Because an educated person must justifiably believe or seriously entertain statements that pertain to all subject-matter areas and rest on justifications that include all the methods and principal reasons there are, he or she must have a comprehensive understanding of justifiably believed or seriously entertained statements that are more than just numerous and profound.

In reaching this conclusion, we have failed to clarify several matters. We have spoken of statements as being numerous and profound without explaining what that means; and we have talked about subject-matter areas, methods of justification, and the principal reasons involved in justifications without specifying what those areas, methods, and reasons are. To remedy these omissions, it will be helpful to discuss the latter items first.

Subject matter, method, and principal reason are analytical features of any intellectual discipline; that is to say that any intellectual discipline is distinguished by a subject-matter area (that which the discipline investigates), a method (how it goes about investigating its subject-matter area), a set of basic principles (those concepts and statements by which all other concepts and statements belonging to the discipline are explainable), as well as an end (that which is to be attained by the discipline in the investigation of its subject-matter area according to its method and basic principles). A kind of discipline recognized by virtually all schemata for organizing the intellectual disciplines is labeled traditionally "theoretical." The members of this class are characterized by the fact that each has publicly justifiable statements for its end. Some intellectual disciplines commonly acknowledged to be theoretical are philosophy, mathematics, the natural sciences, and the social sciences. To be sure, there are various schemata for organizing the theoretical disciplines. Thus, the schema of P. H. Hirst and R. S. Peters[16] lists disciplines concerned especially with the subject-matter area of the intersubjective whereas the schemata of Plato,[17] Aristotle,[18] Comte,[19] and many others do not. The schema of Plato lists dialectic as the method of philosophy; the schemata of Aristotle, Comte, Hirst and Peters, and many others do not. In his schema, Thomas Aquinas[20] incorporates basic principles not found in Comte's. Despite the variety of such schemata, however, they all concern intellectual disciplines that have as goals the justification of statements. Two other sorts of intellectual disciplines widely, but perhaps not generally, acknowledged by the extant schemata of the intellectual disciplines are traditionally denominated the "productive" and the "practical." According to Aristotle, whose analysis of intellectual disciplines has been a reference point for many subsequent analyses of them, the productive and the practical disciplines are alike in that they share the same method, namely, deliberation; they differ from each other in their subject matters, basic principles, and ends. For instance, the productive disciplines—such as the fine arts, the useful crafts, and technology—have material products for their ends whereas the practical disciplines—such as those of prudence, morality, home management, and statesmanship—have right action for their ends.

With reference to the features of the theoretical disciplines, one may understand what was meant above by subject-matter areas, the methods of justification, and the principal reasons to be used in justifications. The subject-matter areas are those specified by some schema of the theoretical disciplines; the methods of justification are the methods listed by some such schema; and the principal reasons used in justifications are the basic principles pertaining to such a schema. When, therefore, we say that an educated person must have a cognitive perspective of justifiably believed or seriously entertained statements that pertain to all subject-matter areas and that these justifications must include all the methods and the principal reasons that there are, we intend that the subject-matter areas, the methods, and the principal reasons be taken as those of some schema for organizing the theoretical disciplines.

Moreover, it is with reference to the features of the theoretical disciplines that what is meant by the numerousness and depth of statements comprehensively understood by educated people may be grasped. How many statements are to be comprehensively understood depends upon the number of basic principles there are for the theoretical disciplines as well as the number of lesser principles and facts there are about the various subject matters of such disciplines.

The depth of statements pertaining to a theoretical discipline involves four kinds of statements: statements of the discipline's subject matter; statements of method; statements of the discipline's principles and any relevant facts; and statements of the discipline's end, including its conclusions. A set of statements belonging to a theoretical discipline has depth when it contains all four types of statements, when those of the subject matter describe it at its different levels, when those of conclusions cover the subject matter at its several levels, when those of principles and whatever facts might be relevant are at the levels of specificity and particularity needed to support the statements of conclusions, and when those of the method describe the operations required to reach the statements of conclusions. In maintaining that the statements an educated person comprehensively understands have depth, we do not mean that all such statements by an educated person have to have depth; but we do intend that at least some of them must have depth, which is to say that some of them constitute a set of statements of the kinds just described.

The claim that an educated person logically must be cognizant of the theoretical disciplines might be regarded as reflecting a special view of education, one that often is described as the "arts and sciences" conception. Yet, even though the claim does seem to be compatible with the arts and sciences theory of education, it is in keeping with the ordinary view of education too. As a matter of historical tradition, grammar schools, academies, the comprehensive high school, and universities have placed an emphasis upon the theoretical disciplines; even today's formal educational institutions, which are sometimes criticized for getting away from the "fundamentals," accord a significant place in their respective curricula to the theoretical disciplines. Moreover, some expressions in educational discourse can be understood only with the references to the theoretical disciplines. For instance, the old-fashioned expression "an educated gentleman" refers to not just any male member of some upper socioeconomic class but to one who is acquainted with the humanities and sciences. Another example is the derogatory term "an educated fool," which refers to a person who is schooled in the theoretical disciplines but is foolish in everyday affairs. Finally, nobody totally unfamiliar with the theoretical fields of study may be described in common speech as "educated"; and any person who is unacquainted with one or another theoretical discipline normally may be spoken of as having an educational deficiency.

Indeed, the weight that has been given to the theoretical disciplines can help to explain a well-known fact about education: there is a historical relativity in what counts as being educated. For his day Aristotle was highly, if not completely, educated; for this era he would have enormous educational gaps. This relativity could not be accommodated if our conception of being educated were tied to an ahistorical schema of the theoretical disciplines. As already indicated, however, our conception treats education as being relative to any schema of the theoretical disciplines; and no schema of these disciplines is utterly free of historical influence. Plato's schema is remarkably different from that proposed by Comte, and Comte's differs from the schema proposed by Hirst and Peters. A reason for the disparity between schemata formulated in separate historical periods, of course, is that new schemata are conceived frequently to take into account historical changes. Thus, Comte's schema recognizes the prominence of empirical science in modern times whereas Plato's allows for the importance of nonempirical thought in ancient society; and Hirst and Peters's schema reflects the prominence of linguistic analysis in twentieth-century philosophy. None of this means, to be sure, that a schema conceived in one era cannot be adapted to another; nor does it intend that people living in the same historical period cannot devise diverse schemata. Hence, Aristotle's schema has been adapted to both the medieval era and the twentieth century;[21] and while Philip H. Phenix is a contemporary of Hirst and Peters, his schema differs notably from theirs.[22] Our position on what counts as being educated allows, then, that what counts depends partly upon the historical circumstances with reference to which a schema of the theoretical disciplines is developed and applies.

A comprehensive understanding, however, is not the only educational learning object. To believe or scrutinize a statement with respect to actual or possible evidence for its acceptability, people have to see the statement in relation to the evidentiary material; and in order to do this, they must recognize that some matters within their cognition have value as evidence. Because justifiably believing or earnestly examining a statement presupposes the search for evidentiary materials and the actual or possible drawing of an inference, justifiably believing or seriously entertaining a statement involves such acts, which means that the cognitive perspective necessary for being educated presupposes such acts. Moreover, because the justified belief in or earnest inspection of statements presupposes a public defense of the given statements, it is also presupposed that anyone who justifiably believes or seriously entertains statements must have the ability to discuss the statements according to the canons of public argument (e.g., those of deduction or induction). The kind of knowledge necessary for being educated, therefore, requires this ability. The relations that one might grasp in having a cognitive perspective might be of diverse sorts (e.g., spatial, temporal, cause-effect, end-means, general-particular, and similarity-difference). But even if the perceived relations are of one kind only, they have to be comprehended according to a cognate relational concept. For instance, it cannot be perceived that two matters are connected by being similar or different unless what it means to be similar or different is understood. An educational comprehensive understanding, consequently, presupposes a grasp of some relational concept (i.e., a concept by which one classifies and distinguishes matters as having a certain relation). Drawing inferences, seeking evidentiary materials, being able to argue publicly, the cognition of relational concepts, and the use of such concepts are matters that have to be learned; but the learning of any or all of them need not be educational. When, however, they are learning objects integral to an educational comprehensive understanding, they too are educational learning objects.

That people acquire cognitive perspectives does not imply that they are disposed toward learning them. They could acquire the perspectives passively; they could have passed up numerous opportunities for learning any comprehensive understanding. While it is the case that having a cognitive perspective might be an educational learning object, it also is true that being disposed to have an educational comprehensive understanding is an educational object too. Indeed, people with the disposition to see the connections among things normally are thought to be more nearly educated than those who simply have some cognitive perspective. The disposition to have an educational comprehensive understanding presupposes other dispositions, however. As previously explained, such an understanding presupposes the search for evidentiary materials, the drawing of inferences, the public discussion of statements, and a grasp and use of relational concepts. It follows that there can be no disposition to have an educational cognitive perspective unless there are the dispositions pertinent to these presupposed matters. Because the latter dispositions have to be learned and because they might lead to an educational learning object, they are themselves learning objects that might be educational.

Other learning objects that might be educational are certain appreciations. It is not readily evident that a person with a disposition necessarily values everything or anything involved in the disposition; at least, it seems plausible that a person might be indifferent toward or even detest the matters related to a disposition of his or hers—for instance, the person who wants to but cannot quit his or her cigarette habit. Nevertheless, it is indubitable that a person with a disposition might and often does appreciate matters integral to it. Hence, the disposition to know may be accompanied by a respect for truth, evidence, reasoning, and public argument; and the disposition to see the relations among things may be accompanied by a valuing of connections, relational concepts, and the use of such concepts, including the mental acts in which the concepts are used. That the appreciations of these matters are objects of learning is obvious, for any appreciation has to be learned. That these appreciations might be educational is almost as perspicuous. After all, the person who properly values matters integral to a disposition that he or she must have for an educational cognitive perspective ordinarily is considered more nearly educated than is the person who has the same disposition but has no appreciations of these sorts. Whether or not somebody who appreciates the matters integral to a disposition is as nearly educated as is another person who has the disposition but not the appreciations is not readily clear. It is plain, nevertheless, that people with the appreciations but not the disposition may be viewed as educated to the extent that they have the former. As a matter of fact, commencement addresses and the legends of the seals of educational institutions tend to treat a respect for truth, reasoning, understanding, and so forth, as major educational objects.

The learning objects discussed so far as being possibly educational (beliefs in and serious examinations of statements, cognitive perspective, dispositions, and appreciations) may be described as "mentals" from the standpoint of any theory of mind. It is now in order to consider what nonmental learning objects might be educational. Those that come to mind are certain bodily habits and skills. Of the various bodily habits, some concern physiological elimination;

others relate to nutrition; and still others pertain to physiological maintenance—habits of sleep, exercise, cleanliness, and medical therapy. That people
learn patterns of behavior in these various areas is known by common experience; that patterns of behavior in these areas may be spoken of as educational
can be seen without much difficulty.

Any learning object that helps a person become educated, partially or
wholly, may be described as "educational." Thus, even though primary reading skills and the basic skills of arithmetic might not be educational in and of
themselves, they often enable students to become educated to some extent;
and when they show promise of enabling students to do this, they may be referred to as educational. By contrast, learning objects that seem to interfere
with a person's becoming educated often are called "antieducational"; and
those with no effect upon a person's becoming educated may be spoken of as
"noneducational."

It is quite plain that bodily habits might, and frequently do, make educational contributions. Any teacher of nursery or kindergarten students will testify
to the educational value of proper bathroom habits, and any teacher of health
will admit to the educational importance of current habits of sleep, exercise,
cleanliness, and nutrition. The same may be said about other bodily skills. To
be sure, not all bodily skills have educational importance; but some of them
might and often do. Speech skills, for instance, enhance the possibilities of educational learning by facilitating communication. Dexterity, by involving the use
of tools and other instruments, extends opportunities for investigation and,
thereby, for educational learning.

IV

LEARNING, it should be remembered, takes place as the result of one or more actions, which means that an educational object is learned by virtue of one or more
actions. Just as it was appropriate to consider which objects of learning might be
educational, it is proper to determine which learning actions might be educational, that is, which actions might lead to the learning of educational objects.

A way to identify some actions that result in the acquisition of objects that
might be educational is to recur to the educational learning objects discussed already. One of the objects discussed earlier is a kind of comprehensive understanding. The action that leads to the gaining of a cognitive perspective terminates in an assenting to a proposition about the significant relations of

statements, but that action occurs only in conjunction with previous ones. Assenting to a proposition implies that the assenter comprehends it; this in turn implies that the assenter has interpreted the proposition's meaning. The action by which a person finally gains an understanding of the connections between statements believed or examined and other mentals and experiential objects is an act by which the connections are interpreted to be of certain kinds. Making sense of connections among objects is the application of relational concepts; that is, it is determining which relational concepts that one has fit the relational features of the objects of concern. The application of relational concepts depends, of course, upon possession of them and upon cognition of the relational features to which they are to be applied. To possess relational concepts is to have acquired them, which would have happened as the result of some action; to be cognizant of relational features is to have gained an informed awareness of them, which also would have happened as the outcome of actions. Hence, an interpretation of the relations between believed or entertained statements and one's other mentals and experiential objects presupposes whatever action led to the acquisition of the relational concepts with which the interpretation is made and to the acquisition of the cognition of the relational features to which the concepts are applied.

Other possible educational learning objects that have been discussed are the disposition to have an educational cognitive perspective and certain bodily habits and skills. That some of these objects are gained by actions is manifest. Habits and skills are, by definition, outcomes of actions; for habits are dispositions acquired by repetition of similar actions, and skills are abilities to perform relatively demanding tasks that are gained by practice. In what sense a disposition to perceive the connections among things is acquired through actions is not immediately clear, however. The disposition to have an educational comprehensive understanding is complex; it consists of a cluster of subdispositions. Even though we normally talk about the disposition to understand relations, we do not refer thereby to any single disposition. What is referred to, instead, is a pattern of dispositions by which one comes to perceive connections among things. The dispositions constituting the pattern are dispositions to perform the various actions that lead to one's having a cognitive perspective. Those actions were mentioned earlier. They include assenting to propositions, reasoning from evidence to conclusions, perceiving information as evidence, the interpreting of relations among mentals and experiential objects, the actions by which one comes to acquire relational concepts, and those by which one gains a cognition of relational features. Accordingly, in holding that the disposition of having an educational cognitive perspective is a result of actions, we emphasize that it is such a result only in that it is a complex of subdispositions that are outcomes of actions. At any rate, insofar as actions effect educational bodily habits and skills and result in dispositions to see relations from an educational cognitive perspective, the actions themselves are educational.

We can be more specific about which learning actions might be educational. Of the various sorts of learning actions, some aim at shaping beliefs whereas others aim at shaping behavior.[23] Of the former type, one that seems especially amenable to being educational is discussion. As used here, "discussion" refers to actions within a kind of pedagogical situation. The discussant tries to get the learner to believe a statement that the former finds justifiable; but far from being closed-minded on the statement's justifiability, the discussant is prepared to change his or her conviction about its justifiability when confronted by the learner or anyone else with overriding reasons. In presenting the statement to the learner, the discussant provides evidence for its justifiability and attempts to get the learner to see the statement as grounded on the evidence; this means, in part, that he or she tries to assure that the learner comprehends the statement, the evidence, and the method appropriate to the justification of the statement. In addition, the discussant invites objections from the learner. One reason why the learning actions of discussion lend themselves to being educational is that they encourage learners to believe statements justifiably and examine them seriously. Another reason is that they acquaint learners with various methods and evidence appropriate to the justification of different statements. Still another reason is that they, by assuring that the presented statements are comprehended by the learner, make it possible for the learner to relate the statements' meanings to beliefs and other mentals he or she already has and to objects of his or her experience. "Training," too, is used here to refer to actions in a kind of pedagogical situation. The trainer attempts to get the learner to develop some habit or skill of behavior that the former regards as justifiable. While the trainer might use any of several approaches to reach the goal of concern, he or she tries to ensure, whatever approach taken, that the learner understands what the habit or skill involves and why the habit or skill should be learned. Hence, the trainer is receptive to questions, suggestions, and objections from the learner. One way in which the learning actions of training are conducive to education is that, by emphasizing the justification of behavior, they foster in the learner a disposition toward and appreciation of justification. Another reason is that, by helping to ensure that the learner comprehends the habits or skills being developed, they help prepare the learner to relate the habits or skills to statements that he or she believes or entertains, to other mental matters of his or hers, and to objects of his or her experience.

Discussion and training, however, might not be suitable to all learners (e.g., the very young, the untutored, and the retarded). When they are not appropriate, other learning actions may be used. Discussion may be replaced by instruction, for instance; and training may be replaced by rational conditioning, for example. The instructor attempts to get the learner to understand and believe a statement that the former regards as justifiable; moreover, the instructor is open-minded about its justifiability. Because of deficiencies in the given learner, however, the instructor might not present the statement as resting on evidence; and if the instructor does, he or she might oversimplify the evidence or in some other way alter it to fit the intellectual abilities or background of the learner. Also, while the instructor is not to expect the learner to raise many questions or to offer serious challenges to the statement's justifiability, he or she is to respect the questions and the challenges put forth and to stimulate, where proper, the learner to ask questions and pose objections to the statement's justifiability. Like the nonrational conditioner and unlike the trainer, the rational conditioner tries to get the learner to develop some habit or skill of behavior by relying upon rewards and/or punishments; but unlike the nonrational conditioner and like the trainer, the rational conditioner looks upon the habit or skill as justifiable and is open-minded about its justifiability. If questions, suggestions, and objections are posed by the learner, they are regarded by the rational conditioner as occasions for rewards (if they are cogent) or punishments (if they are not cogent). If, therefore, the learner develops the habit or skill, he or she does so fundamentally not because his or her developing it is justifiable but because his or her developing it was reinforced. Neither instruction nor rational conditioning in and of itself necessarily produces much that is relevant to an educational comprehensive understanding. Each of them might enable a learner to obtain some insights into justification and the connections among things, but neither of them necessarily furnishes such insights. Nevertheless, instruction and rational conditioning might contribute indirectly to an educational cognitive perspective. When learners are not ready for discussion and training, they might be ready for instruction and rational conditioning; and what they learn by virtue of instruction and rational conditiong might help them to become ready for discussion and training. Because of its positive bearing toward questions and objections from the learner, instruction might get the learner to develop intellectual habits and skills pertinent to the justification of statements and the perception of relations among things. Because of its reinforcement of cogent questions, suggestions, and objections, rational conditioning also might get the learner to develop intellectual habits and skills relevant to justification and the perception of relations among things. It was something like this that Aristotle had in mind when he remarked that a youth cannot profit from moral teaching until he has a moral character, which is to be had by conditioning. Insofar as instruction and rational conditioning do prepare learners for discussion and training that lead them to educational cognitive perspectives, instruction and rational conditioning are educational.

Although discussion, instruction, training, rational conditioning, and perhaps other sorts of learning activities are amenable to being educational, no learning activity is educational in and of itself. If discussion or instruction is to lead to an educational comprehensive understanding, it must lead to the learning of statements that pertain to all the theoretical disciplines and have some depth. And if training or rational conditioning is to lead to an educational cognitive perspective, it has to produce habits and skills that contribute to the learning of such a perspective. Neither discussion nor instruction, however, necessarily leads to the learning of statements that concern all the theoretical disciplines and have depth; and neither training nor rational conditioning has to produce habits and skills that contribute to the learning of an educational comprehensive understanding. Discussion and instruction could be used to yield nothing more than narrow-minded specialists and dilettantes, and training and rational conditioning could be employed to produce people with habits so ingrained and skills so isolated that they cannot adapt their behavior to new circumstances relevant to learning an educational cognitive perspective and cannot see the connection between their skills and other matters in their lives. In short, if a learning activity is to be educational, it has to be utilized for the learning of matters that are educational, that is, matters that contribute to or constitute an educational comprehensive understanding. So, lying, which aims at the learning of beliefs for reasons of deception rather than their justifiability, shows no promise of being even indirectly educational; and physical threat, which seeks to get a person to do or not to do something for reasons of fear rather than because of the action's justifiability or unjustifiability, shows little promise of being even indirectly educational.

V

WHILE OUR VIEW of the practice of education appears to agree with the ordinary notion of the matter, it might provoke several criticisms. Even so, it may be defended against them.

One possible criticism is that our theory ignores the social and cultural.

From ancient times to the present, it might be insisted, educational theorists have conceived education as being intimately linked to society and culture. They have held that to be educated is to be qualified to occupy positions in the institutions of one's society and to be familiar with the artifacts and symbol systems of one's culture. Thus, Plato, Thomas Jefferson, and others in the meritocratic tradition have proposed that the different levels of education attained by the members of a society should determine to a major extent which levels of social positions they occupy; and the view of those in the progressive tradition on the close link between education and society has been reflected by the titles of some of their works (e.g., John Dewey's *School and Society* and George Counts's *Dare the School Build a New Social Order?*). Indeed, as already indicated, many sociologists define education simply as socialization. Common opinion long has held an educated person to be a cultured person. Some educational theorists have maintained that culture should be the content of education. And anthropologists and some other social scientists define education simply as enculturation. Because our view of the practice of education says nothing about society and culture, it neglects, so the criticism might continue, to accord them any significance in education; hence, it is a view that is devoid of much that usually has been respected as educationally important.

In response to such a criticism several points may be made. Even though it is true that many educational theorists have held that educated people should be able to occupy social positions and should be familiar with their culture, it is not the case that they typically have regarded education essentially as socialization or as enculturation. Giovanni Gentile and others, for example, have distinguished sharply between education and enculturation, the former having knowledge for its end and the latter having a way of life for its goal.[24] Still further, it must noted that, despite the inclinations of social scientists, it is doubtful that education should be defined as socialization or as enculturation. Let us suppose that members of a primitive group are both socialized and enculturated. They would not be referred to as "educated" simply on that account.[25] In fact, upon learning that people are socialized or enculturated, we do not describe them as "educated" unless we believe that their socialization or enculturation is of a kind that embodies their being educated. We may say of a person, "He is socialized and enculturated, but is he educated?" Finally, it has to be explained that, while our conception of the practice of education makes no explicit reference to society or culture, it certainly is not exclusive of either of them; as a matter of fact, it provides for the inclusion of each. In its emphasis upon the theoretical disciplines, it is compatible with socialization and definitely inclusive of enculturation. Over the centuries there have been educational theorists who have insisted that the theoretical disciplines help prepare a person for society. For instance, the mediaeval proponents of the seven liberal arts contended that these seven disciplines were not only intrinsically valuable but socially useful as well;[26] and Herbert Spencer argued that science is the most useful of all disciplines to learn in the modern era.[27] In addition, it should be recognized that a study of the subject matters, basic principles, and methods of the theoretical disciplines involves a study of some of the artifacts and symbol systems constituting a culture. The artifacts examined are products of those disciplines, and the symbol systems learned are the languages of those disciplines. Far from restricting education to just the intellect, our position allows the educated person to cultivate all aspects of his or her mind and to have a life of rich experience: it holds that educated people must relate their intellectual lives to the other aspects of their minds and to the objects of their experiences. The position is mute on what those other aspects and those objects are specifically. What they are specifically will turn partly on one's theory of mind and metaphysics and partly on the circumstances in which a person exists.

The next criticism that might be advanced is that our view of the practice of education is impractical. According to this criticism, it is commonly assumed that education, being a practical matter, is something attainable and, therefore, that a theory of education is a theory of something attainable. Our conception of education, however, so the argument might continue, does not present education as something attainable. The theory, it will be remembered, maintains that an educated person has *inter alia* a cognitive perspective of justifiably believed or earnestly inspected statements that refer to all subject matters of the theoretical disciplines and whose justifications involve all basic principles and all methods of these disciplines. If this is what an educated person is, then it means that no one is likely to be educated. A comprehensive understanding, educational or not, seems unattainable by the majority of people. Not only does it require a high level of intelligence, but it excludes the simple inconsistencies and the neuroses that most people exhibit. Moreover, it is doubtful that more than a few of the statements present to somebody are ever justifiably believed or seriously entertained. Yet again, to expect people to be acquainted with all subject-matter areas, all basic principles, and all methods of the theoretical disciplines is to expect what never was and never will be except for some, but not all, geniuses. When these several doubts are compounded, they strongly suggest that nobody, except for an occasional Aristotle, Thomas Aquinas, and John Stuart Mill, will become educated.

While this criticism is interesting, it expresses doubts about our theory that themselves are doubtful; and, what is more important, it fails to recognize the sense in which the theory is practical. How high a level of intelligence is needed for a comprehensive understanding is an issue that has not been settled yet by psychologists. It might be that only a normal level is needed. That people with normal levels of intelligence do not have cognitive perspectives does not mean that they are incapable of having them. They might not have them because they were not encouraged to learn them. A similar point may be made about the criticism's other expressed doubts. It might be that many people do not justify or seriously examine their held statements not because they are incapable of doing so but because they have not been taught to do so; and it might be that most people are not familiar with all subject-matter areas, all principal reasons, and all methods not because they are incapable of learning about them but because they have not been taught about them. There have been experimental research projects that show that most children are capable of benefiting from a study of critical thinking,[28] and there is a long history of liberal education that indicates that most students can learn about the various theoretical disciplines.[29] Besides raising questionable doubts, the possible criticism of concern also overlooks the sense in which our view of education is practical: the view provides a goal by which activities may be organized and directed and which learners may strive to reach. Even if learners cannot attain the goal, which is far from known, they can approach it and, insofar as they approach it, be more or less nearly educated. If the goal is unattainable, it is an ideal, of course; but it is not less practical for being an ideal. It still functions as an organizing principle and a goal to be approached. It would be impractical only if it failed to guide action.

The last criticism that might be lodged against our idea of the practice of education is that it does not contain a normative criterion. According to this line of criticism, education is ordinarily regarded as something worthwhile. To describe people as educated is to allow that they, from the standpoint of some set of normative principles, possess a valuable quality. Education, in other words, is good as a matter of conceptual necessity; thus, it can be neither bad nor normatively neutral. The claim that education has a positive normative quality has been stated well by Peters:

> "Education" does not imply, like "reform," that a man should be brought
> back from a state of turpitude into which he has lapsed; but it does have
> normative implications, if along a slightly different dimension. It implies
> that something worth while is being or has been intentionally transmitted
> in a morally acceptable manner. It would be a logical contradiction to say
> that a man had been educated but that he had in no way changed for the

> better, or that in educating his son a man was attempting nothing that was
> worthwhile. This is a purely conceptual point. Such a connection between
> education and what is valuable does not imply any particular commitment
> to content.[30]

Our position, the present criticism would point out, is mute on the normative
dimension of education. It surely does not expressly say that educational learning objects or activities must be valuable from some normative standpoint, nor
does it assert that any of the learning objects that it deems educational is worthwhile. Our position, then, is either oblivious to the normative facet of education
or takes education to be normatively neutral. In either case, it is flawed.

It is conceded that this criticism is correct in noting that we have yet to
state anything explicit about the worthwhileness of education, and it is granted
that education logically is estimable from some viewpoint. It is maintained,
however, that those who look upon education as a positive normative concept
do so at times for the wrong reason. Peters, Hirst, and others averring that
worthwhileness is a conceptual criterion of education each admit that theirs is
not the only normal conception and that, furthermore, there is even a normal
conception that is negative about education; but they insist that the positive
normative conception is that of people "in the main educated" and "professionally concerned with education," whereas the other conceptions belong to the
majority.[31] In response to this stance it may be pointed out that identifying the
use of the positive normative conception with those "in the main educated" and
"professionally concerned with education" both begs the question and does not
prove much. The identification presupposes the conception of being educated
that is supposed to be at stake, and those professionally concerned with education should be expected to have a pro-attitude toward it. It also may be argued
that why people berate or esteem matters that they call "education" is irrelevant
to their being uneducated or educated or to whether or not they are "professionally concerned with education." People esteem or condemn education for the
reason they might esteem or condemn something else: they see it as agreeing or
disagreeing with standards they hold. Hence, the members of a fundamentalist
religious group might condemn education because they might see it as conflicting with the values of their way of life; and the members of an upperclass group
might praise education because they might see it as agreeing with the values of
their way of life.

From the perspective of our moral theory, education logically would have
to be regarded as normative if it could be shown that being educated conceptually involves being voluntary. If an educated person logically had to be regarded

as a voluntary agent, such a person necessarily would have to be viewed as having the same qualities—voluntariness, purposiveness, and perhaps evaluativeness—that he or she would have to value as a voluntary agent and that any other voluntary agent would have to appreciate. Accordingly, an education would have to be looked upon as normative from the standpoint of any voluntary agent. Let us now consider whether or not being educated involves being voluntary. A voluntary agent, it will be remembered, knows what he or she is doing and does it freely. To be educated, we have maintained, is to have a cognitive perspective based upon the theoretical disciplines. That an educated person knows, or at least is disposed to know, what he or she is doing is indisputable. By virtue of having an educational comprehensive understanding, a person is disposed to learn what he or she is doing and, more specifically, disposed to relate the theoretical disciplines to the action and thereby gain insight into the latter. Also, that an educated person freely does, or at least is disposed to do freely, what he or she is doing is unquestionable. By virtue of their theoretical knowledge about action, educated people know what it means to justify actions, namely, to establish the worth of the ends of action and to determine the value of actions as means. And because of their dispositions to seek and utilize truth, evidence, understanding, intellectual skills, and other matters involved in having a cognitive perspective resting on the theoretical disciplines, educated people would be inclined to act not under compulsion but from judgments they themselves have formed, which is to say that they would be inclined to act freely.

For our moral theory, however, education is not normative only in a nonmoral sense; it is good and right in a moral sense. More specifically, it concords with the moral principles that we have advanced, mainly, the RPGC and the RPP (Chapter 2, Parts IV and V). In gaining an educational cognitive perspective, one is to become acquainted with the various subject-matter areas, basic principles, and methods of the theoretical disciplines; and in becoming acquainted with these matters, one will become familiar with some judgmental standards and their significances, will learn about methods of deliberation, will absorb some facts and learn about methods of empirical investigation, and in other ways become somewhat prepared to be an agent of voluntary actions, especially those with valued aims. The RPGC, consequently, maintains that education is morally right insofar as it prepares people to be agents of voluntary actions with prized goals, and it indirectly acknowledges that education is morally good in that it involves goods that approximate necessary conditions of the performance of such actions. From time to time it has been mentioned that education is a matter of degrees: people become more or less nearly educated. How nearly educated a person might become depends upon different factors, which include his or her intellectual capabilities and achievements, other mental capabilities and achievements, and experiences. Thus, those with greater mental capabilities and achievements and greater experiences relevant to attaining an educational cognitive perspective can become more nearly educated than those with lesser capabilities and achievements and lesser experience. This point has a positive significance for the RPP, according to which those who can become more nearly educated have a moral right to a greater degree of education than those who cannot become as nearly educated have.

In showing that education necessarily is a normative concept from the viewpoint of the voluntary agent, we have raised the issue of whether or not it logically is a normative concept from the standpoint of the involuntary agent. Our impression is that an involuntary agent, who need not be made to esteem educational matters, is not necessarily committed to using "education" in an approving way. It follows from this impression that education is only conditionally, not categorically, normative: whether or not it is normative depends upon the stance from which it is viewed. While the impression might be mistaken, it need not be defended here. It is enough to know that voluntary agents logically treat education as a normative concept.

The Role

I

HAVING FORMULATED THEORIES of morality, democracy, and education, we now are prepared to define education's moral role in the democratic commonwealth. A procedure for arriving at a statement of the role involves several steps. The first is to formulate the function of the practice of education as a social institution of the democratic state. The next is to specify what elements of this function are morally obligatory for the practice of education. And the last is to determine what else is morally obligatory for the practice of education in democratic society.

II

KNOWING what education's institutional function is in a democracy will not tell what education's moral duties are in the society, but it will give a reference point by which to specify these duties. A social institution is "a relatively stable, standardized arrangement" for pursuing some purposive function that is "socially approved on the ground (whether justified or unjustified) of its value for a society."[1] It involves, among other things, positions. Each position is occupied by an individual, and each is under certain rules that assign rights and duties to its occupant. The actions prescribed for an occupant by a position's rules constitute a social role. While an institution has some purposive function, it might also have a nonpurposive one—an end actually brought about even though it was not intended. A nonpurposive function is not assigned to an institution, whereas a purposive function might or might not be assigned. A member of a society may hold one or more institutional positions; and if the member is to perform various institutional roles, he or she has to possess the knowledge, skills, appreciations, and other qualities the performance of the roles requires. The process through which the members of a society might learn to perform institutional roles is a part of what is usually called "socialization." Some institutions (for instance, the school and the college) might have socializing functions assigned to them, whereas others (for example, the family and the military) might have socializing functions that have not been assigned. An institution's positions pertain to its functions, and the roles governing the positions do the same. Accordingly, a social institution—unlike a practice, law, or custom—is organizational; it includes structured groupings of persons associated so as to fulfill its purpose and to enforce its rules. The various roles of a social institution are tantamount to a system, and the various social institutions of a society also make up a system.[2]

The social institutions of a body politic may be classified as civil and noncivil. The former are the institutions with assigned functions of governing, whereas the latter are those without such functions. Civil institutions are necessarily integral to the state's government while noncivil institutions need not be. Thus, legislatures, judiciaries, monarchies, and military forces, all of which have assigned functions of governing, are integral to governments; while marketplaces, churches, families, and hospitals, which do not have such functions, are not integral to governments. There are occasions when a commonwealth's government directly owns, controls, and operates one or more of the society's noncivil institutions; but when it does, it does not thereby transform any of them into a civil institution. The ownership, control, and operation of a social institution is quite distinct from its function. Hence, a marketplace or a church is not assigned a governing function by virtue of its being directly owned, controlled, or operated by a state's government. Like any other kind of state, democracy has civil institutions that carry on legislative, judicial, and executive functions; but unlike some other types of state it also has a civil institution with the function of electing governmental officials.

A noncivil social institution that any democratic commonwealth logically has is the practice of education. By its nature education can provide, through educational learning activities, a comprehensive perspective based on the theoretical disciplines; and the members of such a society need an understanding of the kind. Knowledge of philosophy, biology, and the behavioral sciences is necessary for fundamental insights into the major features of voluntary action. Knowledge of history, political science, and economics is vital for a basic grasp of government. And knowledge of the theoretical disciplines alone, by virtue of their principles and methods, prepares people to anticipate and grasp the new existential conditions and new interests that any political society will have. The only way, it will be remembered, by which an educational comprehensive perspective can be attained is through educational learning activities. Because education in a democracy must be reliable in furnishing the society's members with their educational perspectives, it must be stable and somewhat standardized, which is to say that it must be institutionalized.

Of course, knowing that each and every democracy has to institutionalize education so as to socialize its members is not knowing what education can do specifically to enable the members to play their institutional roles. To see what education can do specifically, we will focus upon the two major aspects of education—comprehensive understanding and learning activities. By explaining what education can do specifically, we might soften, if not eliminate, the skepticism of egalitarians about the value of the study of the theoretical disciplines for the operations of a democratic society.[3]

There are two sorts of ingredients in an educational comprehensive understanding: *necessary* and *contingent*. The necessary ingredients are *(a)* the statements that pertain to all subject matters of the theoretical disciplines and whose justifications include all methods and all basic principles of such disciplines and *(b)* the acts, abilities, dispositions, and appreciations involved in any educational cognitive perspective. The contingent ingredients are both *(a)* the other mentals and bodily skills and habits and *(b)* the objects of experience that the person with the given educational comprehensive understanding has. The former are necessary in that what they specifically are logically has to be included in any educational cognitive perspective. The latter are contingent in that what they specifically are is not conceptually connected with what such a perspective is. The identity of the contingent ingredients of an educational comprehensive understanding, such as who one's parents and acquaintances are, what one's health and career aspirations are, and where one lives, depends upon the biographical circumstances of the person with the understanding. What an educational cognitive perspective can do specifically to prepare the members of a democratic commonwealth for their civil duties can be regarded from the respective standpoints of these necessary and contingent elements.

Let us begin from the standpoint of the contingent ingredients. The members of a democracy are citizens and noncitizens. The citizens are those who have occurrently or upon maturity the legal rights to vote and to hold governmental office; the noncitizens are those who do not have these rights, occurrently or upon maturity. Both the citizens and the noncitizens of a democratic state share certain civil duties—most notably, to obey the laws of the land and to support their society in times of crisis. Citizens, however, have civil duties that noncitizens do not have—most notably, the duties of voting and those of holding office. While it is the case that the mentals and the objects of experiences that the members of a democracy have might be, as a matter of fact, of little or no significance for their respective civil duties, it also is true that the members require certain mentals, including experiences of sensorial objects, closely connected with their society if they are to perform their several civil duties. To be able to obey the laws of the land, the members of a democracy have to know what the laws are. To be able to support the society in times of crisis, the members must be acquainted with its existential conditions and, besides its laws, the other factors determining its interests—its central principles and its ideals. To have a positive motivation for obeying the society's laws and supporting the society in times of crisis, the members have to see that the laws and the society's interests are in the public interest, which means that they have to perceive that the laws and the interests are at least compatible with the major features of their voluntary actions.

In performing their duties as voters, the citizens of a democratic body politic are not to vote for just any individuals or approve referenda indifferently; they are bound to vote for persons who will look after the state's interests and to approve referenda favoring its interests. This entails that they must be informed of the qualifications the various candidates have for looking after the state's interests and of the significances any referenda have for its interests; and this in turn implies that they have to be cognizant of the relevant principles, ideals, laws, and existential conditions that shape the state's interests. In addition, they logically must be familiar with the public interest; for to be aware of the state's interests, they logically have to be aware of the public interest. It will be remembered that a democratic society is workable only if its citizens, especially in their capacity as voters, see its interests as being in the public interest, which means that its interests conceptually have to be in the public interest. Instruction on the duties of both citizens and noncitizens may rely upon various sources: textbooks in the geography, history, government, and current problems of the given students' society; newspapers, magazines, and television; topical movies and novels; parental role models; and public service jobs. Whatever sources it uses, however, the instruction must concern itself ultimately with students' identifying and appreciating their society's public interest.

As occupants of governmental offices, citizens need many of the same mentals especially related to their society that they require as voters. They have to be cognizant of the state's interests and, therefore, its basic principles, ideals, laws, and existential conditions; they have to be informed of the public interest; and they must have the dispositions appropriate to acquiring this information and appreciate this information and these dispositions. Yet the occupants of governmental office in a democratic commonwealth also require mentals that the voters of the society do not have to have. They need the technical knowledge and skills for understanding the technical complexities of problems facing their state. They must have the ability and disposition to anticipate the impact of laws and policies upon state interests. They have to be able and inclined to view the public interest impartially; that is, they need to regard the state's interests as they relate to the major characteristics of the voluntary actions of all members of the society, not the voluntary actions of just some members. They require the ability and inclination to explain the problems of their state to its members, which entails that they must be as honest as the public interest allows. Finally, they need to value the public interest above all else. While the knowledge and intellectual skills mentioned above can be learned through academic experience supplemented by continuing education and on-the-job training, some of the mentals mentioned are likely to be, at least partly, products of happenstance. It simply is not altogether clear how to produce people who have an abiding passionate concern with public affairs or who have personalities that facilitate communication.

The information, dispositions, and appreciations that are especially suitable to the members of a democracy in their civil institutional roles are contingent, not necessary, elements of an educational cognitive perspective; they are not the sorts of things that each and every person must have in order to have such a perspective. Thus, the information, dispositions, and appreciations appropriate particularly to the members of England are not entirely pertinent to members of Ireland and the United States let alone India. Preparing the members of a democratic state to obey the laws of the land, to support the state in times of crisis, to vote wisely, and to serve competently in office—this is plainly in the state's interests. It is in the public interest as well, however; for it helps the members to perceive the relationships between the state's interests and the major characteristics of their voluntary actions. Insofar as those relationships are perceived, members are placed in a position to harmonize the former with the latter.

Some of the information, skills, dispositions, and appreciations particularly significant of the civil institutions of a democratic society are relatively stable while others are quite temporary. Examples of stable elements are the society's central principles, its ideals, its constitutional law, and the major features of voluntary action. Instances of temporary elements are laws dealing with particular problems of the society, the names and records of particular candidates and officials, and the features of voluntary action at a given time and place. The stable elements may be taught to members when they are students in schools, colleges, and other institutions of formal education, whereas the temporary elements may be learned by members from the public media, from face-to-face discussion, and from other sources of informal education. Apparently, then, a part of the political role of educational practice in a democratic commonwealth is to supply the society's members with the information, skills, dispositions, and appreciations particularly important for their civil institutional duties.

It should not be thought that the quality of learning activities is unimportant for this part of education's political role in a democracy. During the history of democratic states, noneducational learning activities have been used to ready the members of the states for their civil institutional responsibilities. Mind-numbing propaganda, for instance, has been employed frequently to prepare members to support their respective societies in times of emergency; and nonrational conditioning has been utilized often to habituate members to obey the laws of their several societies.[4] Because noneducational learning activities have been used to prepare the members of democratic commonwealths for civil institutional roles, it might be concluded that it is not important to employ educational learning activities to this end. The reasons why this conclusion would be wrong are twofold. The first is a conceptual point. As previously emphasized, the practice of education includes educational learning activities in addition to educational learning objects, which means that one cannot learn the objects without engaging in the activities. Hence, to think that the practice of education can get the members of a democracy to learn certain objects without engaging in educational learning activities is to be confused about the practice of education. The second reason is political. While propaganda, nonrational conditioning, and other noneducational learning activities sometimes have been successful for democratic states, they have created problems for such states too; for by imbuing the members of democracies with information, skills, dispositions, and appreciations in an unreflective way, noneducational learning activities have tended to make it difficult for these members to alter their minds as the interests of the states have changed. Hence, the eminently successful propaganda of the two world wars has left many Americans incapable of viewing Japan and West Germany as allies of their country even though the United States has had much to gain in recent decades by becoming allied to these two states.

If learning the contingent ingredients of an educational comprehensive understanding can provide the members of a democracy with the information, skills, dispositions, and appreciations particularly significant of their civil institutional roles, it seems to render otiose the learning of the necessary elements of such an understanding. What could the learning of the necessary ingredients furnish that would be important to the society and still not be a duplicate of those matters supplied by the learning of the contingent elements? What the learning of the necessary ingredients can provide are matters that are relevant to the civil institutional responsibilities of a democracy's members in only a quite general way but that, when coupled with those things furnished by the learning of the contingent elements, are highly important to the society. Quite obviously, an acquaintance with the subject matters, basic principles, and methods of the theoretical disciplines will help citizens grasp issues and problems related to state interests, especially issues and problems of a technological nature. The disposition to search for materials and assess them evidently prepares citizens to look critically at the claims of the candidates for office and at the claims concerning given referenda. The disposition to discuss according to the rules of public debate enables them to make sense of and to weigh claims about the state's interests, including the public interest.[5] The disposition to relate matters to one another helps them to compare and contrast the state's principles, ideals, laws, and existential conditions with claims about the state's interests and to compare and contrast the major characteristics of the voluntary actions of the state's members with claims about its interests. Finally, appreciation of these dispositions as well as of a cognizance of the theoretical disciplines will help motivate the members of a democracy to keep abreast of developments in these disciplines and, thus, to enhance their grasp of the issues and problems facing the society and their critical reflection upon the public discussion of these issues and problems.

It is therefore important for education's institutional role in a democratic commonwealth that members of the democracy learn the necessary elements of an educational cognitive perspective. The activities by which those elements are to be learned—discussion, instruction, training, rational conditioning, and other educational learning activities—are also important. It is true that one can learn about the theoretical disciplines in some noneducational way (e.g., indoctrination); and it also is the case that one can learn habits and values related to such disciplines in a noneducational way (e.g., nonrational conditioning). Nevertheless, if information, habits, and values pertinent to the theoretical disciplines were learned by means of noneducational activities, they would not be learned as elements of an educational comprehensive understanding. Educational learning activities enable people to understand why certain beliefs, dispositions, and appreciations should be had and, moreover, enable them to relate these beliefs, dispositions, and appreciations to each other and to other matters. Noneducational learning activities, however, do not prepare people in these ways; they only assure that beliefs, dispositions, and appreciations will be learned regardless of their justifications and relationships. It follows, then, that if the members of a democracy learn information, dispositions, and appreciations by noneducational activities, they will not be prepared to relate them to the information, dispositions, and appreciations particularly relevant to the institutional duties of the members' society.

In socializing the members of a democracy to perform their noncivil institutional responsibilities, educational practice can do things that are markedly similar to what it can do in socializing the members for the civil institutional duties. It is impossible to give an exhaustive and precise accounting of the noncivil institutions pertinent to a democratic state, but it is possible to provide a general inventory of the noncivil institutions that often have existed in democratic states. They are economic (such as manufacturing, agricultural, and extractive industries), health (such as medicine and sanitation), communicational (such as books, the press, and the electronic media), religious (such as churches and theological studies), educational (such as families, schools, and colleges), and others (such as leisure and recreation). Yet, whatever noncivil institutions a democracy has, the positions of each can be served by information, habits, and values especially relevant to its positions but only contingently relevant to an educational comprehensive understanding. This is patently the case for doctors, lawyers, clergymen, scientists, and other professionals who need information, dispositions, and appreciations that are specific to their respective professions but that an educated person does not necessarily have. It plainly holds also for engineers, practitioners of the fine arts, and skilled tradesmen; but it is the case too for unskilled workers. Whether educated or not, a maid, busboy, or itinerant farm worker needs information special to his or her job, dispositions for getting the job done properly, and appreciations that help ensure the correct performance of the job. In addition, the positions of each noncivil institution in a democratic society can use the information, dispositions, and appreciations that are the necessary elements of an educational cognitive perspective. The occupants of noncivil institutional positions in a democracy have to have more than competence for satisfying the role expectations of the positions. As a part of having to perceive the relationship between the state's interests and the major traits of their voluntary actions, they must be able also to relate the state's interests to the duties of their positions. Not only will the information, dispositions, and values necessarily integral to an educational cognitive perspective help the occupants of noncivil institutional positions grasp the theoretical and technological problems involved in performing their duties, but it also will aid them in perceiving the connections between their duties and their society's interests. It should be clear that an acquaintance with the theoretical disciplines, a disposition to relate things to one another, a respect for evidence and public discussion, and so forth, will at least help them grasp these connections. So, even though a garbage collector in a democracy, unlike a scientist, does not have to be learned in theoretical disciplines in order to do his job, he, like a scientist, who does not have to be educated in order to do science, will be prepared to make sense of his job in the society if he is educated.

While it is an educational cognitive perspective that ultimately will prepare the members of a democracy to carry out the specific responsibilities of the noncivil institutional positions they occupy and to see the political significance of their responsibilities, it is educational learning activities such as discussion and training that logically must be the means for getting the members to learn the perspectives appropriate to their respective positions. Hence, educational learning activities as well as educational learning objects are involved in education's socializing role for the noncivil institutions of the democratic state.

III

A QUESTION NOW ARISES: Is education's role as a social institution in a democratic state agreeable with its moral role in the society? Is the practice of education morally bound to enable the society's members to occupy the positions of its civil and noncivil institutions? More specifically, is the practice morally obligated to prepare the members to obey the laws of a democracy, support it in times of crisis, vote in its elections and referenda, holds its offices, and perform the roles of its various noncivil institutions? It should take only a modest amount of reflection to recognize that education's role as a social institution in a democratic society is consistent with its moral role in the society. There are two reasons why.

The first concerns the fact that the practice of education is, with reference to the moral theory we have propounded, morally correct. From the standpoint of that theory, a practice is morally right if it is governed by rules that are consistent with the Revised Principle of Generic Consistency, and the practice of education is subject to such rules. The practice has the end of getting a person to learn an educational cognitive perspective and utilizes educational learning activities as means. As explained previously (Chapter 5, Part VI), an educational comprehensive understanding involves enabling factors of voluntary action, especially those with valued purposes; and educational learning activities encourage voluntariness, purposiveness, and evaluativeness. Consequently, anyone who engages in the practice of education necessarily follows rules that respect the rights of all to the major features of voluntary action, which is to say, rules that are compatible with the RPGC. So, because educational practice is subject logically to rules that agree with the RPGC, it is, according to our moral position, morally proper in whatever it does and, thus, in performing its role as a social institution in a democratic society.

The second reason relates to the point that the democratic state is, by our moral theory, morally right in at least several respects. Any democratic commonwealth, it has been argued (Chapter 4, Part V), follows certain rules that agree with the RPGC, namely the rules of participation, inquiry, and popular will. These rules allow that educational practice in a democratic body politic has the social institutional role of preparing the society's members to occupy the positions of its civil and uncivil institutions. In turning out members inclined to vote intelligently and to hold office, the practice will follow the rule of participation. In providing members disposed to public discussion of matters of public interest, the practice will satisfy the rule of inquiry. And in furnishing officials who will tend to make decisions in view of the public interest, the practice will agree with the rule of popular will. Because, therefore, educational practice as a social institution in a democracy follows rules of the society that are compatible with the RPGC, the practice follows rules that are morally correct and, insofar, is itself morally right.

Despite these reasons, however, it might be objected that the moral rectitude of educational practice as a social institution in a democracy is a contingent, not a necessary, matter—even from the standpoint of our moral theory. A law of a democratic state, it might be noted, need not reflect the RPGC in a positive way, as the laws of invidious religious, racial, and sexual discrimination in the history of the United States, England, and other actual democratic states testify. If, therefore, education is to turn out members of a democracy who are to obey its laws and elect officials who will enforce its laws and make decisions consistent with its laws, it will furnish members who will obey, enforce, and make official decisions according to laws that might be morally wrong. Hence, education's socializing role in a democratic state is morally right only if the laws of that state are consistent with the RPGC.

This possible objection, however, ignores an important point. In discussing the nature of the democratic state, we recognized (Chapter 4, Part II) that a law of a democratic society might be morally wrong; but in stating that education in such a society is to produce members who will obey, enforce, and make official decisions according to its laws, we did not say that education is to provide members who will do these things in a morally blind way. Admittedly it was claimed that educational cognitive perspectives would *incline* members to do these things; but it was not stated that the perspectives would *compel* them to do these things. Moreover, we explained that the perspectives would dispose the members to relate their society's laws and official decisions to the chief characteristics of voluntary action and, in so doing, to be perceptive of and respectful of each other's rights to these characteristics. Accordingly, the members would be reluctant to obey, enforce, or decide according to immoral laws. How they should act in the face of immoral laws depends upon various factors, among which are the degree of moral gravity of the laws, the moral sensitivity of incumbent officials, and the available governmental mechanisms for changing and abolishing laws. It might be that an immoral law will be unenforced and, thus, can be disobeyed with impunity; that it can be modified by legislative action; that the officials who enacted, enforce, and make decisions according to the law can be removed from office; or, among other possibilities, that the law and related decisions should be subject to disobedience with punishment. In any event, members of a democracy who have educational comprehensive understandings will have preparation to deal with the question of immoral laws from the moral position that we have advocated even though they might actually deal with it from another moral position.

If it were the case that those who are members of a democratic state would do nothing of moral significance other than perform the duties of the civil and noncivil institutional positions they occupy, it necessarily would be the case also that education's moral role in the state would be coextensive with its socializing role therein. But those who are members of a democracy surely may do more of moral importance than perform their civil and noncivil institutional duties. Being rational agents, they morally may do whatever they want to do that is in keeping the the RPGC; and they may desire to do some morally correct things that are not matters of their institutional duties. Rational agents, for instance, are given to leisure pursuits and friendships, which typically, if not conceptually, are not regarded as institutional duties; and the rational agents who are members of a democratic commonwealth well might want to engage in leisure activities and friendships as well as other matters that are not parts of their institutional roles. Moreover, because any democratic state has the intentions of establishing conditions conducive to free action by its members and removing the negative and positive constraints of voluntary action, it has a commitment to permit, if not help, its members perform whatever morally correct actions they might want to perform. In fact, it is not unusual for states of various kinds to have institutions that facilitate activities by their members that are not integral to the performance of the members' institutional duties. Ancient Athens had its theater and its agora; Rome had its circus; and modern nations have their museums, parks, music concerts, and athletic events.

Obviously, there are some things that the practice of education can do to help the members of a democracy participate in those morally acceptable activities which lie beyond the pale of the members' institutional duties. Insofar as the practice familiarizes the members with the theoretical disciplines, it can contribute to their grasping the theoretical and technological problems of the activities in which they might participate. Insofar as the practice provides the members with a cognitive perspective of their mentals and objects of experience, it enables them to have a comprehensive understanding of their activities outside their institutional roles with respect to the other mentals and experiential objects of their lives. By preparing the members to grasp the theoretical and technological problems of those activities, educational practice will help ready them to exercise their rights to voluntary action; and by giving the members cognitive perspectives of their activities, it will induce them to have knowledge about the activities that they well might need to engage in them voluntarily, that is, wittingly as well as freely. It is, then, morally right for the practice of education to help ready the members of a democratic society to engage in activities beyond their institutional positions. It is in fact more than morally correct; it is morally obligatory as well. Not only can educational practice help enable the members of a democracy to engage in morally proper activities extraneous to their institutional roles, but it is a necessary part of the members' preparation to participate in such activities. Only educational learning activities can assure that whatever information, habits, and appreciations are required for this participation will be learned by the members in a way that will induce them to engage in the activities of concern with a practically full freedom and knowledge. Only educational learning objects can assure that the members will have the information, dispositions, and appreciations needed for the members to perform the activities of concern with a practically complete freedom and knowledge. Other learning activities, such as indoctrination and irrational conditioning, will encourage the members to acquire unjustifiable beliefs, blind habits, and unsupportable appreciations, all of which will tend to prevent free and witting action. A cognitive perspective not grounded in the theoretical disciplines will not help the members of a democratic state to have insights into the theoretical and technological aspects of their activities, and an acquaintance with the theoretical disciplines that does not involve a comprehensive understanding will not enable the members to view their activities fully in relation to the other factors of their lives.

The view that education's moral role in the democratic state is more extensive than its role as a social institution of that state certainly is not new in the history of political and educational theory, but it surely is not a commonplace in the history of such theory either. A position agreeing with ours was held by John Dewey. According to Dewey, a democracy, while distinctively having self-government, has the same purpose as a state of any other kind: to protect the interests shared by the members of its public.[6] The public of a state consists of all people affected by the indirect consequences of given transactions to such an extent that "it is deemed necessary to have those consequences systematically cared for";[7] but far from being all inclusive, a public is only one among the other groups constituting the social whole, or great society or great community, to which its members and other people belong.[8] In a democracy, therefore, education has the institutional role of preparing the citizens and other members of the society to identify and look after the public interests of the state. This, however, is not just an institutional role; it is a moral one too. For Dewey the ultimate and central moral value is growth in experience (i.e., the having of as many as possible novel and meaningfully connected experiences of which a person is capable),[9] and the morally correct way to obtain growth in experience is inquiry.[10] To identify and look after the public problems of their society, the members of a democracy must employ inquiry; and by resolving these problems, which present obstacles to and opportunities for the use and development of their capabilities, the members foster conditions favorable to their growth in experience as individuals. So, in performing its role as a social institution of the democratic state, education performs a moral role too: it prepares members of the state to obtain the ultimate and central moral value through the morally correct means. Education in a democratic commonwealth, however, is morally bound to do more than to enable the members of the society to identify and look after their public interests. The politically significant is not all that might contribute to one's growth in experience. An understanding and appreciation of the intellectual disciplines in their own right, aesthetic expression, personal relationships, vocations, religious experiences—these are only some of the sectors of experiences that might lie beyond the political and that might be ingredients in a person's growth. Education in a democratic state, therefore, is morally obligated to help the society's members grow in all areas of experience, not in just the political sphere.

A position contrary to ours was taken by Thomas Jefferson, who was acutely aware that a political society of a given kind needs members of a given type and can best obtain them through education. According to Jefferson's political thought, the goal of democracy is to enable its members to exercise their natural rights and, thereby, obtain happiness. This end suggests that the role of education as a social institution of any democratic commonwealth is to provide the society's members with the knowledge, skills, and appreciations that will help them to recognize and exercise their natural rights in both the public and the private sections of the society. Moreover, a democratic state, in order to achieve its end, needs leaders with superior intelligence and moral virtue. Consequently, the role of education as a social institution of a democracy is threefold: to furnish all members with the information, skills, and values that will enable them to pursue happiness as private persons; to prepare all citizens to exercise their rights of self-government; and to provide the knowledge, abilities, and appreciations that will enable the superiorly gifted citizens to make full use of their intellectual and moral powers, especially with respect to the exigencies of leadership.[11] The reason why this view of education's institutional role in a democracy includes all that its moral role in such a society comprises is that Jefferson makes the interests of a democratic state as broad as the moral rights of its members. A person's moral rights and duties, which are determined by the moral laws of nature, are the person's natural rights and duties. The interest of any political society is to protect the natural and, hence, the moral rights of its members. The point of education is to ready people to exercise their natural rights and, thus, to obtain happiness. Consequently, when education functions in a democracy as a social institution, it does all that it is morally bound to do in the society. By contrast, neither Dewey's nor our political theory regards the interests of a democratic society as coincidental with whatever is morally valuable or right for its members. Dewey's theory does not because it restricts any state's interests to only a portion of the moral values (i.e., the growth in experience) of its members; whereas ours does not because, while it conceives of a democratic society's interests as possibly being compatible with the chief moral goods and rights of its members, it does not look upon such interests as being necessarily coextensive with such goods and rights.

IV

EVEN THOUGH EDUCATION as a practice is only one of several senses of the term, it is, we have argued (Chapter 5, Part II), basic to the other meanings. It may be presumed, therefore, that what has been determined about the moral role of educational practice in a democratic commonwealth has significance for the moral role of education in any of its other senses in such a commonwealth. For convenience, we will see what the significance is for only two of the other senses, namely, an intellectual discipline and a profession.

As an intellectual discipline, it will be remembered, education has three branches: pedagogy, research, and recommendation. Pedagogy prepares persons for positions in the practice and the study of education (e.g., teacher, researcher, and administrator). Hence, in the democratic or any other kind of state, pedagogy has the social institutional purpose of readying the society's members to occupy positions in the practice and the intellectual discipline of education. This, however, is not only its purpose as a social institution in a democracy; it also is its moral role in the society. Several reasons may be given to support this claim. First, because a democracy requires the practice of education, it must have members who occupy positions within the practice. Second, because a democracy must have institutions that study the practice of education in the society and set policies for the practice, it must support the research and recommendation branches of the discipline of education. These branches are, by their nature, the only agencies that can serve as such institutions. Third, pedagogy is the only agency that can provide a democratic or any other type of society with members qualified for positions in the practice and the study of education. Fourth, it would be morally right for members of a democracy to be prepared to occupy positions in the society's institutions of the practice and the intellectual discipline of education. As maintained in our discussion of education's social institutional role in a democratic state, being prepared to be an occupant of any social institution of such a state involves a person's being educated, which is consistent with the RPGC. It follows that pedagogy in a democracy—rather than being a matter of narrow, fragmented, and isolated information, skills, and attitudes—is to be educational. More specifically, the content of the pedagogical curriculum is to be closely tied to the theoretical disciplines and related to other factors within the lives of prospective teachers, researchers, administrators, and others of the sort in the given society. Moreover, the learning activities of the pedagogical curriculum, far from being indoctrination and blind conditioning, are to be discussion, training, instruction, rational conditioning, and other educational learning activities. It also should be emphasized that the teachers in the pedagogical field of a democratic society are themselves to be educated as well as skilled in teaching methods. Their being educated will be to their own moral and political good, but it will help them as well to perform their role of contributing to the education of others. In other words, teacher education in a democracy must have a knowledge base as well as a performance base.

The research component of the study of education, through empirical and nonempirical means, seeks facts and theories about education in its various senses. In a democratic commonwealth, whose members have to learn to perform their political duties, the social institutional role of educational research is to determine facts and theories concerning the practice, the study, the profession, and whatever other kinds of education there might be in that society. This also is the moral role of educational research in such a democracy. As already mentioned, such a democratic state needs an institution to provide an understanding of the practice and the study of education; educational research logically is the only agency that can be that institution. In addition, it would be morally proper for educational research to determine facts and theories about the practice and the other senses of education in a democracy; for in achieving this goal, such research would help the members of the society to become educated, which would be morally worthwhile. It must be noted that, for reasons similar to those explaining why teachers in the pedagogical branch of the study of education are to be educated, the members of a democracy who need to learn to perform their political duties and who occupy positions in the research branch of the discipline are to be educated. Being educated will redound to their moral and political benefit, but it also will help them in their research tasks. It will give them cognitive insights into and appreciations of the problems they will investigate, and it will help make them sensitive to conditions in need of investigation. The educational researcher in the democratic commonwealth, therefore, is not to be a narrow specialist.

Similar points may be made about the recommendation aspect of the intellectual discipline of education. In the democratic state, the social institutional role of educational recommendation is to formulate policies, programs, and plans for the practice and study of education in that society; and its moral role is the same. As previously indicated, any democratic state requiring education has to have an institution that furnishes direction for the practice and the study of education in that society; the recommendation component of that study conceptually is the only agency that might qualify as that institution. Moreover, it would be morally correct for it to assume the purpose of such an institution; for in giving direction to the practice and study of education in a democracy needing education, recommendation will help the members of the society to become educated and, thus, will aim at something morally estimable. The claim that educational recommendation in a democratic body politic is morally bound to furnish directives for the practice and the study of education does not intend, of course, that such recommendation is obligated to supply perfect directives only (these sometimes might be practically impossible to conceive), or to produce stupid directives at all (these would not assist anyone in becoming educated). What the claim purports, rather, is that this recommendation is morally obligated to put forth directives that, in view of their social context, are morally, as well as educationally and politically, defensible. Hence, those who determine educational directives in a democracy not only should be educated but also should be especially well-informed about the findings of educational research in the society, about the society's interests, and about the major features of voluntary action in the society.

As a profession, education is an organization of those holding positions in the practice and the study of education. The purpose of the organization is to look after the interests of its members as teachers, administrators, students, and occupants of other related positions. That every democratic state would need education in that sense of a profession is doubtful. In a small society, for instance, where each group's, if not each concrete person's, interests might be commonly known and respected, a profession of any kind might be redundant. However, in a democracy where the interests of educators and students are not publicly understood well or, at least, are not commonly respected as relevant to the public interest, there is a need for the society to have an educational profession. If the interests of the educators and students in a democratic state are harmed or neglected by its government, there will be a tendency for the educators and students to feel alienated from the workings of the society and, insofar as they do, to be reluctant to participate in its government; there will also be a tendency of the society's members not to take positions in educational institutions. When a profession of education becomes needed by a democracy, it assumes the institutional role of looking after the interests of its members within the context of that society; this means that it is to look after the major features of the members' voluntary actions vis à vis the society's interests. In other words, the profession is to protect the members' professional interests to the extent that they are integral to the state's public interest. Thus, the profession might concern itself with the salaries and pensions of teachers, researchers, and administrators; the health care of its members, including students; the working conditions of teachers, researchers, and administrators and the study conditions of students; and the academic freedom of its members.

The moral role of the educational profession in a democratic state also includes looking after the professional interests of the profession's members insofar as they are related to the society's public interest; but it includes, in addition, protecting the members' professional interests even in the respect that they are related to matters other than the state's interests. This is so for various reasons. Because the members' professional interests are positively connected with the practice and the study of education, which are regulated by rules compatible with the RPGC, they are morally worthy. And being morally worthy, they must be secured, by morally legitimate means, against any threats and they must be advanced, by morally legitimate means, in the face of any opportunities—regardless of the sources of those threats and opportunities. Thus, the educational profession in a democratic state might have the moral duty to take action with regard to threats to academic freedom in another society and to encourage favorable working and study conditions of educators and students in other societies. Finally, the educational profession of a democracy, as it would have in any other kind of state, has the special moral duty of lending assistance to protect the rights of educators and students in any country whenever it is appropriate and practically possible to do so. Despite their possible political and cultural differences, the educators and students of one society are especially knowledgeable of the moral rights of educators and students in any other society; therefore, they are liable more than other persons in their society for being concerned with the protection of the moral rights of educators and students in any other society.

The Curriculum

I

EDUCATION'S MORAL ROLE in the democratic state, which is to prepare the members of the society to carry out their institutional duties and to help them learn to participate in morally acceptable activities lying beyond their institutional duties, cannot be performed without the benefit of a curriculum. It is far too complex for its performance to succeed by happenstance. But what course of studies will help the practice of education fulfill its moral role in the democratic commonwealth?

This question has much relevance to discussions about learning in democracies during the past several decades. After World War II a position popularly ascribed to Progressive Education was that curricula should center around student interest.[1] During the 1950s and early 1960s this position was attacked in favor of the proposition that the intellectual disciplines should constitute the heart of curricula.[2] By the later 1960s this proposition gave way to a revival of the student interest position,[3] which in turn yielded, in the 1970s, to one of vocationalism.[4] Subsequently, the vocationalist view was joined by arguments advocating a return to traditional subjects.[5] Of course, none of these proposals, which apply to courses of study in general, reflects the various stands taken on curricula for special groups of students (e.g., socially disadvantaged, retarded, physically handicapped, and female).

As the variety of all these proposals indicates, they have been supported by a diversity of principles: individual interest, national interest, material success, normal academic achievement, and justice. That a curricular proposal is based on a set of principles is desirable, but that the proposal be founded on an adequate set is much more desirable. Unfortunately, the principles undergirding the proposals of recent decades frequently have suffered a major difficulty, which is that the body of principles underlying a given proposal usually has been too narrow: typically, none of the principles supporting a particular proposal has been political, educational, or moral. When a set of principles has been overly narrow in this sense, it has not been able to answer some of the questions raised by the recommendation its supports. Thus, the student-interest curriculum position has rested mainly on the principle of individual interest,[6] but that principle has not been able to explain whether or not a curriculum that satisfies the various interests of a democracy's students is also politically and morally worthwhile. The intellectual-disciplines curriculum standpoint has relied heavily upon the principle of national interest,[7] but that principle has not been able to settle whether or not a curriculum favorable to a democracy's interests is educationally and morally important as well. The curricular recommendations for correcting past moral wrongs done to the socially disadvantaged, the retarded, the physically handicapped, and females have been based largely upon the principle of justice,[8] but that principle has been unable to show whether or not a curriculum trying to rectify past moral wrongs in a democracy is educationally or politically sound. The curriculum of vocationalism has been founded to a large extent on the principle of material success,[9] and the curriculum of traditional subjects has been grounded primarily upon the principle of academic achievement.[10] The former principle has been incapable of clarifying whether or not a curriculum that prepared the students in a democracy to gain material success is morally, politically, or educationally significant; and the latter principle has been unable to determine whether or not a curriculum that helps the students in a democracy to make and raise that society's average on standardized academic tests is morally, politically, or educationally significant.

So a statement of a curriculum that rests upon our conception of education's moral role in democracy has a distinct advantage: it rests upon political, educational, and moral principles.

II

IT IS RECOGNIZED generally that a question to which any statement of a curriculum is subject is that of its purpose, or the end that the course of studies is intended to attain. Obviously, the end a democracy's curriculum ought to have is helping the practice of education fulfill its moral role in the society.

This statement may be supplemented by more or less specific goals suggested by our discussions of education and the democratic state. Preparing the members of a democracy to fulfill their institutional duties and to engage in extrainstitutional activities that are morally correct incorporates the less general goals of imparting to the members information about the subject matters, basic principles, and methods of the theoretical disciplines and about the fundamental principles, ideals, laws, and existential conditions of their society as well as the chief characteristics of voluntary actions in their society. Moreover, the aim embodies the less general objectives of getting the members to learn the skills, dispositions, and appreciations especially integral to having a cognitive perspective within the state and those especially pertinent to being a member of the state.

Precisely which information, skills, dispositions, and appreciations are to be learned in a democracy will depend largely upon several factors: the schema of the theoretical disciplines that is being employed; the historical circumstances of the given society; and the talents, development, interests, and background of the particular students of concern. Hence, the goals may be made more definite by formulating them with reference to these factors. Regardless of how much they are to be delimited, however, they must be formulated with a view to the highly general purpose of the curriculum. Being intimately related to education's moral role in the democratic state, that purpose is the ultimate and overall aim of any curriculum meant to help education perform this role. It is ultimate in that any specific objective of such a curriculum will make sense only if that specific objective is seen as being finally for the sake of the general goal, and it is overall in that it is the framework within which the specific aims of any such curriculum are to be coordinated with one another. From another standpoint the highly general goal may be seen as the long-range goal for the curriculum, whereas the more or less specific purposes may be looked upon as the intermediate and short-range goals for the curriculum.

Another issue that a statement of what morally should be the curriculum in any democracy must address is the curriculum's content. That is, the statement has to indicate what information, skills, dispositions, and appreciations are to be presented to and studied by the members of the society.

The principles of action that underpin our statement of the morally proper curriculum in democracy strongly suggest that the members of a democratic state should be encouraged to study the concepts and principles associated with rational agency. More specifically, they should be encouraged to distinguish between voluntary and involuntary action; to be disposed toward and prizing of voluntary action; to be inclined toward establishing and being appreciative of actions with valued goals; to acquire facts, skills, dispositions, and standards involved in deliberating about courses of action; and to grasp and be inclined to apply and see the worth of the Revised Principle of Generic Consistency and the Revised Principle of Proportionality. The statement's principles of democracy indicate that the members must become versed in the operations of their government and in the public interest. That is, they should learn about and become positively inclined toward participation in their government, which includes their acquiring the civic virtues of truthfulness, lawfulness, loyalty, tolerance, and community. Moreover, they ought to learn about and become positively disposed toward the public interest, which means not only that they should comprehend and prize the major features of voluntary action but also that they should grasp the basic principles, intentions, laws, and existential conditions of their state. Besides the operations of their government and the public interest, the principles of democracy indicate too that the members ought to be encouraged to learn about the familial, economic, religious, artistic, and other noncivil institutions of their state and about their own individual capabilities, abilities, and interests. The statement's principles of education plainly suggest that the members of a democratic commonwealth must become familiar with and appreciative of the theoretical disciplines and that they have to learn about and to use relational concepts whereby they may develop cognitive perspectives.

While a democratic commonwealth's curriculum ought to have the content described above, that curriculum might have to comprise as well other matters intimated by the principles of action, democracy, and education. The membership of a democratic state logically need not be human. While it is the case that the only members of such a state with whom human beings are familiar are human beings and the corporations they have created, it is conceptually possible for the members of a democracy to be nonhuman. There is nothing about the concept of democracy that precludes its members from being agents from another planet. To become educated, as we have suggested already (Chapter 5, Part III), human beings need to learn the skills, dispositions, and appreciations of physical health, namely, those of bodily function, rest, nutrition, exercise, and medical care. To engage in the activities pertinent to an educated member of a democratic society, however, human beings should acquire more than physical health; they should gain also the skills, dispositions, and appreciation for psychological health and proper social manners. Sound physical health enables a person to engage in a greater breadth and depth of activities than unsound physical health habits permit. Good psychological dispositions do the same thing, but in addition they tend to promote social harmony among the members of a group. Proper social manners also contribute to group harmony, and they serve to make social interaction efficient. When, therefore, a democratic society has a human membership, it will do well to have a curriculum containing matters on physical and psychological health and correct social manners.

It is obvious that the content of one democracy's curriculum need not be identical with that of another's curriculum in particulars. The laws of the one state might differ from those of the other. The existential conditions of the one society, including its historical development, geographical circumstances, and demographic aspects, are likely to vary significantly from those of the other. The governmental operations of the two states might be dissimilar; thus, one government might be parliamentary while the other might involve a sharp separation of and strong balance among the executive, legislative, and judicial powers. The noncivil institutions of the states might be diverse. The talents and interests of the members of the one society are as likely to differ from those of the members of the other as they are likely to vary among the members of the same society. And even though the standards of good physical and psychological health and correct social manners in a democratic society ought to reflect whatever pertinent natural regularities there might be, and even though they should be compatible with the principles of morality, they nevertheless will also reflect the historical and cultural circumstances of the society. What passes as health in one era or culture might count as illness in another; what passes as graciousness in one era or culture might count as extravagance in another. Yet, despite the diversity that must be allowed in the curricular content from one democracy to another, it should not be regarded as meaning that the elements of the content described above are not important. All that the diversity signifies is that the ingredients well might differ in emphasis and particularity from one democracy to another; it does not signify that they must vary in kind. Knowing what the elements are in kind will be useful in constructing a democracy's curriculum: it will help to determine what sorts of particular matters should be included in the curriculum, what matters are different mainly by way of emphasis, and the categories in which the particulars should be placed.

Even though the theoretical disciplines are the only intellectual disciplines that so far have been mentioned explicitly as ingredients in a democracy's curriculum, they should not be regarded as the only disciplines to be included in the curriculum. A field of inquiry long recognized as an intellectual discipline is the practical; its subject matter is voluntary action, its method is deliberation, and its end is right action. This field is to be involved where the curriculum of a democratic society is concerned with rational agency as well as with governmental operations, the public interest, noncivil institutions, personal interests, health, and manners, all of which allow for deliberations aimed at right actions, whether moral, political, prudential, or some other sort. Another area of intellectual activity long viewed as an intellectual discipline is the productive; its subject matter is material objects, its method is deliberation, and its end is products, fine or useful. This area will be embodied in a curriculum wherever it takes the state as an object to be produced by means of deliberation; and it evidently will be contained in the curriculum where it deals with economic and aesthetic institutions, with career, hobby, and other personal interests concerned with production, and with health and social interaction wherever they are seen as products.

Yet even if it is clear that the theoretical fields are not the only intellectual disciplines to appear in the content of a democracy's curriculum, it is not certain which organization of the theoretical disciplines will be pertinent to the content. As already explained, the theoretical disciplines have had various schemata of organization during their history; and any schema they are given is important. One mode of organization might treat the theoretical disciplines as having only a single kind of method, whereas another mode might view them as having a diversity of methods. One type of organization might regard the theoretical disciplines as resting upon a common body of basic principles, whereas another sort might view them as resting upon different bodies of fundamental principles. One schema might present logic and mathematics as mere auxiliaries to the other theoretical disciplines, whereas another might show them to be as substantively significant as any of the others. The schema or schemata that will be relevant to the curriculum of a given democratic state will depend upon the history of the theoretical disciplines and upon the historical circumstances of the states. Different modes of organization have prevailed at different times, and different historical circumstances have made some modes more acceptable than others. Hence, the Platonic mode prevailed during the Middle Ages before the Aristotelian mode gained ascendance during that era. And John Dewey's schema seems much more pertinent to a twentieth-century democracy than does Hegel's, which was conceived in a period when metaphysics was viewed widely as the queen of the intellectual disciplines and industrial democracies were not yet in existence. It might be that some organization of the theoretical disciplines is necessarily incompatible with the workings of each and every democratic state. Which organization or organizations are incompatible in this respect is not readily apparent, but any that is must be excluded as a positive ingredient from the curricular content of any such state.

It is one thing, however, to know what the content of a curriculum is and quite another to know what the organization of the content is. Knowledge of the former extends no farther than identification of the curriculum's ingredients. Knowledge of the latter covers institutional responsibilities for the various elements and the relationships among the elements within the institutions to which they belong.

Which institutions should have what responsibilities for the several factors of a democracy's curriculum has received much attention for the past two decades and more. Sometimes the issue has been construed as reflecting the distinction between formal and informal education; at other times it has been depicted as reflecting the distinction between scholastic and nonscholastic institutions.[11] Thus, so-called "educational romantics" have charged that education has traditionally been too formal and should be much more informal. Members of the "moral majority" have held that piety should be taught by scholastic institutions as well as by churches. And radical social critics have contended that schools and colleges have been instruments of social oppression and their curricular duties should be reassigned to nonscholastic institutions. But regardless of the guise under which the issue has been discussed, it frequently has not been settled on solid ground; as often as not, it has been resolved on ideological grounds and without appeal to pertinent facts. Which responsibilities are to be given to which institutions of a society is a question that may be answered partly by theoretical considerations, but it also is one that must be answered with the benefit of certain factual considerations. So, in determining which curricular factors should be given to which institutions of a democracy, a person will do well to refer not only to moral, political, and educational theories but also to some pertinent facts, namely, the relative efficiencies of the institutions in dealing with the various factors, major problems facing the society, and any legal and cultural restrictions that the society imposes upon its institutions.

According to our own theories, the theoretical disciplines and a grasp of the public interest are so vital in education's moral role in any democracy that they ought to be placed in the hands of institutions that will assure that they will be provided to all students. And in view of the importance of technological problems in this day and age, the theoretical disciplines of mathematics and the sciences and the productive discipline of engineering must be put in institutions that will accord them special consideration. For some time the institutions that have been able to assure availability of these subjects to all students have been schools and colleges. Moreover, since World War I schools and colleges in actual democracies have been fairly successful in teaching masses of students the academic basics, the theoretical disciplines, and career exploration. These institutions alone might not be adequate for instilling students with a sense of public interest, but they could be supplemented in this task by military and civilian service institutions.[12] By contrast, the mass media have been somewhat effective in providing continuing education about the theoretical disciplines, the public interest, and civic morality. The family in twentieth-century democracies, despite recent lapses, has been more or less efficient in enabling its members to develop personal interests and to learn civic morality; and industry has been the trainer of legions of workers in vocational areas. In the United States and other democracies, scholastic institutions have suffered some legal and cultural prohibitions on what they might offer in the way of religion, but they have acquired increasing legal and cultural freedom in what they might offer about sex education. So, because the assignment of curricular elements to a democracy's various institutions must be undertaken with an appeal to facts, and because the facts to be examined are relative to each society of concern, the assignment should be undertaken ultimately on a society-by-society approach.

The curricular content belonging to a society's nonscholastic institutions need not have a distinct organization, but that belonging to the scholastic institutions is to have a specifiable order. This is neither a moral, a political, nor an educational requirement; it is simply a conceptual necessity. To describe a curriculum as both scholastic and without order is to utter a contradiction or to express a doubt about the quality of a so-called "school," "college," or other "scholastic" institution. Because the curricular content pertaining to a democracy's scholastic institutions must be determined through a case-by-case approach, the order that should be assumed by the curricular content of these scholastic institutions can likewise be comprehended thoroughly only through such an approach. Even so, something worthwhile can be said about the organization of the curricular content of any democratic state's scholastic institutions insofar as that content is presently known.

What we have established is that the scholastic institutions of a democratic commonwealth must contain studies oriented toward the theoretical disciplines, the public interest, and a comprehensive understanding, plus courses in any academic basics requisite for participation in these studies. It should be quite apparent that these blocks of curricular content ought not to be totally separated from each other. Learning about the theoretical disciplines and the public interest in isolation from one another runs completely counter to acquiring the concepts, skills, dispositions, and appreciations constitutive of a cognitive perspective. This is not to say that every class dealing with a theoretical discipline has to address itself to the public interest, but it is to say that connections between the theoretical disciplines and the public interest must occupy a portion of the curriculum sufficient to help assure that the students of concern will develop a comprehensive understanding. There are different modes of organization whereby these connections might be made in a serious way. For convenience only five will be cited.

1. The theoretical disciplines may be initially taught apart from references to the public interest and then used as sources of concepts, principles, and findings in courses dealing with the public interest.[13]
2. The theoretical disciplines may be taught interactively with courses about the public interest. That is, the theoretical disciplines may be used as sources for understanding the public interest while courses on the public interest may be utilized as sources of problems for the theoretical disciplines.[14]
3. Problems of the public interest may be employed as focal points around which to teach each of the theoretical disciplines.[15]
4. Problems of the public interest may be used as focal points around which to teach some theoretical disciplines, whereas other theoretical disciplines are taught without special concern for the public interest.[16]
5. Personal interests of students may be employed as focal points around which to study the theoretical disciplines and the public interest.[17]

Which mode or modes of ordering the curricular content of scholastic institutions in a democracy ought to be utilized depends, among other things, upon the relative suitability of the various modes to the students of the society. One mode of organization might be much more suitable to students at a certain stage of intellectual development than to those at another stage. Thus, (1) seems more appropriate to students ready to learn the theoretical disciplines systematically and in depth than to those still guided largely by fantasy. A mode of order might be quite appropriate to students with career interests of one kind but not very appropriate to those with career interests of another kind. Hence, (4) appears to be pertinent to students specializing in one sector of the theoretical disciplines but who still need to learn more about the other sectors; and (3) seems suitable to students not specializing in the theoretical disciplines. A mode of organization might be highly pertinent to students with intellectual aptitudes of one sort but only marginally pertinent to those with intellectual aptitudes of another kind. Thus, (5) might be quite relevant to primary students but only slightly relevant to college students.

In what manner the academic basics are to be related to the theoretical disciplines and the public interest is problematic too. Reading, writing, and arithmetic may be presented separately from the theoretical disciplines and the public interest. They may be integrated into the former, they may be integrated into the latter, or they may be presented partly separately and partly integrally. Separation might be best for beginning students, partial separation might be best for high school students, and total integration might be best for graduate students. Whereas the study of the theoretical disciplines and the public interest is not necessarily the same as career education, it does provide the opportunity for some career education, to wit, exploration of and preparation for a career specifically connected with the theoretical disciplines and the public interest. (Such careers might include those of a scientist, scholar, lawyer, or physician.) Career education, we have mentioned, need not be a curricular content of scholastic institutions. But whether it takes place within or without scholastic institutions, it needs to occur from the standpoint of a comprehensive understanding. This means that the information, skills, dispositions, and appreciations constituting a vocation must be presented as they relate to the theoretical disciplines, the public interest, and the other factors within the lives of the given society's students. Historically, this has been a task not well performed whether career education has been a scholastic or nonscholastic enterprise. University-trained engineers and accountants, for instance, have been regarded generally as bereft of education in the humanities; and on-the-job training in industry has been notorious for its lack of cognitive perspective. Nevertheless, career education is an important educational task for a democracy and should be performed well.

A curriculum is not normally regarded as comprising learning activities, but is conceived usually as being closely connected with them. After all, its content is to be learned; and learning results from activities on the part of the learner (Chapter 5, Part II). An advocate of a curriculum, therefore, is liable to indicate the activities whereby its content is to be learned. While we will not attempt to specify any learning activities appropriate to the curriculum we have proposed for the democratic body politic, we will state three of the major conditions that any learning activity in any democratic society should satisfy.

First, any such activity must be educational. This condition obviously follows from two points: that the general issue of this inquiry is education's moral role in democracy; and that a person becomes educated only by engaging in educational learning activities. To say that the learning activities of a democracy are to be educational is to allow that they will not result in mindless or fragmented learning. Hence, the activities may be those involved in discussion, instruction, training, and rational conditioning but not those involved in indoctrination, propaganda, and irrational conditioning.

Second, the learning activities of a democratic state may or may not need to be coordinated with teaching activities in the state. As explained earlier, educational learning typically takes place in conjunction with teaching, but it may occur apart from teaching. When it occurs with teaching, it follows directly, we have suggested, not from any action of the teacher but from some action by the learner. Nevertheless, the learner's action is usually shaped—commanded, prompted, elicited, stimulated, or whatever—by some action of the teacher.

When, accordingly, learning activities in a democracy are to occur along with teaching, they well might need coordination with teaching activities. When, however, they are not to happen in view of teaching, they need not and, perhaps, cannot be tied to teaching activities. Educational learning activities may be random, spontaneous, learner-directed, or they may have some other feature that puts them beyond the control of the teacher.

Third, when learning activities are to be evoked by teaching activities, they must be learning activities within the capabilities—intellectual, emotional, and physical—of the given students. It is simply a conceptual truth that students cannot learn by activities that they are not capable of performing. In this sense teaching logically has to begin where the student is. This does not mean, however, that it must leave the student where he or she is. Students, generally speaking, can learn new capabilities for learning; and they have to in order to become increasingly educated as they go from childhood to adulthood. In the democratic state especially, the passage from childhood to adulthood should involve an increase in intellectual and moral autonomy: it should allow for students' becoming increasingly capable of learning on their own as they approach adulthood. Teachers in a democracy, consequently, are bound to determine that their students develop new capabilities for learning activities and, moreover, that they eventually develop capabilities for independence in learning.

III

TO SHOW that our sketch of curriculum in democratic society is adequate to serve as a set of standards for helping to assess curricular proposals for particular democracies, we will apply the sketch to two proposals for the United States. One is from the 1950s and the other is from the 1980s.

The earlier proposal comes from the President's Science Advisory Committee's report of May 24, 1959. The report states that the nation's educational system "must always have as its primary objective the development of men and women of noble character and high moral purpose who have also the intellectual capacities and the sense of values to lead fruitful and satisfying lives in modern society."[18] In addition to stating this objective, the report lists major existential conditions of the United States: the nation has a great variety of needs, or problems; it is a democracy; and it is undergoing rapid change.[19] It is in view of these conditions that the report further specifies the role of America's scholastic institutions: in order to provide citizens capable of solving the nation's problems, the schools and universities must fully cultivate the special talents of each student; and to enable each citizen to participate in the molding of all public decisions, the schools and universities must prepare him or her to have an understanding of the nation's problems not directly related to his or her special competencies.[20] Following this recommendation, the report addresses itself to the curriculum of these institutions. First, it argues that science should receive special attention in schools and universities.[21] Education in the sciences will furnish the scientists and engineers required to solve the nation's technological problems, and it will give all citizens a comprehension of such problems. Moreover, the report notes, education in the sciences will help train all citizens to respect the search for truth, to be intellectually honest, to appreciate natural beauty, and to understand many of the problems of other nations. Second, the report recommends ways to improve scholastic education in general and science and engineering education specifically.[22]

1. Scientists and scholars of the country are to establish intimate contact with experienced teachers at all levels so that the curricula, as well as the teaching and learning aids, in scholastic institutions may take account of the new facts and the new points of view that scientific progress has established.
2. A research program should be established to design more adequate curricula planned to give all educated citizens an adequate introduction to those areas of science and technology essential to an understanding of the problems of modern society.
3. Textbooks and other reading materials are to be brought into line with the most modern scholarly research in each discipline represented in the curriculum.
4. Teaching and learning aids of all appropriate kinds and laboratory equipment and materials of all suitable kinds are to be developed and supplied to scholastic institutions.
5. Engineering colleges are to modernize and otherwise improve their offerings in all of their fields to insure that their students will be given adequate training to meet the engineering and technological problems of tomorrow.
6. A nationwide effort should be made to pay more attention to the academically talented students ("those in the upper 15 to 20 per cent of their age group in intellectual ability") and to the unusually gifted students ("those in the upper 3 per cent of the age group").

There is little question that the report's curricular proposals receive some support from our position. The report's plea for special attention to the sciences in the nation's scholastic institutions receives backing on two counts. For one thing, our view of a democracy's curriculum maintains that the theoretical disciplines should be included in the offerings of schools and colleges. For another thing, the view, which allows that the emphasis to be given to each of the theoretical disciplines in a democracy's scholastic institutions depends partly upon that society's existential conditions, agrees that the sciences in American schools and colleges should be stressed as long as the nation's existential conditions justify the emphasis. Thus, the report's recommendation that the sciences should be part of the education of all students is approved by our position, which holds that all students should study the theoretical disciplines including the sciences. The proposals that engineering programs and instructional materials in science education should be improved are applauded in that our view implicitly recognizes that there are standards for educational programs and instructional materials and that whenever such programs and materials fail to meet their respective standards, they must be upgraded. Finally, the recommendation that the academically gifted must be given special consideration is supported to the extent that our position rests upon the Revised Principle of Proportionality and to the extent that scientists and engineers have to be academically gifted (whether or not they have to be appears to be an empirical question).

Despite this agreement, however, our view finds the report's recommendations lacking in several respects. Even though the report advocates a strong emphasis upon science education, it is silent on the other theoretical disciplines (e.g., philosophy, history, and the other humanities). It does not say even that others should be taught in scholastic institutions, and it certainly does not state what emphasis ought to be given to each of the others. According to our position, the other theoretical disciplines should be offered in America's schools and colleges; and the priority to be given to each of them is to be determined partly by the nation's existential conditions. Thus, the report should have considered not simply whether or not science should be emphasized in scholastic institutions but what priority it ought to have relative to each of the other theoretical disciplines. It follows that while our view approves the proposal to improve engineering programs and instructional materials in science education, it faults the report for being mute about other programs and materials. After all, engineering programs can be improved at the expense of others; and instructional materials in science education can be upgraded while those in other areas remain inadequate. Finally, there is an objection concerning the recommendation to give special attention to the academically gifted: while our view rests upon the RPP, it also recognizes that each and every moral agent has a right to certain moral goods, including those involved in education, and that the goods of a society should be distributed in society in such a way that *inter alia* the society itself will benefit and its more disadvantaged members will benefit. It is granted that giving special attention to America's academically gifted students is quite likely to benefit the nation, but it is not evident that giving special attention to them is likely to benefit the academically average and subaverage students. It might be, of course, that the academically gifted are the more disadvantaged, for they might not have the opportunity to develop their academic capabilities fully whereas the average and subaverage might have such an opportunity. Unfortunately, the report does nothing to clarify that the academically gifted are more or less disadvantaged than other students in the nation.

The curricular proposals of the 1980s to be considered were advanced in the report by the National Commission on Excellence in Education. Even though the report does call for the improvement of education in science, it is not a new edition of the one whose recommendations were just now scrutinized; for unlike the report from the 1950s, the more recent report aims at improving much more than just science education. It seeks to generate a reform of America's educational system in "fundamental ways and to renew the Nation's commitment to schools and colleges of high quality throughout the length and breadth of our land."[23] Lying behind the report's proposals is its perception of America's existential conditions, namely, that the nation faces the prospect of losing its competitive edge in world markets and that many individuals in the nation face the prospect of being "effectively disenfranchised, not simply from the material rewards that accompany competent performance, but also from the chance to participate fully in our national life."[24] To maintain and increase its economic competitiveness, the report argues, America must reform its educational system; for learning is the "indispensable investment required for success in the 'information age' we are entering."[25] To ensure that all its citizens will be able to understand the complex issues confronting itself, the report argues further, America must provide a high level of "shared education," which is essential "to a free, democratic society and to the fostering of a common culture, especially in a country that prides itself on pluralism and individual freedom."[26] The specific curricular inadequacy that the report regards as crucial concerns secondary schools: "Secondary school curricula have been homogenized, diluted, and diffused to the point that they no longer have a central purpose. In effect, we have a cafeteria-style curriculum in which the appetizers and desserts can easily be mistaken for the main courses."[27] With respect to its analysis of the condition of America's scholastic institutions, the report makes this recommendation for the secondary school curriculum: all students seeking a diploma must take four years of English, three years of mathematics, three years of science, three years of social studies, and one-half year of computer science. College preparatory students are to take, in addition, two years of foreign language.[28] Besides this proposal the report recommends that the high school curriculum should provide programs requiring effort in subjects that advance students' personal, educational, and occupational goals, such as the fine and performing arts and vocational education, and that the curriculum at the elementary school level should provide a sound base for study in high school in such areas as "English, computational and problem solving skills, science, social studies, foreign language, and the arts."[29]

There is no doubt that the report presenting these proposals contains much that is attractive. Its forthright inclusion of the theoretical disciplines in elementary and secondary curricula is certainly consistent with our views on the curriculum of a democratic society. Its insistence that other intellectual disciplines, personal development, and vocational studies are to be a part of the curriculum of scholastic institutions agrees with our position. And its contention that America's schools and colleges must help ensure that its members attain a common understanding relevant to their functioning as citizens also agrees with what we have said. Even though the report says nothing explicit about morality in its recommendations, it does make some statements, both as curricular proposals and as commentary related to them, that are compatabile with our principles of morality. For one thing, the report formulates and favors a view of equal educational opportunity that is in keeping with the Revised Principle of Generic Consistency and the Revised Principle of Proportionality.[30] For another, it declares that education is a right, which is a claim in line with our discussion of the RPGC.[31] For still another, it holds that special considerations must be given to the different learning abilities of individual students.[32]

Yet regardless of these features, the proposals have some unattractive aspects. None of the recommendations calls for the concepts, skills, dispositions, and attitudes constitutive of a cognitive perspective. It is true that the report formulates its curricular proposals with respect to providing a common understanding for all citizens, but it is the case also that a common understanding is not necessarily a comprehensive understanding. Indeed, the understanding urged by the report is the grasp by all citizens of the complex problems facing America; it is not a grasp by each citizen of the significant relationships among all of his or her mentals and objects of experience. Thus, while the report is concerned that each student study science partly with a view to comprehending the nation's technological problems, it is not concerned that the student should relate other theoretical disciplines to the sciences and to the nation's technological problems. It is noted further that the report envisions America as "a learning society"—a society committed "to a set of values and to a system of education that affords all members the opportunity to stretch their minds to full capacity, from early childhood through adulthood," inside and outside school and college, so as to improve the general quality of the members' lives as well as contribute to their career goals.[33] Yet it must be remarked also that the report does not even hint whether or not the members of a learning society are necessarily individuals with comprehensive understanding. Learning, it will be remembered, does not imply being educated.

In addition the report's recommendations fail to provide a specific statement concerning the priority it places on the theoretical disciplines as opposed to curricular items related to personal development. The report does object that the nation's schools assign equal value to studies in the theoretical disciplines and studies in automobile driving and in cooking, but it conspicuously fails to state how much more worth should be given to the former than to the latter. Finally, the report largely ignores the question of the relative suitability of various scholastic and nonscholastic institutions for the different subjects to be offered in America's curriculum. There is no question that schools and colleges are the institutions most appropriate for offering studies in the theoretical disciplines, but are they the ones best suited for offering courses in personal development and vocational education? It is largely because the report does not take up this question that it is able to tell how to administer its strong dose of theoretical disciplines at the secondary level only by proposing that both the school day and the school year be lengthened. If the report had discussed the issue, it well might have been in a position to recommend that some subjects be removed from the school curriculum.

IV

OUR VIEW of the democratic society's curriculum, however, does more than provide standards to evaluate curricular proposals for particular democracies; it also furnishes guidance for formulating curricula in special areas of study in a democracy. In support of this claim, it will be shown what direction the view gives concerning the shaping of a curriculum for teacher preparation in a democracy. Teacher preparation is chosen as a focal point for two reasons. First, such preparation, having been a subject of much dispute in various democratic states during the past several decades,[34] is markedly more relevant to current interests than some other special areas of study are. Second, teacher preparation is associated with curricula. While the learning of some elements of a curriculum might not involve teaching, the learning of others might. For instance, the learning of those within the domain of scholastic institutions typically includes teaching.

A person, of course, cannot conceive of a program of teacher preparation for a society of any sort unless he or she has some understanding of what it means to be a teacher. As normally understood, a teacher is the agent of a voluntary action, which means that the teacher performs an action, or acts freely, and knows what he or she is doing. It is common for teachers to be held responsible for their respective acts, and a person not regarded as acting both freely and wittingly cannot be looked upon as responsible for the action. Because a teacher is the agent of a voluntary action, he or she is a rational agent and, therefore, is subject, absolutely or contingently, to the theories of morality, democracy, and education that have been set forth. The purpose of teaching, which is to get someone to learn something, is rationally held. Far from being an objective that is had by whim or by some other nonrational factor, the objective of a teaching act is had by the teacher on the basis of evaluation, which is a rational ground for the goal. Because a teacher necessarily esteems the end of his or her teaching, he or she perforce possesses, if only dimly, standards by which to assess prospective and occurrent teaching aims. One such standard a teacher has to have is beneficence; that is, the goal of any act of teaching must be taken by the teacher to be worthwhile for the student.[35] Thus, whenever an individual states that he or she is trying to get students to read and understand *Hamlet,* that teacher is liable to explain what value reading and understanding the play has for the students; and if he or she cannot show any such worth, he or she is subject to being regarded as perhaps a fraud or a charlatan but, in any case, not as a teacher. From a moral perspective, the standards by which a teacher is to evaluate a learning purpose are the moral goods and rights entailed by the concept of moral action (Chapter 2, Part IV). From the perspective of a democratic state, the standards are the major characteristics of voluntary actions of the society's members, including the occurrent and prospective voluntary actions of students insofar as the actions fall within the pale of the public interest (Chapter 4, Part III). From a strictly educational perspective, the standards to be used are the elements of what it means to be educated: knowledge, understanding, perceiving relationships, and so forth (Chapter 5, Parts III–V).

Because an act of teaching is voluntary, its agent must regard it as a means for attaining its purpose. Accordingly, a teacher must be capable of using a means-end schema in his or her thinking and be cognizant of the principles of deliberation. In view of this claim several observations may be made. A teacher has to be well versed in the subject matter being taught. This is so because he or she must know both what aspects of a subject matter serve his or her purposes and what purposes are suggested by his or her subject matter. Moreover, a teacher must have information, skills, dispositions, and appreciations constitutive of communication.[36] This is so because any teaching act is a communicative act: it is an act whose point is to get something across to somebody. In order to get students to learn what they are intended to learn, a teacher has to be capable of revealing to students what they are to learn, to present the subject matter of teaching to them so that it makes sense to them, to explain to them why they should learn what they are to learn, to get their attention, and in other ways to communicate with them. Hence, teaching acts may be (among others) speech acts, bodily gestures, facial expressions, and the use of technological devices. In any event, the communicativeness of teaching helps to explain why the theoretical disciplines and pedagogical methods are highly important for teachers: they are devices for communicating. The theoretical disciplines provide languages through which ideas may become public information,[37] and pedagogical methods are formal ways for presenting subject matters to students so that they are likely to learn what they are supposed to learn about each subject matter. Finally, a teacher must have standards whereby to decide upon an act for attaining his or her goal. To be sure, one of the standards has to be efficiency. After all, insofar as an action is more efficient than any other action in attaining an objective, it is, in that respect, preferable to any other action. Efficiency, however, is not the only standard that may be employed in a teacher's deliberations. Being rational agents, teachers, as well as their students, are subject to the precepts and rules of morality. Teachers, therefore, have to utilize moral principles, such as the RPGC and RPP, in determining their actions. Also, because teachers are rational agents, they may be members of political societies; and when they are, they need to be aware of their respective societies' basic principles so that they may consider which possible teaching acts are politically correct. Still further, when teachers aim at educating their students, they are bound by the principles of education in determining which acts to perform. By those principles they may engage in acts of discussion, instruction, training, and rational conditioning; but they may not perform acts of propaganda, lying, nonrational conditioning, intimidation, and physical threat.

The foregoing analysis of the qualities of teachers strongly indicates what some of the content of teacher preparation should be in a democracy. With reference to the qualities that teachers must have in order to evaluate goals, teacher preparation in a democratic state ought to include a study of morality reflecting the RPGC, the RPP, the moral goods associated with voluntary action, and the specific rights of moral agents. Moreover, it should ensure learning about the society's public interest, which involves its underlying principles, its ideals, its laws, and its existential conditions as well as the major features of the voluntary actions of its members. Still further, the program ought to provide study about the nature of education. Teacher preparation in a democracy should encourage development of the qualities that teachers have to possess in order to decide which acts to perform. It ought also to ensure that teachers learn about the subjects they will teach; develop a facility in language and interpersonal relations; and master pedagogical methods—especially discussion, instruction, training, and rational conditioning.

Our theories of democracy and education, however, have additional significance for the preparation of teachers. In a democratic commonwealth a teacher has duties and rights pertaining to areas of his or her life other than that of teaching. There are duties and rights relating to citizenship, parenthood, and recreation, among others. Accordingly, a teacher in a democracy must have the information, skills, dispositions, and appreciations that enable him or her to perform and exercise these other duties and rights as well as those integral to teaching. To have these qualities, a person must be imbued with the state's basic principles, its ideals, and its laws, and be familiar with its existential conditions and the major features of voluntary action within the state; moreover, the person must have had an opportunity to learn about the roles of nongovernmental institutions and develop his personal interests. It is not enough, however, for a teacher in a democracy to know how to teach and to perform and exercise the duties and rights associated with the other areas of his or her life. It is required that the teacher have a definite comprehensive understanding, a grasp of the connections between the pedagogical and the other areas of his or her life. To have this understanding is for the teacher to be educated, which is (among other things) for him or her to be familiar with the theoretical disciplines. In a democratic body politic, therefore, a teacher preparation program must include the study of the principles, ideals, laws, and existential conditions of the state; familiarization with roles in both governmental and nongovernmental institutions; explorations and developments of personal interests; and a grounding in the theoretical disciplines. None of these subject areas should be presented in isolation from the others; each should be offered in conjuction with the others so as to enhance the likelihood of the prospective teacher's acquiring a cognitive perspective. Indeed, each ought to be presented also in relation to the student's pedagogical studies with the same goal in view.

Some observations may be made, without benefit of an empirical investigation, concerning which social institutions in a given democracy should be responsible for its teacher preparation program. Because of the importance of morality, citizenship, the theoretical disciplines, and pedagogical methods in the program, it seems advisable for at least some of the content in each of these areas to be provided by the society's scholastic institutions. While it is apparent that scholastic institutions should be responsible for all offerings in pedagogical methods, it is dubious that they ought to be responsible for all studies in the other subjects. For instance, the family, the church, and the mass media in a democratic state might be very effective in providing studies in morality and citizenship; and the media might be very effective in presenting aspects of the theoretical disciplines. Yet, placing morality, citizenship, and the theoretical disciplines in scholastic institutions will help ensure that they will be offered in an organized and enriched way. Regardless of the institutions to which the various curricular components of the program are assigned, however, it is crucial that the institutions are interactive with each other in their respective curricular offerings. To the extent that they are, they will encourage students to see the relationships among what they learn in the different instituitons and, thus, to gain a comprehensive understanding; to the extent that they are not, they will foster among students fragmentary learning and thereby no cognitive perspective. Dewey is famous for having said that the school and society should not be separate from each other. He said this because he recognized that education can flourish only in a society where all institutions are interactive.

Even if those elements of a democracy's teacher preparation program which are to be the responsibility of scholastic institutions are identified, the issue of how those elements are to be organized remains. (*a*) Should prospective teachers study morality, citizenship, and the theoretical disciplines more or less than others study them? (*b*) Are morality, citizenship, and the theoretical disciplines to be finished by prospective teachers before they undertake subject specialization and the study of pedagogical methods? (*c*) Is subject specialization for prospective teachers to be completely separate from any such specialization by other students? It is important to consider these questions.

(*a*) That prospective teachers should study morality, citizenship, and the theoretical disciplines less than all other students is highly doubtful. Prospective teachers have to learn the minimum of morality, citizenship, and the theoretical disciplines that any citizen of a democratic state has to learn. In addition, because teachers in a democracy have to make pedagogical judgments and decisions that depend upon a familiarity with morality, citizenship, and the theoretical disciplines, prospective teachers in such a society ought to have more than a minimum acquaintance with these subjects. Finally, because teachers in a democracy are responsible for helping students to be grounded in morality, citizenship, and the theoretical disciplines, those who are to become teachers in the society must possess more than a minimum competence in these areas. This does not mean that elementary and secondary school teachers have to be experts in these areas, but it does intend that they must be provisional experts in the areas relative to the content they are teaching to their students and their students' levels of development. It means also that Performance Based Teacher Education, which emphasizes performance at the expense of knowledge in teacher education, is wrong.[38]

(*b*) It is dubious that the study of morality, citizenship, and the theoretical disciplines should be totally finished by prospective teachers before they begin to learn their subject specialities and pedagogical methods. In preparing specifically to be teachers, students have to learn to make judgments and decisions relevant to morality, citizenship, and the theoretical disciplines; hence, they must learn how these subjects relate to the making of pedagogical judgments and decisions. But there is another reason too: any division between the presentation of morality, citizenship, and the theoretical disciplines and the curricular offerings special to teacher prepraration would tend, as a matter of fact, to undermine the chances of students to gain a comprehensive understanding as teachers in a democratic commonwealth. Hence, the Holmes Group is wrong for proposing separate pedagogical study from liberal education by placing the former mainly at the graduate level and leaving the latter mainly at the undergraduate.[39]

(*c*) It is questionable that subject specialization for prospective teachers should be entirely separate from subject specialization by other students. The subject matter, method, principles, and conclusions of any subject area are the same regardless of their vocational applications. Thus, any subject specialization for prospective teachers that is wholly divided from but the same as any subject specialization by other students entails a duplication of effort and, thus, inefficiency. What is more, it will encourage the individuals of each student group involved to believe that what they are studying is different from what those in any of the other student groups is studying and thereby will weaken their opportunities to acquire a cognitive perspective.

Whether a teacher preparation program is for a democracy or some other type of society, it is, of course, necessarily different from any other kind of vocational preparation (e.g., law, engineering, or carpentry). The information, skills, dispositions, and appreciations distinctive of one vocation are different from those distinctive of any other. Hence, preparation for the one includes the learning of information, skills, dispositions, and appreciations not found in preparation for any of the others.

Nevertheless, a teacher-preparation program for a democratic body politic is not entirely different from any other vocational-preparation program for such a society; for some of the information, skills, dispositions, and appreciations required of teachers in a democracy are the same as those needed by the members of any other vocational group in the society. Our discussion of teacher education in the democratic state is, in the following six areas, also significant for any other vocational-preparation program in the state. First, any vocational-preparation program in a democracy must offer instruction in the special information, skills, dispositions, and appreciations pertinent to the vocation with which the program is concerned. Second, any such program must allow studies in morality reflecting the moral goods of voluntary action and reflecting the RPGC and the RPP. Any member of a vocation in a democratic society is a rational agent and consequently must have moral standards for evaluating the ends of his or her action and deliberating about the means for attaining the ends. Third, a vocational program in a democratic commonwealth must contain instruction in citizenship, which includes study of governmental institutions as well as the public interest. This is so that the members of a vocation can perform their duties and exercise their rights as citizens but also so that they can place their respective jobs within the context of the society. Fourth, any vocational-preparation program in a democratic state has to give its students the opportunity to learn about nongovernmental institutions and to engage in personal development. Thereby, the students will be in a position to participate in areas of their lives other than those of their jobs and citizenship. Fifth, the students in each vocational program in a democratic body politic must study the theoretical disciplines and master the common language of the society. After all, they have to be able to communicate not only with the members of their respective vocations, but with all other members of the society as well. Sixth, because any member of a democratic state should be educated, the curricular offerings of any vocational-preparation program in such a society ought to enhance the likelihood of the students enrolled in that program becoming educated. This means, among other things, that the offerings should contain the theoretical disciplines and encourage the learning of comprehensive understandings.

Morality, citizenship, personal development, common language, and other things integral to a vocational-preparation program in a democratic commonwealth may be learned to some extent within nonscholastic institutions. It is historical fact that families, churches, guilds, neighborhoods, and the mass media have been very effective on occasion—through example, face-to-face discussion, training and conditioning, and the publication of news—in fostering the learning of matters relevant to vocations in democracies. Scholastic institutions, on the other hand, also have been known to encourage, especially through systematic and concentrated presentations, the learning of vocational subjects in such societies. As already emphasized, which curricular content in vocational preparation should be scholastic and which nonscholastic is an empirical contingency—a point that applies to the content specific to a particular vocation as well as that general to all vocations. (There was a time when medical and legal studies and automobile driver training were conducted exclusively by nonscholastic institutions.) In any case, it is important in a democracy that a student's vocational learning experiences in scholastic institutions be connected, with a view to his or her gaining a cognitive perspective, with those the student has in nonscholastic institutions.

What organization of courses should be followed by scholastic institutions for a vocational-training program is equally uncertain. Some subjects (e.g., morality, citizenship, personal development, and common language) might be presented as offerings both in the theoretical and in the practical disciplines and studied jointly by all students regardless of their individual vocational interests. Others, those significant specifically for a particular vocation, might be taught in special courses for only the students interested in that vocation. Yet empirical conditions in a democracy might speak against either of these possibilities. Whatever organizational mode is used, it should be one that helps to turn out not just good workers but good workers who are morally sensitive, democratically oriented, and educated. There is no room in a democracy for lawyers who are morally obtuse, engineers who are politically naive, and mechanics who are uneducated.

V

THERE WELL MIGHT BE READERS who will object that our discussion of curriculum in the democratic state has ignored an important issue, one that lately has received such names as "the hidden curriculum," "the implicit curriculum," and "the latent curriculum."[40] The issue arises from the point, both logical and empirical, that students may and often do learn many things other than formal subjects that are systemic in scholastic institutions. Thus, it has been observed: "Schools socialize children to a set of expectations that some argue are profoundly more powerful and longer-lasting than what is intentionally taught or what the explicit curriculum of the school publicy provides."[41] Two major qualities that students learn from schools, according to critics, are compliance and competitiveness. Another thing they learn, according to others, is to recognize that the time and place given to the study of a subject are standards by which to judge the worth of that subject and, by extension, the value of other matters. It well might be objected, therefore, that we have failed to address the question of what should be the hidden curriculum of scholastic institutions in a democratic commonwealth.

In response it must be said that a related issue has been taken into account. Sometimes labeled "the paracurriculum," it is the question of what ought to be the curricular content of nonscholastic institutions that will complement the proper curricular content of scholastic ones; and this question has been explicitly discussed by us in several contexts. Yet it must be said also that we do not believe that scholastic institutions in such a society should have a hidden curriculum let alone that we should argue what that curriculum ought to be. A curriculum is hidden, implicit, latent, or whatever because it has not been discovered, articulated, made apparent, or whatever. In the respect that it is obscure, it is beyond the scope of cognition and, consequently, interferes with voluntary action by the teacher and by the student; and to the extent that it runs counter to voluntary action, which is crucial to morality, democracy, and education, it is morally, politically, and educationally bad in the democratic commonwealth. Hence, what we propose is not that scholastic instutions should have hidden curricula with one content or another but that they ought to be vigilant in guarding against hidden curricula and, upon discovering them, bringing them under their control. The institutions thereby will be able to eliminate the undesirable elements of the implicit curricula and incorporate the desirable elements they detect into their explicit curricula.

It might be charged, however, that this conclusion itself contains a curriculum with an objectionable hidden function. According to the conclusion, the only components a curriculum should have are those that are educationally, democratically, and morally correct; and according to the philosophical framework propounded in this inquiry, the criteria of educational, democratic, and moral rectitude are rationalistic: they place a premium upon intellectual analysis, the theoretical disciplines, intellectual talent, and rational agency. As a matter of historical record, however, rationality has not been perceived as paramount by many disadvantaged groups; it actually has been regarded by some as the ideological basis for their oppression. Moreover, rationality has been an ideological tool with which people of the dominant class preserve their power and social status. Consequently, by insisting that the elements of a curriculum should be kept only if they are rationalistic, are we not in effect advocating a curriculum which has a hidden function of suppressing disadvantaged groups and furthering the interests of dominant-class people?[42]

Whether or not this charge is sound depends partly upon the accuracy of its historical claims. It is acknowledged that many disadvantaged groups have been held down in the name of reason and, thus, have been made suspicious of social programs advanced in the name of reason. In addition it is conceded that dominant-class people have benefited very much from social programs declared to be rationalistic. Nevertheless, we must insist that these points are largely irrelevant unless the rationality they address is genuine and is specifically, not just generally, the sort that has been advocated. One of our impressions about appeals to rationality to defend oppressive social programs is that they sometimes have not been serious. As indicated by Pope Urban VIII's, Hitler's, and Stalin's treatments of science, they occasionally have served to cover up nonrational factors undergirding the programs. They have reflected rationalization, not rationality. Another impression is that none of the forms of rationality historically underlying oppressive social programs has fit with the principles presented here. For instance, neither the rationalistic ideologies of ancient society, nor the rationalistic ideology of mediaeval Europe, of the Protestant middle class, or of corporate liberalism has followed consistently the principles we have set forth. Even though each has approximated them at times, each has violated them at other times. They variously have defended slavery, advocated religious intolerance, denounced intellectual freedom, overemphasized property, and discounted the rights of all rational agents to the enabling factors of voluntary action. The soundness of the charge that our curricular proposals embody an invidious partiality suffers also from its ignoring the safeguards for the disadvantaged built into our philosophical framework. Those safeguards, which will be discussed in the next chapter, propose that preferential consideration be extended to the disadvantaged. They thereby function to protect such groups from oppression by dominant-class people.

8

Equality

I

A TOPIC TRADITIONALLY ASSOCIATED with education in the democratic state is equality.[1] One reason for this is that equality, both in the sense of sameness and in the sense of fair treatment,[2] is interwoven into the notion of democratic society. Theories and ideologies of democracy regard all members of political society as the same in that, despite their having individual differences, they all are rational agents. Moreover, such theories and ideologies hold that the members of a commonwealth should be viewed equally in the allocation of goods and services and in the assignment of social positions. In other words, goods and services are to be distributed to each member according to relevant standards; and social positions are to be assigned to members according to appropriate criteria. Still further, democratic theories and ideologies claim that the life ambitions of all members of political society must be respected equally in the sense that each member must be permitted to live as he or she wants to live within the bounds of social order. Another reason for the pertinence of equality is that education or something like it is the institution in a democracy with the responsibility for assuring that each member of society will acquire and develop the knowledge, talents, dispositions, and appreciations pertinent to obtaining society's goods and services, holding social positions, and fulfilling his or her life ambition. Thus, government-supported mass education has been a feature of modern democracies. Still another reason is that equality is part and parcel of the notion of access to education, schooling, or whatever else of the sort in a democratic body politic. Hence, it is rare that a discussion of education in democracy does not mention equality of educational opportunity.

Our inquiry into education's moral role in the democratic state has raised already, directly and indirectly, the topic of equality. It has held that all members of political society are the same in that they are all rational. The investigation has contended that all members of such society are subject to the Revised Principle of Generic Consistency. It has maintained that each member has a right to certain moral goods, that each shall occupy institutional roles according to his or her qualifications, and that each has a right to whatever personal pursuits he or she wants to undertake within the bounds of the RPGC and the ideals and laws of the given society. The inquiry has emphasized that education is to help the members of a democratic society acquire moral goods, become qualified as occupiers of institutional roles, and become capable of undertaking legitimate personal pursuits. And the investigation has suggested, at least, that each member of a democracy is to have equal access to education in the society.

Yet while the topic of equality has been posed, it has not been discussed seriously as it relates to education's moral role in the democratic state. We have failed to describe in a concerted way how education, in performing its moral role in a democracy, will promote social equality and to explain what will count as equal educational opportunity in such a society. Also, we have not discussed the various issues that face any treatment of equality as it pertains to education in a democratic commonwealth. An attempt will now be made to remedy those shortcomings.

II

TO UNDERSTAND how education will promote social equality by performing its moral role in the democratic state, one should begin by considering the special conditions that must obtain if a democracy is to foster a morally correct social equality. Determining what these conditions are will enable a person to relate education's performance of its moral role especially to social equality in a democratic commonwealth. We will look specifically for the conditions presupposed by a morally proper equality in the distribution of goods and services, in the assignment of institutional positions, and in the fulfillment of life ambitions.

There are at least two reasons why any democracy morally must distribute its goods and services. First, it has to dispense them so as to maintain security and order in a fashion that promotes voluntary action by its members. Second, it must allocate them in order to eliminate negative constraints upon voluntary action (e.g., hunger and ignorance).

But whether or not a democracy has to disburse its goods and services for other moral reasons, it must dispense them in a morally fair way. With respect to the maintenance of security and order, there is a general rule applicable to any democratic state: goods and services are to be allocated so that they will protect, as far as is necessary and no farther, the members of the state from those and only those who threaten the main traits of their voluntary actions (Chapter 4, Part VI). Because this rule directs the expenditure of resources for security and order with regard to the intentions of any democracy, it is especially appropriate to the democratic state; and because it aims to protect the rights of a democracy's members, it also is morally correct. This general rule supports two specific ones: priority will be given to those members who occupy positions crucial to the workings of a democracy; sameness will be accorded, relative to the resources available for the purpose and relative to the degree of severity of threat to the various members' rights, to all members not occupying crucial offices. Thus, heads of state will receive as much military and police protection as is needed for their safety and for which resources are available; whereas ordinary members, depending upon the resources remaining for the purpose, may or may not receive as much military and police protection as is needed for their safety. In any event, no ordinary member is to receive any more protection for a given degree of severity of threat to a right than any other is to receive. The priority rule rests upon the general, or protection, rule in that the former, recognizing that the workability of a democratic state is essential to the protection of its members' rights to voluntary action, calls for the allocation of goods and services to do whatever is necessary to protect those rights. The sameness rule depends upon the general one in that the former, recognizing that all members of a democracy are rational agents and, to that extent, are the same, demands that all ordinary members be treated relatively the same. Being consistent with the general rule, which is quite proper for a democratic state and morally correct, these specific rules also are especially fitting for a democracy and are morally right.

The rules governing the dispensing of goods and services for the elimination of negative constraints also have some logical order. One of the rules is general: goods and services should be allocated for the removal of only those negative constraints that are remediable—for example, unemployment where jobs or maintenance can be made available and alcoholism where treatment can be provided. Moreover, one of the specific rules is closely connected with this general one. It says that goods and services should be expended to discover and develop means for eliminating negative constraints that presently are not eliminable—for instance, many forms of cancer and the anomy of the underclass. The other specific rules also rest upon the rule of remediable negative constraints. The rule holding that priority is to be given to removing any remediable negative constraints suffered by members occupying crucial offices follows partly from the idea that the workability of a democracy is essential to the elimination of negative constraints, but it also follows partly from the rule of remediable negative constraints. The rule maintaining that second priority is to be given to those whose remediable negative constraints are the result of state policies (e.g., birth defects caused by pollution from an officially sanctioned nuclear energy program), while following partially from the principle of workability and from the logically necessary intentions of the democratic state, follows partially also from the rule concerned with remediable negative constraints. Finally, the rule insisting that third priority be assigned to aiding members who are not victims of state policy but whose negative constraints, such as mental retardation, are greater than those, such as dyslexia and deafness, of the other members who are not victims of state policy follows partly from the point that any democracy must aim at removing remediable negative constraints but partly also from the distribution rule about such constraints. Regardless of how these rules are related to each other, however, they plainly are pertinent to democratic society and are morally proper. They are the former in that they aim at removing negative constraints, which is an intention embodied in the concept of the democratic state. They are the latter because the elimination of negative constraints is consistent with the RPGC and because the recognition of levels of priority in the removal of negative constraints is likewise consistent with the RPGC.

The main reason why a democracy or any other kind of political society must disburse offices is to enhance its interests. If it did not allocate them, it would hinder its institutions from serving its interests as it sees them; and if it does fill them, it will help its institutions to serve its interests. It follows that the offices a state should distribute depend upon the institutions it needs, which in turn depend upon its interests. Because a democratic society requires institutions that, among other things, facilitate self-government, maintain security and order with a view to voluntary action among its members, and eliminate the negative constraints suffered by its members, it should allocate those, and only those, offices that are integral to its proper institutions. It ought not to dispense positions just to keep the cronies and relatives of governmental officials employed or just for purposes of make-work.

A chief principle whereby positions in a democracy are to be distributed with moral equity is qualifications. Because any office in a political society has duties, it requires certain qualifications of its occupant. Social institutions may be civil or noncivil. The former is an institution with an assigned function of governance, whereas the latter has no such assigned function. Moreover, institutions may be vocational, nonvocational, or a mixture of both. But whether an institutional position is civil or noncivil, vocational, nonvocational, or a mix, it is under rules that assign rights and duties to its occupant. The rules of an office prescribe actions for its occupant, and the actions that they prescribe constitute the occupant's role in that position. Accordingly, to be able to fill an office, such as that of fire marshall, computer operator, parent, or citizen, a member of a state must have the qualifications that enable him or her to perform the role associated with the position. Indeed, it may be said that the rules of an office establish its qualifications. Even the formal qualifications of a job such as age, citizenship, sex, and place of residence make sense as qualifications only if they are relevant to the performance of the job's duties. It may be noted that the rules of some positions might be easier to follow than those of other positions, and the rules of some offices may have a greater significance for the state's interests than those of other offices. Accordingly, the office of citizenship in a democracy may be filled by the majority of its members; and while the job of garbage collector is vital to any modern democracy, it is not as important for the public interest as that of judge. That it is morally equitable for a democratic state to fill offices with a view to qualifications is clearly evident. Like other aspects of morality, moral fairness conceptually must be rational; and the assignment of jobs with a consideration of qualifications is rational. The point of placing people in offices is to have them play the roles of the offices, which is to say that they rationally cannot be put in positions without considering whether or not they are qualified for performing the roles. The fact that qualifications have to be considered in the morally fair allocation of any job by a democracy means that they are a major principle for such distribution.

The other chief principles are the public interest, the major traits of voluntary action, and moral disadvantage. Some offices, as already explained, are more important for the public interest than others; some (e.g., that of president) might be so important that all precautions must be taken to ensure their successful performance while others (e.g., poet and athlete) are minimally important so that fewer precautions have to be taken to ensure their successful performance. When a role is of the former sort, it should be filled by only the best qualified; and when it is of the latter type, it may be filled by the lesser qualified. Or so it would seem. Because the members of a democracy are agents of voluntary action, they normally should not be compelled to accept positions in the society. There are times, however, when there might be a morally relevant reason for compelling them to accept positions. Thus, physicians may be called into national service to cope with an epidemic or some other urgent public health problem, and all able-bodied members may be drafted into a nation's armed forces in the face of a war. Given the significance of voluntariness for the members of a democracy, however, they may be impressed into service only under two conditions: the service they are being compelled to perform must be sine qua non for the public interest, and there must be no viable alternative for getting the service performed. The crucial need for the service means that the service will help preserve the basic moral goods of the society, including the voluntariness and purposiveness of the members' actions. Moreover, the members of a democracy who are qualified for given positions do not have a moral right to withhold their service at a crucial time; for in withholding them, the members would violate the RPGC. Their action, despite its intent, would endanger the basic moral goods of their society and, thus, would endanger the rights that all other members, future as well as present, have to those goods. It could be argued that there is a condition under which the withholding of vital services from a given democracy might be morally proper: the withholding of the services, which would mean the dissolution of that state, would be morally acceptable if it would not violate the members' moral rights as seriously as the continued existence of the state would. However, under such a condition the society of concern would be only a sham or a shell of a democracy. At any rate, the performance of vital services for a democracy should be made involuntary only when there is no viable alternative.

Even if the members of a democracy who are best qualified to perform a given role are willing to perform it, however, they are not necessarily the ones who ought to perform it. It might be that the office is not so vital to the society that it has to be done by only the best-qualified, willing or not; and it might be that there are members who are less qualified, perhaps only marginally qualified, but who are willing to take the job in order to overcome some moral disadvantages greater than any suffered by the best-qualified. A moral disadvantage, it has been suggested (Chapter 2, Part V; Chapter 4, Part VI), is the absence of some proximate necessary condition for a voluntary agent's performance of any and all of his or her voluntary actions; it is brought on by a positive or negative constraint. Thus, it might be that some less-qualified members of a state might seek certain jobs mainly in order to get paychecks for purchasing adequate food, clothing, and shelter; whereas the best-qualified members might already have adequate food, clothing, and shelter and want the positions only as means to fulfill their career ambitions. If a democracy does have willing members who are not the best-qualified for a lesser role but suffer moral needs greater than those suffered by the best-qualified for the position, and if the former members can satisfy their moral needs by holding the position, the society morally should assign it to the former rather than to the latter members. The justification, quite simply, is that in a situation of this sort the former members' moral disadvantages outweigh the latter's and outweigh any need the society might have for expertise in the office, and that, moreover, the best-qualified may seek a role more nearly commensurate with their talents.[3] The same point applies *mutatis mutandis* to the whole range of job qualifications among all willing members of a democratic commonwealth: lesser positions should be parcelled out to members according to the society's need for expertise in the various offices, according to the moral disadvantages of the society's members willing to perform the roles, and according to the relevance of the individual members' having the positions to the removal of their respective moral disadvantages. As a rule of thumb, then, the poor ought to receive preferential treatment over the rich in the assignment of lesser jobs in a democracy. This does not mean, of course, that the rich should receive preferential treatment over the poor in the assignment of a democracy's more important offices.

Each member of a democratic state, it has been argued, has a moral right to whatever personal pursuits he or she wants to undertake within the bounds of the RPGC and of the basic principles, the ideals, and the laws of the society. As a rational agent each member has a right to undertake voluntarily personal pursuits; as a moral agent he or she has a right to undertake voluntarily any personal pursuit that is in keeping with the RPGC; and as a member of a democratic commonwealth he or she has a right to undertake voluntarily any personal pursuits that are consistent with the society's major principles and its ideals and laws. The most general kind of restriction that morality and democracy place upon a pursuit of personal interests is that the pursuit cannot interfere with any other agent's right to the major features of voluntary action.[4] Thus, the objects of some personal interests (such as firearms and pornography) may be pursued but within the confines of attentive social regulation; the objects of some personal interests (e.g., children as sex objects) may not be pursued at all; and the objects of some personal interests (such as cabinet making) may be pursued with a minimum of social concern. A more specific type of restriction is put on life ambitions by the distinction between evaluative and nonevaluative voluntary actions, the former being those whose ends are esteemed by the involved agents and the latter being those whose ends are not esteemed by the involved agents.

All other matters being equal, the agent of an evaluative voluntary action has a greater right to his or her action than does the agent of a similar voluntary action that is nonevaluative. In a democracy, therefore, members whose morally correct life ambitions entail only evaluative voluntary actions have a greater right to pursue their life ambitions than do members whose life ambitions comprise nonevaluative voluntary actions. Democracy does not regard the whimsical life as equal to the serious life.[5] Still another specific restriction is placed upon life ambitions by the RPP. According to this principle, it will be remembered, any agent whose qualifications for performing a morally correct action are greater than those of another for performing a similar morally right action has, in that respect, a claim to performing the action that is superior to any claim by the latter agent. So, while the members of a democratic society all have the right to undertake whatever morally acceptable life ambitions they want to undertake, they all do not necessarily have the same degree of claim to the right. Those with superior qualifications for pursuing a given morally proper personal interest have, with respect to qualifications, a stronger claim to the pursuit of the interest than do those with inferior qualifications. This does not necessarily mean that lesser-qualified members should never get to undertake life ambitions similar to those undertaken by the greater-qualified; but it does mean that when only the lesser- or the better-qualified members (not both) can undertake a similar life ambition and no greater moral considerations are at stake, the better-qualified are to receive preferential consideration. Hence, the democratic state does not view the incompetent member as equal to the talented member in personal pursuits.

But what is the priority relationship between the preference for evaluative voluntary action and that for superior qualifications? Does the former preference carry heavier weight than the latter? Is a lesser-qualified agent of a morally correct evaluative voluntary action to receive preference over a better-qualified agent of a nonevaluative voluntary action that is otherwise the same? An answer to the question can be had only if it is understood in what respect the former agent is lesser-qualified than the latter. Plainly, the former is *not* lesser-qualified in selecting the given action's goal; for in choosing the objective by evaluation, or rationally, instead of by whim or some other irrational factor, the former obviously is better-qualified as a rational agent for selecting the purpose. Accordingly, the respect in which he or she must be lesser-qualified is determining or employing the action as a means to its goal. The question, therefore, is whether or not a rational agent who is better-qualified for choosing the objective of a given action by virtue of being evaluative, but who is lesser-qualified for determining or performing the action as a means to achieve the objective, has a stronger claim to perform the action than does a rational agent who is lesser-qualified for selecting the purpose of the action but who is better-qualified for determining or utilizing the action as a means to fulfill the purpose. An answer that easily comes to mind is that each has a stronger claim to do what he or she is better-qualified to do: one agent has a stronger claim to establish the end of the action while the other has a stronger claim to determine or perform the action as a means to the end. In truth, this answer is especially apt for actions of social significance. Because of their various qualifications, some members of a society occasionally are given the task of formulating the goals of the society's actions impinging upon its interest if not its public interest; others are given the job of establishing means for attaining the goals; and still others are given the task of putting the means into operation. This is a division of labor widely recognized since the time of Plato. The difficulty with the answer is that it does not respond to the question as it bears upon actions that have significance mainly for individuals. These are actions where a division of labor of the sort just mentioned often is not feasible, even if conceptually possible. It does not help answer, for instance, this question: All other things being equal, who has the stronger claim to play a private game of chess, a person who understands and prizes the point of the game but is only an average player or a person who has no regard for the point of the game but is a superior player?

An answer that does address the question insofar as it relates to actions of private importance is that the agent of the evaluative voluntary action has the superior claim. One justification for the answer was suggested in our original discussion of morality (Chapter 2, Part IV): Any morally proper evaluative voluntary action is more fully rational than is any morally proper nonevaluative voluntary action and, thus, is more fitting as an object of performance by a rational agent than is any such action of the latter sort. Another justification concerns the logical point that a morally right evaluative voluntary action is more valuable to its agent than a morally correct nonevaluative voluntary action is valuable to its agent. This is because the former agent appreciates the purpose that he or she is to fulfill by the action whereas the latter does not. Because of this greater worth, the former agent has a larger interest, as a rational agent, in the action he or she performs than the latter has, as a rational agent, in his or her action. Hence, participation in the game does not matter as much to the superior chess player of the above example as it does to the inferior player. The superior player will gain or miss something in playing or not playing the game, but so will the inferior player. On the other hand, the inferior player will miss or gain something in achieving or not achieving the end of the game that the superior player will not miss or gain. A society, of course, might not have to face the prospect of treating agents of morally right evaluative voluntary actions preferentially to agents of morally correct nonevaluative voluntary actions. The resources of the society might be so abundant and the members of the society might be so cooperative that no conflicts between such agents would ever arise and, therefore, that no official policy or action regarding such conflicts would ever be called for. If, however, a society, democratic or otherwise, has to show preference between the two sorts of agents and does so according to the position that has been argued here, it gives no one cause for charges of morally unfair treatment. The agents of the nonevaluative voluntary actions may say that they have been treated worse than those of the evaluative voluntary actions, but they may not say that they should have been treated better than or even the same as the latter.

To show further the importance of valued aims in extending preferential treatment, let us examine a somewhat complicated case.[6] John, reared in a home of classical musicians, loves classical music, sees its cultural meaning, and wants to be a concert pianist; but despite much training he cannot play exceptionally well. Barbara, reared in a ghetto and with no acquaintance with classical music, was exposed to the piano in school and turned out to have extraordinary talent for the instrument, even being able to play and interpret very well whatever music is put before her. A conservatory receives applications from John and Barbara. Which applicant should be preferred? Barbara should be if the conservatory believes that she can learn to esteem the point of classical music and that John will never learn to play well enough. John should be preferred if the conservatory believes that the piano world has no need for any more technicians; that Barbara will never be more than an excellent technician with a whimsical respect for her craft; and that John can learn, under the conservatory's tutelage, to play competently. There are conditions, of course, under which John and Barbara should be ranked equally. For instance, if the conservatory believes that John will never learn to play well enough and that Barbara will never learn to appreciate classical music, it should rank them both as equally unacceptable. And if it believes John will learn to play well enough and Barbara will learn to appreciate classical music, it should rank them both as equally acceptable. So even though the conservatory, by the nature of its institutional function, must emphasize the actual and potential talent of its applicants, it still, also by the nature of its institutional function, must assess that talent as it relates to the individual applicants' appreciations of the point of the talent.

Plainly, however, there can be no morally equitable distribution of a democracy's goods, services, and offices and no equality of life ambitions for the society's members unless certain conditions obtain.[7] To the extent that goods, services, and offices are to be allocated with reference to the value of the various institutional roles played by the members of a democracy, the members must be informed of and appreciative of the significance of the goods, services, and offices for the society's public interest. Otherwise, those members responsible for allocating these matters will not know or care about the right way for disbursing them, and the other members will not be able to know or care when these matters are dispensed correctly. This condition in turn presupposes that all members be informed and appreciative of the society's intentions to provide security and order—the providing of which embodies the removal of positive constraints— and to remove negative constraints. Otherwise, the distributors of goods, services, and offices might not give these intentions the priority that they deserve; and the other members might not understand or care about the priority. Insofar as the goods, services, and offices of a democratic state are to be allocated with respect to its members' moral disadvantages, whether incurred because of state policy or not, all members must be aware of and concerned with the disadvantages, including the degrees of severity among them. Otherwise the members responsible for distributing the goods and services might neglect the disadvantages in performing their roles, and other members might not care about or might even resent the distribution of the goods and services with regards to the disadvantages. The conditions just described, however, presuppose other conditions. The members of a democratic state cannot obtain information relevant to their society's ideals, policies, and actions and pertinent to their moral disadvantages unless they enjoy the freedom of inquiry and of expression; and to employ inquiry and expression to garner relevant information, they must guide that inquiry and expression by the moral and political principles of the democratic commonwealth. Accordingly, the morally fair disbursement of goods, services, and offices in a democracy depends upon a freedom of inquiry and expression guided by moral and political principles. Neither a value-neutral science nor a disinterested press will do here.

The conditions that must hold if there is to be equality of life ambitions in a democratic commonwealth are somewhat different from the ones prerequisite to an equitable allocation of goods, services, and positions in such a society. First, the members of a democracy must recognize and be disposed to esteem the voluntariness, purposiveness, and evaluativeness of each other's voluntary actions; for if they do not, they will not perceive and value one another's personal pursuits, which are a mode of their voluntary actions. Second, they have to understand and appreciate that the right to voluntary action belongs to each other not just because they are members of their society or of a society of a democratic form but also because they all are rational agents. Otherwise, any equality of their life ambitions would be legal or political only; it would not be moral. Third, and last, they have to recognize and prize the talents requisite for voluntary actions; for if they do not, they will neither comprehend nor accept the RPP as applicable to the equality of personal pursuits. These three conditions, of course, are features that previously have been shown to be logically embedded in the concept of rational agency; hence, they are conditions that should be expected to obtain in a democracy, whose members are supposed to be rational agents. The same is true of our description of the conditions that have to obtain if there is to be a morally fair disbursement of goods, services, and offices in a democratic commonwealth; that description too is largely, if not completely, tautological. The point in specifying all of these conditions, therefore, is not to state anything that has not already been declared at least implicitly, but it is to show something of practical significance. While the members of an ideal democracy necessarily are rational agents and only rational agents, those of an actual democracy, as we have explained, might not be rational agents at all times and places. Actual democracies, therefore, will have moral equality only to the extent that their members are rational agents. So, in spelling out how moral equality in a democracy logically depends upon rational agency, we have specified those conditions that actual democracies must establish if they are to have moral equality.

III

IT IS ONE THING TO EXPLAIN what social equality is in the democratic state; it is quite another to explain how education might contribute to social equality by performing its moral role in democracy. The problem, it should be noted, is quite different from the input-output problem of schooling and equality in America discussed a decade or more ago by sociological analysts. The problem they addressed was whether or not increased expenditures on schooling would improve the distribution of incomes and social status among the products of schooling.[8] Our question is one to be answered by logical argument while theirs was to be answered by empirical investigation. Moreover, ours concerns education and equality, not just schooling and equality.

The central and ultimate learning object of education, it will be remembered, is a comprehensive understanding based on the theoretical disciplines. And this understanding has both necessary and contingent elements (Chapter 6, Part II). Both kinds of elements can be furnished to the members of a democracy in such a way that they will help promote an equitable distribution of goods and services among the members.

One of the theoretical disciplines that can be very useful in this regard is philosophical morals, which seeks mainly to determine, by an appeal to fundamental reasons, basic standards of moral conduct. Through a study of philo-sophical morals the members can learn about the meaning of rational agency, the importance of evaluativeness and voluntariness for rational agents, the kinds of disadvantages that rational agents might suffer, and the cannons of moral discussion. Insofar as they understand these things, the members of a democ-racy will be prepared to understand themselves, individually and collectively, as rational agents, to esteem evaluativeness and voluntariness for themselves and all other rational agents, to be cognizant of the possibility of moral disadvan-tages among themselves and others; and to engage in discourse with one another about moral problems. And to the extent that members accomplish these goals, they will be in a position to comprehend, shape, and regard as worthy policies of their state to allocate goods and services so as to remove positive and negative constraints and to give priority in so doing to those members with the greater moral disadvantages. The study of philosophical morals may and should be re-lated, with the aid of contingent elements, especially to the members' lives. With reference to such elements, students may examine specific possible pur-poses (e.g., becoming school teachers or corporation lawyers) for their worthi-ness, weigh specific alternative courses of action (e.g., borrowing money or working to finance a college education) for their moral rectitude as well as their efficiency, effectiveness, and other qualities as means, and become aware of pos-itive and negative constraints in their own society (e.g., poverty, drug abuse, and physical handicaps). Thereby, students will become cognizant of and mor-ally sensitive to the major features of voluntary action in the society. While the study of philosophical morals and of moral cases is quite appropriate to formal educational institutions, it may and ought to be supplemented and reinforced by necessary and contingent ingredients learned within informal educational in-stitutions. Families, churches, neighborhoods, literature, cinema, television, and the like can furnish information and help mold habits and values that con-tribute to an awareness of and respect for voluntariness and evaluativeness in the context of a particular democracy, a sensitivity to positive and negative con-straints in that society, and skills for and appreciation of public discussion of oral problems in the society. In any event, informal learning about morality in a democracy is likely to begin before formal learning about it. This means, as al-ready suggested (Chapter 7, Parts II and IV), that the formal and the informal educational institutions of a democracy must be interactive with one another.

Other theoretical disciplines that can be quite helpful are political philoso-phy and political science. The former seeks principally to establish, by an appeal to basic reasons, fundamental standards of social organization while the latter strives mainly to provide, by an appeal to facts as well as to fundamental reasons, general descriptions and explanations of social organization. Through the study of these disciplines, students can gain an understanding of democracy that will enable them to comprehend its primary principles, intentions, and institutions. To the extent that they do, they will be in a position to understand and appreciate why a democracy needs to disburse its goods and services according to certain intentions and according to the individual importances that institutional roles have within the society. With the aid of courses in history, government, and social problems, students can learn the particularities of their own society's principles, ideals, institutions, and existential conditions. Thus, they will be able to have a grasp of the relative weights that need to be given to the society's expenditures on military defense, police activities, health services, food, clothing, housing, and so forth. Further information, habits, and attitudes concerning the society's principles, ideals, and institutions can and should be gained from experiences in informal educational institutions. For instance, parents can relate to their children an understanding of the society's particularities; and the media can provide a continuing education to the society's members, including those who are parents, about changes relevant to the allocation of goods and services within the society.

With regard to understanding the morally equitable distribution of positions in a democratic commonwealth, the necessary ingredients of the practice of education are rather helpful. Studies dealing with the subject matters, basic principles, and methods of the natural and social sciences will help members grasp issues and problems related to state interests, most notably issues and problems of a technological nature. Hence, they will help prepare members to occupy the roles of voters and public officials and help qualify them to hold positions in economic and other noncivil institutions. In addition, studies in social theory (e.g., political philosophy, political science, and sociology) will help members to grasp that each role in a society has a value for that society, that the occupant of a role has to have the qualifications called for by that role, that some roles are crucially important to a society while some are not; that the crucially important ones require occupants with the highest qualifications available, whereas those not crucially important need not be occupied by the best-qualified; and that the occupant of a role has the social value that he or she has because of the role itself, not merely because of any personal qualities that he or she has. To the extent that these concepts are grasped, the members of a democracy will recognize that they should seek to occupy positions only if they want to contribute to their society in the ways that the positions individually are supposed to contribute, that they should be cognizant of the relative priorities that qualifications and moral disadvantages have in the assignment of offices, and that even though the social value of a member to a morally proper democracy might not be high, it is of moral value and, for that reason, deserving of moral respect from all other members of the society. The contingent elements of the practice of education in a democracy also are able to contribute to the morally fair allocation of offices in the society. They can provide and instill information, skills, dispositions, and values particularly relevant to the positions of the given society. They are able to give an understanding of the particular problems of the society's public interest and of how particular positions within the society contribute to its public interest. They can indicate what qualifications are needed for various positions within the society. And they are able to furnish a comprehension of the particular moral disadvantages present in the society.

It has to be stressed that the necessary and contingent elements ought to be taught in such a way that the relationships among the different elements may be grasped by students. There are various ways in which this may be accomplished, as suggested already (Chapter 7, Part II). The necessary ingredients do not always have to be taught in the same classes with the contingent ones, nor do the contingent elements always have to be taught along with necessary ones. But the two sorts must be taught together with regularity and for significant periods of students' lives.[9] Moreover, it has to be emphasized that the necessary and contingent elements should be offered by formal educational institutions interactively with informal educational institutions, which are able to reinforce and add to what the formal ones do in contributing to a morally just assignment of offices in a democracy. Some informal educational institutions, such as families, can introduce members to the notion of moral respect, roles, qualifications, and moral disadvantage. Others, such as institutional agencies, can provide informal training for positions. And still others, namely the mass media, can keep members informed of current happenings and trends related to institutional roles.

Some of the contributions that the formal practice of education can make to a morally equitable disbursement of personal pursuits in a democracy should be rather obvious. Studies of the theoretical disciplines can lead to information, skills, dispositions, and appreciations of general significance for careers, hobbies, recreation, and other modes of personal pursuits. Course work bearing on the given society's existential conditions can provide information and stimulate interest in the sorts of personal pursuits available in the society. And vocational studies, ranging from those about the professions to those about manual trades, are able to furnish and encourage information, skills, dispositions, and values of particular importance to personal pursuits in the society. Other contributions by formal education are less obvious. Student performances, insofar as they are matters of discussion, instruction, training, and rational conditioning, can enable students to become aware and appreciative of evaluativeness, purposiveness, and voluntariness. Such performances also can help students to become cognizant of their respective academic talents and, thus, of personal qualifications for tasks. Still further, such performances can enable students to learn to value qualifications for tasks by allowing them to experience satisfaction in successful activities as well as dissatisfaction in unsuccessful activities. For those students suffering moral disadvantages, formal educational institutions can provide diagnostic services and institute corrective programs for remedial disadvantages.

The contributions that can come from informal educational institutions are partially similar to the ones coming from formal educational institutions. Families and mass media can be sources of information and values on what specific careers, hobbies, recreational activities, and other personal pursuits are available in a given democratic society. Informal institutions can help members of the society to discover their talents and interests by providing them with opportunities for voluntary action. And on-the-job training and other informal institutions can furnish particular information, skills, dispositions, and values required for engaging in personal pursuits in the society. One contribution that might be made by the family is different from those mentioned with reference to formal educational institutions. To young members of a given democracy, parents can be models of what it means to have a career, of what it means to make a sensible use of leisure time, and of what it means to have qualifications for an activity.

IV

BECAUSE OUR DISCUSSION of how education's moral role in the democratic state promotes social equality makes important references to the notion of qualifications, it strongly suggests that the role encourages a meritocratic policy for education. The role, it is admitted, does do this by calling for education to identify and develop talents that will be serviceable to the civil and noncivil institutions of a democracy. Nevertheless, the discussion is not liable to the criticism usually heaped upon meritocratic education in recent times. This is because these criticisms are aimed at meritocratic education of a bad sort, not at meritocratic education in general, even though they are meant to pertain to the latter.

A philosopher who has regarded meritocratic education as essentially opposed to moral justice is John Rawls. According to Rawls's conception of the matter, meritocratic education is education in a meritocratic society, which society distributes positions according to talents and aims at wealth and power;[10] and meritocratic education has the primary function of identifying and developing the socially useful talents of the society's members. Plainly, then, equal educational opportunity is important in such education; for it is the means whereby the socially useful talents of each member of the society may be spotted and trained. But equal educational opportunity in meritocratic education has a special significance: it means that all members have an equal opportunity to compete with each other in proving their respective socially useful talents. Those whose talents show themselves worthy of further development receive more education than do those whose talents do not show themselves deserving of further development. As Rawls states, meritocratic society allots its educational resources "according to the return as estimated in productive trained abilities"; it does not distribute, in a major way, such resources "according to their worth in enriching the personal and social life of citizens, including here the less favored."[11] Consequently, equal educational opportunity enables students to prepare themselves, according to their talents, in the personal pursuit of "economic prosperity and political dominion" while preparing themselves for social roles. The students proving to have greater socially useful talents qualify to occupy roles with greater benefits than the roles suitable to the students with lesser socially useful talents.

For Rawls meritocratic education suffers three faults. First, it promotes self-esteem at the expense of others because, in its effort to identify and develop the socially useful talents of students, it encourages the more successful students to regard themselves as especially socially estimable and to do things worthwhile, and it fosters the attitude in the more unsuccessful students that they are not especially socially estimable and are not capable of doing much of value. Second, meritocratic education violates Rawls's Difference Principle, which holds that "social and economic inequalities are to be arranged so that they are both (a) reasonably expected to be to everyone's advantage, and (b) attached to positions and offices open to all."[12] By helping to develop the socially useful talents of students, equal educational opportunity puts students in a position to pursue personal wealth and personal political power. Moreover, because the wealth and power to be obtained will be commensurate with the talents developed, the highly successful students will be able to become much more wealthy and powerful than the markedly less successful ones. Hence, meritocratic education will enable the more talented to acquire wealth and power that will not benefit the least talented. Third, Rawls views meritocratic education as rationally unacceptable. Before entering a meritocratic society, people would not be able to know that education in it would give them self-esteem at the expense of others or vice versa; nor would they be able to know if education in the society would enable them to accumulate personal wealth and power while others do not or vice versa.

Even though these criticisms apply to meritocratic education as conceived by Rawls, they do not apply to all conceptions of it; and they certainly do not apply to the meritocratic aspects that we have proposed for education in a democracy. First, the charge that meritocratic education promotes self-esteem at the expense of others holds only because Rawls has ignored the significance of morality for such education. While education in a meritocratic society does spot and develop the socially useful talents of students, it also may identify and develop moral traits in students; and if it assumes the latter task, it may encourage in all students the attitude that any socially useful talent not only constitutes a basis for self-esteem but makes the subject of that talent important to the society. Thus, it may foster the attitude among the members of a democratic commonwealth to respect not only themselves individually as rational agents but also one another for the contributions that they severally make to the society. Second, the claim that meritocratic education will enable highly successful students to become much more wealthy and powerful than the markedly less successful ones and, therefore, acquire wealth and power that will not benefit the least talented stands up only by ignoring that the training of talents might guide students to become devoted to the public interest. This, it will be recalled, is the direction that our conception of education's moral role in democracy will take students. Third, the point that meritocratic education is rationally unacceptable is allowable only if one discounts the place of morality in education. Before entering a meritocratic society, a person can distinguish between a meritocratic education without morality and one with morality, and between meritocratic education with morality that does not foster self-esteem in all members and does not advocate the Difference Principle and one with morality that does promote self-respect in all citizens and other members and advocates the Difference Principle.

Besides rebutting these criticisms, however, we also must stress that Rawls's conception of meritocratic education is questionable. Such education, Rawls says, serves to identify and develop socially useful talents in a meritocratic society, which society distributes its offices strictly according to talents and aims at wealth and power. The difficulty with this conception is twofold. For one thing, it insists that meritocratic education must belong to what Rawls calls a meritocratic society. What is wrong here is that education may be meritocratic (i.e., may identify and develop socially useful talents) while belonging to a society that does not satisfy Rawls's description of a meritocratic society. Thus, education in England and the United States has been meritocratic; but even if these nations have wealth and power as ideals, which is somewhat dubious, they do not distribute positions according to talents and talents only. Social connections, family, disadvantage, and the popular will are criteria also used in allocating offices. For another thing, Rawls's conception maintains that a meritocratic society aims at wealth and power, which is highly doubtful. The societies envisioned by Plato and Thomas Jefferson, to name only two, are generally regarded as meritocratic: both are understood widely to take socially useful talents as a major criterion for disbursing positions. Neither society, however, has wealth or power for an objective. Plato proposes for society's purpose a life lived according to reason, and Jefferson sets forth for society's goal a life lived according to the moral natural order. It is submitted, therefore, that Rawls castigates meritocratic education only because he conceives it as belonging to a society that employs talents as the only standard for distributing offices, and that poses wealth and power as its ideals. Such a society is morally bad and wrong for Rawls; thus, if meritocratic education has to be integral to such a society, it has to be morally bad and wrong too. But, as we have argued, it does not have to pertain to a society of the sort.

Although it might be conceded that our view of what education can do, in performing its moral role in a democratic state, to foster social equality is not subject to the criticisms directed by Rawls at meritocratic education, it might also be insisted that our position is seriously flawed. More specifically, it might be argued that our view could encourage social inequality just as much as it could foster social equality. This possibility has to do with the inequality of results that are likely to flow from the practice of education.

According to our discussion, so the argument might go, we have allowed that those who become educated do not necessarily become educated to the same degree. Some might learn more about the theoretical disciplines than others might; some might relate more thoroughly or more accurately what they know about the theoretical disciplines to their other mentals and to the objects of their experiences. So, to the extent that the practice of education in a democracy turns out products with different levels of quality, it will produce members with various levels of qualifications for performing the society's institutional roles and with various levels of capacities for pursuing life ambitions. What will happen, then, is that the best-educated will get the best offices and engage in the most worthy personal pursuits, whereas the less-educated will occupy the lesser positions and undertake less desirable life ambitions. Of course, none of this would be a case of unjust inequality if the students who turned out less educated did so willfully. Moreover, none of this would be an instance of unjust inequality if those turning out less educated did so because of forces beyond the control of their society. Nevertheless, any member of a democratic state who receives a lesser education that is involuntary on his part and that results from circumstances controlled by the society is a case of unjust inequality; and the history of education testifies that societies, democratic ones included, do allow or even encourage some of their members to receive, in a compulsory way or unwittingly, lesser education. One need look no farther than contemporary America, where the disparity between the education obtained by the students of affluent suburbs and that obtained by the children of migrant workers is an indisputable mark of unjust inequality.[13] To be sure, it might be better that those suffering moral disadvantages as a result of the practices of educational institutions in a democratic commonwealth receive preferential treatment in the allocation of goods and services and of positions in the society than that they receive no compensation; but such preferential treatment, which is at best a poor substitute for social justice, might come to function as a mollifier of the disadvantaged and, thus, as a perpetuator of social inequality in a democratic state. Perhaps then such preferential treatment is morally wrong in a democracy.

In response to this argument it is acknowledged that the practice of education in a democratic commonwealth is likely to have uneven results. While it is possible that some students voluntarily will not seek to be educated as much as others, it is likely also that more students will be less educated than others apart from any volition on their part. Some students might be born with genetic defects that inhibit their being educated as much as others. Some might have family situations that discourage or at least do not foster interests in education. Some might associate with peers who prize noneducational matters more highly than educational ones. And some might attend formal educational institutions that have teachers and programs inferior to those of other such institutions.[14] Indeed, it is quite possible that a portion of the students in a democracy might suffer inferior educations not because of their individual circumstances but because of certain existential conditions of the society, to wit: that segment of students belongs to a group that historically has been treated unjustly in the society and, insofar, has been handicapped in its educational experience. The vestiges of past racial, ethnic, and sexist injustices persist today in democratic states; and they have burdened their victims in the field of education. Moreover it is acknowledged that the forces bringing about unequally educated students in a democracy might be within the society's control. We cannot concede, however, that any of this shows that our view of what education can do, in performing its moral role in a democratic state, to promote social equality allows education to foster social inequality as well.

The reason why it does not demonstrate this has to do with the objectives of the democratic state. Being subject to the principle of the workability of self-government, the democratic state must pursue interests and only those interests compatible with the major features of the voluntary action of its members. Thus, it is bound to remove the positive and negative constraints of its members' actions. The educational handicaps suffered by a student may be construed as positive or negative constraints. For instance, if a married woman wants to attend school or college, but cannot because her husband wants her at home, she suffers a positive constraint; and if she cannot because she lacks the financial resources to do so, she suffers a negative constraint. Just as the democratic state is bound to remove all other remediable positive and negative constraints affecting its members, it is obligated to remove all corrigible educational handicaps affecting them. Hence, it has the duty to promote conditions in families, peer groups, and other informal educational institutions that support students in efforts to become educated. It has the duty to ensure that the quality of teachers and programs in all its schools and colleges is as high as is practically attainable. And it has the duty to do what it can to prevent, eliminate, and alleviate genetic educational disorders.[15]

As indicated elsewhere (Chapter 4, Part III), a democratic commonwealth's obligation to remove eliminable educational handicaps does not entail that the society's government logically has to assume direct regulation of education. Whether or not the government should have direct control of education is ultimately a question of which institutions in the society are likely to be most effective in controlling educational activities, which is to say that it is ultimately an empirical question. Thus, an answer to the question is contingent upon an inspection of the facts relevant to each democracy's existential conditions. Moreover, it has to be emphasized that the measures a given democratic state should take to remove educational handicaps are likely to be varied in kind, different in scope, and more or less approximate to educational activities. Some measures might be relatively simple, restricted in scope, and close to the educational scene (e.g., upgrading teacher qualifications and strengthening scholastic and collegiate programs). Others, however, might be relatively complex, pervasive, and distant (e.g., changes in real estate and tax laws, modifications in employment and population policies, alterations in narcotics laws, and changes in cultural values). While the democratic state has a duty to remove the eliminable handicaps of its members, it has other duties too. Accordingly, it has to define the priority to be given to removing the handicaps. Because the abolition of educational handicaps contributes to social equality, it should receive a high priority in a democracy. Indeed, there are very few matters that ought to receive a higher priority in such a society. Emergencies where the existence of the state is threatened obviously should have a greater priority, and problems whose solutions are presupposed by the removal of educational handicaps plainly ought to receive a greater priority. More generally, it is submitted that the elimination of educational handicaps should have a lower priority than do other policies only to the extent that the expenditures on it threaten to weaken the infrastructure on which it rests—namely, a sound educational system, state security, civil order, a healthy economy, relevant scientific and technological progress, and social institutions favoring moral respect.

It is recognized that even if a democratic state were to remedy all corrigible educational handicaps in its midst, it still might witness uneven results among its members, which is to say that some students might become more educated than others. The reasons for this possible outcome are easy to see. There might be students who choose freely and knowingly not to become educated fully,[16] and there might be others who suffer educational handicaps that are not remediable. To be sure, unequal educational results even in a democracy that has removed all remediable educational handicaps from its members will affect the distribution of positions and personal pursuits in the society: the best-educated are likely to receive the best positions and have the most worthy personal pursuits, whereas the less-educated are likely to receive the lesser positions and have less desirable personal pursuits. Nevertheless, uneven educational outcomes are not unjust inequalities in a society that has done all that it reasonably can to eliminate educational handicaps; and the allocation of offices and the personal pursuits shaped by such outcomes are not unjust inequalities either. The uneven educational results are misfortunes, and the distribution of positions and the differentiation among personal pursuits are misfortunes too. Misfortune, however, is not necessarily a sign of unjust inequality. Unjust inequality in a democratic state is not a lack of sameness in condition; it is, rather, a condition that arises from unfair treatment by a society. If a society does nothing to remove the educational handicaps of its members when it can, it acts unfairly; and if it eliminates educational handicaps of some of its members but fails to remove the same kinds of handicaps belonging to other members, it acts unfairly. If, however, a society does all that it can to eliminate all the educational handicaps of all its members, it acts fairly. Any uneven educational results brought about by willfulness of students or by incorrigible educational handicaps are beyond the control of the society and, thus, are not matters of unfair treatment by the society. A similar claim may be made about the distribution of positions and the pursuits of personal interests in the society that are affected by such educational outcomes. In any event, the educational disadvantages that are involuntary for their sufferers but allowed by society demand justice; and preferential consideration is an appropriate way to deal with them justly.[17]

Moral Education

I

WHILE IT HAS BEEN STRESSED that the learning of morality is essential for the members of a democracy, it has not been explained what the learning of morality in a democracy is. More specifically, we have not examined, among other issues, the connection between moral education and education, whether or not moral education is necessary for the learning of morality in a democratic state, whether or not morality in a democracy is to be learned formally, whether or not the members of a democratic commonwealth have to be educated in our moral theory, and whether or not moral education in a democracy is developmental. These issues will now be discussed.

II

IF MORAL EDUCATION IS UNDERSTOOD, as it is here, to be a matter of education rather than any enculturation in any set of moral beliefs, it has to consist of a kind of comprehensive understanding learned through certain types of learning activities. Moral education, to be sure, is not one and the same thing as education. The educated person is morally educated, but the morally educated person might not be educated in all respects. Albert Schweitzer, who was eminent as a missionary, concert organist, physician, and moral philosopher, was a thoroughly educated person. If, however, he had been a moral philosopher and humanitarian who was largely ignorant of atomic physics and classical music, he would have been morally educated but educationally deficient in some areas.

The sense in which moral education is an aspect of education has to do especially with the cognitive perspective involved in the former. The comprehensive understanding of an educated person is his or her relating certain statements to his or her other mentals and the objects of his or her experiences—statements that the person justifiably believes or seriously entertains, that pertain to all subject-matter areas of the theoretical disciplines, and that can be justified by including all the methods and basic principles of these disciplines. By contrast, the cognitive perspective that an educated person has in the respect that he or she is morally educated emphasizes moral matters. The statements related to other mentals and objects of experience may be moral statements—namely, judgments, rules, or precepts of interpersonal actions, or statements simply of moral import (e.g., factual claims about interpersonal actions). The other mentals to which statements are related may be moral statements or statments of moral import only; or they may be skills, dispositions, and appreciations of moral significance.[1] The experiential objects to which the person relates statements might be interpersonal actions, concrete moral agents, physical resources, or societies and their institutions. Thus, the statements related to one another may pertain to any or all of the subject matters of the theoretical disciplines; what is significant about them for the morally educated person is that they are moral statements or at least have moral significance. That statements concerned with the subject matter of moral philosophy might be moral statements is trivially true, and that statements about the subject matters of the sciences and aesthetic theory often have been regarded as having moral significance barely needs mention.[2] At any rate the related statements integral to a moral comprehensive understanding, including any conclusions determined through the understanding, must be justifiable by the methods and basic principles of the relevant theoretical disciplines. If the statements are moral, they must satisfy the methods and basic principles of moral philosophy; if they are mathematical or scientific, they must follow the methods and basic principles of mathematics or the sciences.

Our insistence that the theoretical disciplines occupy a key spot in moral education appears to pose a difficulty. Schemata of the theoretical disciplines may be diverse. They may relate these disciplines to one another in different ways, and some of them may omit intellectual fields that others include. Thus, Aristotle's schema allows for more than one ranking of the theoretical disciplines whereas August Comte's permits only one; and Aristotle's schema contains philosophy and mathematics while Comte's schema, which recognizes only the natural and social sciences, does not. Yet, no one type of schema is essential to our conception of education; any may function as a basis of

education.³ It is possible, therefore, that a specific idea of education will include
a schema of the theoretical disciplines that leaves out moral philosophy; and if
an idea of education were to incorporate a schema of this sort, it would seem to
exclude any theoretical foundation for morality and, accordingly, exclude moral
education. Accordingly, our claim that moral education is an aspect of education would not hold.

The difficulty raised here, however, has more appearance than reality.
Even if it is acknowledged that some specific conception of education might rest
upon a schema of the theoretical disciplines that excludes moral philosophy and
any other field that might provide normative principles of action, it is not conceded that such a concept of education logically excludes moral education as an
aspect of education. Moral judgment involves a grasp of relevant facts in addition to a knowledge of appropriate standards of conduct. Just as in jurispru-
dence one must know the facts of a given case as well as what law applies to the
case, so in moral understanding one must know the facts of a given situation as
well as what precepts or rules apply to the situation. A morally educated person,
consequently, must comprehend both the facts and the precepts and rules relevant to moral situations. A theoretical understanding of facts necessarily rests,
wholly or partially, upon the sciences, natural or social. And while a theoretical
comprehension of moral precepts and rules might rest, according to some schemata of the theoretical disciplines, partly upon moral philosophy, it does rest,
according to each and every schema of such disciplines, at least partly upon the
sciences—especially the social sciences. This is because any moral principle,
whether it is justifiable or not, is a statement and, in that respect, is a matter of
fact; as such it can be explained from the standpoint of some science. For instance, the logical positivists and others of this century who expunged moral
philosophy from the theoretical disciplines showed how moral statements could
be interpreted as emotive expressions and how moral reasoning could be regarded as a kind of persuasion.⁴ Accordingly, if education embodies a schema of
the theoretical disciplines that omits moral philosophy and anything else like
moral philosophy, it will still contain moral education as an aspect of education
because it will provide for a theoretical comprehension of morality from the
standpoint of the sciences. A theoretical grasp of morality, of course, is not necessarily a comprehensive understanding of morality. A moral education based
upon something like a Comtean schema of the theoretical disciplines logically
embodies more than a scientific understanding of morality. It also includes *inter
alia* relating this understanding to concrete moral situations and learning the
dispositions and attitudes appropriate to such situations. The moral theory
advanced in this inquiry does look upon moral philosophy as a theoretical

discipline. However, because our analysis of education was formulated independently of that theory, our analysis does not logically discount specific conceptions of education that exclude moral philosophy from the theoretical disciplines.

III

WHILE IT IS THE CASE that moral education is an essential facet of education, it is not the case that moral education for a democratic state is an essential aspect of moral education. The person with a moral education suitable to a member of a democracy is morally educated, to be sure; but a person can also have a moral education not appropriate for membership in a democracy. Even if the principles ingredient to his or her education support membership in the democratic commonwealth, which they need not, some of the other statements, the experiential objects, and the skills, dispositions, and appreciations integral to the education might be especially pertinent to an aristocracy or some other kind of nondemocratic society. Although Abraham Lincoln held moral precepts that were compatible with democracy, he also had prejudices about blacks that were incompatible with it. Moral education for the democratic state is moral education with a special orientation to membership in such a body politic. This orientation concerns the given comprehensive understanding; but it relates also to the enabling factors of voluntary action as well as to the skills, dispositions, and appreciation contained by the education. It even concerns the learning activities involved in the education.

Some of the statements integral to an educational cognitive perspective proper to membership in a democracy must recognize that the main characteristics of voluntary action—voluntariness, purposiveness, and evaluativeness—are moral goods and rights. This is so because moral goods and rights are politically crucial for the democratic commonwealth; they are ideals of the society, constitutents of the public interest, and essential goods and rights of the members of that state (Chapter 4, Parts II and IV). While the statements presenting the major features of voluntary action as moral goods and rights must function as moral principles, they need not serve as basic moral principles. In our moral theory, the statements presenting the characteristics as moral goods and rights do function as fundamental moral principles; thus, an educational comprehensive understanding relying upon our moral theory necessarily would contain these statements as basic moral principles. That theory, however, is not the only theory through which the major traits of voluntary action might be viewed as moral goods and rights. It would not be surprising to find these traits regarded as moral goods and rights by, for instance, some theory in the natural law or utilitarian tradition. After all, Aristotle thought of deliberativeness and evaluativeness as excellences of the intellect;[5] and John Stuart Mill took them, along with voluntariness, as elements of happiness.[6] Insofar as an educational cognitive perspective might include statements of these characteristics as less than fundamental moral principles, it does not have to embody the moral theory we have been advocating. Accordingly, while moral education for the democratic commonwealth has to foster values and rights embedded in our moral theory, it does not have to foster them from the standpoint of that theory; it may use some other theory that recognizes the same values and rights.

Statements of the moral values and rights of voluntary action are not the only statements that are elements of a moral education for the democratic state. In a body politic, moral principles may be utilized as standards to formulate and assess the society's laws and other policies. Hence, a moral education befitting a state must give a person the ability to interrelate statements of the moral principles of voluntary action with statements of the society's laws and other policies; and to be prepared to do that, a person must have learned statements of the laws and policies. Being able to interrelate such statements is especially important for the government of a democracy. Accordingly, the teaching and learning of statements of the laws and other policies of the democratic commonwealth are parts of a moral education suitable to the society. Still other statements that must be ingredients in such an education are statements of the society's existential conditions; statements of its various institutional roles, both civil and noncivil; and statements of the noninstitutional activities of the society's members. The members of a democracy or a state of any other kind cannot fully understand its interests unless they relate the last type (statements of the noninstitutional activities of the society's members) to the society's existential conditions—conditions ranging from geographic, economic, and political, to vocational, aesthetic, and religious. Some existential conditions of a society may be known directly by experience; but others, such as historical conditions, have to be known through statements. Moreover, public discussion of the society's existential conditions necessarily involves statements of the conditions, including those that may be experienced immediately. Because, therefore, the members of a democracy cannot have a comprehensive understanding of the moral aspects of the state's interests without possessing statements of the involved existential conditions, they have to learn such statements as a part of their moral education. Although all members of a democratic commonwealth have to learn statements of the society's various institutional roles, they all need not learn the same statements of all the roles. Those who occupy or are to occupy positions not held or not to be held by others will require statements of institutional roles not needed by the others. In sum, the statements of institutional duties that are involved in moral education for a democracy have to vary among members according to the different institutional roles to which the members individually are committed. Similarly, the statements in a democracy's moral education that are about the opportunities, values, and rights relating to noninstitutional activities need to differ among members according to the diverse noninstitutional activities in which the members individually are interested.

While a morally educated member of the democratic commonwealth must be prepared to interrelate statements of the moral principles of voluntary action with statements of the society's policies, existential conditions, instituional roles, and noninstitutional activities, the member also must be ready to relate all these statements to objects he or she might experience (e.g., other concrete members of the society, physical actions, physical possessions of institutions and corporate members of the society, economic commodities, and natural environmental factors). The member surely does not need to apply the statements to an experiential object each and every time it is encountered, but he or she does need to apply them to objects experienced that have moral importance. Hence, the purchase and use of tobacco products call for moral judgment as do the purchase and use of goods imported from an antidemocratic country.

Just as the constituent statements of a moral education in democratic society are somewhat different from those of a moral education in any other kind of state, so the skills, dispositions, and appreciations pertinent to moral education in the democratic commonwealth are special. For instance, rather than allowing members to draw inferences haphazardly, moral education in a democracy must foster skills in making judgments about the society's policies, institutions, and members' moral actions with respect to the moral principles of voluntary action as well as with respect to appropriate facts. Making such judgments requires the members to have a familiarity with the policies, institutions, actions, principles, and facts; it also involves a competence in relating those policies, institutions, and actions to those principles and facts. Rather than skills in searching for just any evidence, moral education in a democracy seeks to help its members develop skills in locating evidence bearing on moral problems, personal as well as social, in the given society. Where evidence is located and how it is to be obtained are likely to differ from one society to another. Rather than skills in the discussion of any moral problem, such education necessarily promotes skills in the discussion of moral problems, personal as well as social, in that society. Different societies are likely to have different protocols for the discussion of their respective moral problems. What values should be fostered by moral education in a democracy? Besides appreciation of the relevant skills and dispositions, they include a member's valuing of the central features of voluntary action as moral principles, appreciation of both the ideals generic to each and every democratic state and those special to a member's particular democratic state, valuing of the morally correct laws and policies of a member's own democracy, appreciation of the morally right actions of the state's members, and valuing of morally proper increased levels of attainment by the members. These and other moral appreciations, it should be emphasized, have an affective dimension: they can cause many feelings including those of joy, sadness, satisfaction, discontent, righteousness, shame, guilt, and contempt.

It is such feelings that constitute, along with moral reasoning, the moral conscience. Proper moral feelings are consonant with correct moral reasoning, and improper ones are disconsonant with it. Thus, if an agent's reasoning justifiably ends in a negative moral judgment, his or her moral feelings should be negative toward the object of the judgment; and if the agent's reasoning justifiably terminates in a positive moral judgment, his or her moral feelings should be positive. If a person's moral feelings are opposed to his or her moral reasoning when it is incorrect, the feelings may be morally right; but because they are a factor in a divided conscience, they do not necessarily lead to morally right action. The moral conscience befitting a democratic state, then, consists of feelings in agreement with correct reasoning about moral problems in the society. This means, among other things, that the reasoning is guided by a consideration of the central features of voluntary action as moral goods and rights and by an examination of factual conditions in the society. The acquisition of this conscience is plainly a part of the moral education suitable to democracy. Acquiring such a conscience includes, among other things, learning to identify the various sorts of moral feelings and learning the objects toward which it is appropriate to express which moral feelings. For instance, while it is important for members of a democratic society to learn to identify feelings of guilt and shame, it is equally important for them to learn that guilt is a feeling that results from one's own violation of another's right to voluntariness rather than from someone else's violation of that right; and that shame is a feeling that one may have toward other people's violation of that right.[7]

Because moral education in a democracy is to provide a comprehensive understanding pertinent to the society, it should ideally exist in whatever educational institutions, informal and formal, the society might have. If there are homes, neighborhoods, churches, workplaces, and mass media with

educational functions, they should help educate the society's members in morality; and if there are schools and colleges, they too ought to help. To the extent
that moral education takes place in all educational institutions, it will encourage
students to see connections among what is learned in the various institutions
and, thereby, to understand morality comprehensively; moreover, it will encourage coordination of educational activities among the different institutions.
By contrast any effort to confine moral education in a democracy to only some of
the society's educational institutions will tend to be self-defeating. If students
learn about morality in only some educational institutions, they might fail to
grasp the moral significance of what they learn in the other educational institutions. And to the extent that educational institutions are divided as to which
ones contribute to moral education and which do not, it will be difficult for
them to integrate their respective educational efforts. Thus, students learning
only in informal institutions about morality might fail to understand the moral
importance of what they learn in schools and colleges about, for instance, social
class structure and genetic engineering; and they might find that what they learn
in informal institutions about morality has little or no connection with what
they learn in schools and colleges about, for instance, economics and political
theory. For similar reasons this caveat against restricting moral education to only
some educational institutions has applications to other matters also. Moral education should not be confined to one area of an educational institution, nor
should it be restricted to any given educational age level of students. If students
learn about morality only in social studies classes, they are likely to miss the
moral importance of what they learn in their science classes and to believe that
there are few or no connections between the two types of classes. And if they
learn about morality when they are children and teenagers but not in later years,
they might come to regard morality, as some morally suspect operators on Wall
Street seem to do, as something peculiar to childhood and youth.

It is held sometimes that only one portion of the disciplinary fields can
contribute to moral education. For instance, it is argued occasionally that the
sciences are value-free and, thus, are inappropriate arenas for moral education;
but that the humanities, aiming mainly at an understanding and appreciation
of human existence, necessarily involve a consideration of values and are therefore especially pertinent settings for moral education. Restricting moral education to only one segment of the disciplinary areas is wrong, however, for moral
education may receive help from most, if not all, of the disciplines. The sciences
highly esteem truth and objectivity; both are qualities pertinent to morality.
The sciences would be very useful vehicles for teaching information, skills, dispositions, and appreciations about truth and objectivity, and perhaps about

other qualities relevant to morality as well. Moreover, because both the natural and the social sciences are concerned mainly with describing, explaining, and predicting natural and social phenomena, they would be appropriate disciplines through which students might learn to understand the existential conditions of their societies. A study of the natural sciences would also be indispensable in students' comprehending the technological problems of their societies. Studying the social sciences could contribute much to students' grasping the ideals, purposes, laws, and interests of their societies. Certainly, learning through both the natural and the social sciences about the existential conditions, technological problems, and the other social factors just mentioned can help students to grasp the significance of the factors for the central features of voluntary action. In sum, the claim that science is impertinent to morality seems to be more a piece of rhetoric than a defensible position on moral education. The humanities, of course, are especially appropriate disciplines for moral education. Not only can study of the humanities provide students with various views of the meaning of human existence, but it also can furnish them with insights into moral problems and familiarity with moral reasoning. Moral philosophy is notorious for doing these things. History and literature are adept at doing them too. The sciences and the humanities, however, are not the only disciplinary fields that might contribute to moral education. The fine arts, without being rendered moralistic, might serve to heighten a student's moral awareness through a sensory and emotionally charged presentation of moral experience. The useful arts can provide students with opportunities to learn about the moral problems involved in the making and use of products. And the practical disciplines can give students opportunities to learn about purposiveness and evaluativeness as well as about prudential, professional, political, and other nonmoral standards for decision making, and about the relationships between such standards and moral ones. Because it is the case that moral education in a democratic state *may* be carried on, in its different aspects, in the various disciplinary fields, it also is the case that it *should* be diffused through them; for by being so distributed, moral education in the democratic commonwealth will encourage students to develop a comprehensive understanding of morality. To be sure, the diffusion of moral education through the disciplines means that extra care and effort will be needed to organize and implement such education; but that does not mean that organizing and implementing such education will be impossible.

By now one well might be wondering if our view of moral education for democratic society is liable to the charge of imposition. The view insists, it will be remembered, that the members of a democracy logically must learn to regard the major characteristics of voluntary action as moral goods and rights; and that

the members must acquire the information, skills, dispositions, and appreciations that will enable them to respect the major characteristics of voluntary action as moral goods and rights. How, then, is one to ensure that the members of
a democratic commonwealth will come to accept the central features of voluntary action as moral goods and rights without imposing, through indoctrination
and irrational conditioning, these features upon the members as moral principles? The question is critical. Like any other aspect of education, moral education excludes indoctrination, irrational conditioning, and other modes of imposition. Hence, if there cannot be moral education in a democracy without
imposition, there cannot be moral education in a democracy. Moreover, there is
a patent conceptual absurdity in compelling anybody, whether a member of a
democracy or not, to regard the main traits of voluntary action as principles for
guiding voluntary action. The charge of imposition, however, does not apply in
a serious way to our view. Far from proposing indoctrination and irrational conditioning as pedagogical methods, our position maintains that moral education
in the democratic state is to employ rational pedagogical methods—mainly discussion, training, instruction, and rational conditioning. The first two, discussion and training, which include justifiable understanding and free assent on the
part of the students, are devoid of all imposition. And while the last two, instruction and rational conditioning, which do not require justifiable understanding and free assent on the part of the student, do involve imposition, they
do not contain it necessarily in an irremediable way. Instruction and rational
conditioning, which are appropriate to students for whom discussion and training (for any of several reasons) are not suitable, may help students prepare for
discussion and training. When students who have learned through instruction
and rational conditioning begin to learn through discussion and training, they
will be in a position to examine and assess whatever has been imposed upon
them through instruction and rational conditioning and make adjustments in
their beliefs and conduct in view of their assessments.

Not all members of an actual democracy, unfortunately, are likely to be
capable of learning through discussion and training; and those who can never
learn through them are beyond the pale of moral education (that is, in the sense
that the term is being used here). Nevertheless, those incapable of moral education should learn, to the extent that they can, to act according to the moral principles of voluntary action as well as the ideals and laws of the society. Conduct
that is merely in agreement with these principles, ideals, and laws is certainly not
as desirable as that following from an understanding of them, but it is far better
than conduct that is in disagreement with them because of ignorance or compulsion. At any rate, students in a democracy incapable of ever benefiting from

discussion and training might learn through instruction and rational conditioning to act according to the principles of voluntary actions and the ideals and laws
of their society. Those who can never benefit even from instruction and rational
conditioning will have to be served by other learning activities—more specifically, activities that will help them learn to act as much as they can in desirable
ways but that will not violate their moral rights except for compelling reasons.
Those incapable of learning to act in desirable ways will have to be placed under
institutional care or in some other way restrained from injuring other members.

IV

THE MORAL EDUCATION PROPOSED by us for the democratic state certainly is
not without its current competitors. During recent decades a variety of theoretical approaches to moral education have been formulated, and some of these
have been regarded by their advocates as quite suitable for democratic society.[8]
Most of the latter approaches differ markedly from ours; and of those that do, a
few have attracted the interest of many educators. In an effort to show in what
ways our proposal contrasts with its contemporaries, we will relate it to two of
those widely noted among educators. One will be dubbed "Values Clarification," and the other will be called "Moral Development."

Values Clarification focuses upon values, which it takes to be the central
fact of moral and civil life.[9] Through and from their experiences, this approach
claims, human beings normally acquire guides of behavior. These guides may
take the forms of purposes, attitudes, feelings, beliefs, and other psychological
factors; and they may be consciously held or not. For Values Clarification a
value is any psychological factor that tends to direct some of the behavior of any
person.[10] The proponents of the approach in general do not claim any set of values a person holds must be acceptable according to a given moral standard, but
they do agree that the set of values held by a person should be internally consistent. For Values Clarification the objective of moral education in a democracy is
to help students to develop internally consistent sets of values and to live deliberately by whatever such sets they individually develop. The method for attaining this objective is values clarification, which enables students to identify their
respective values and to spot and eliminate inconsistencies among their respective values.

It takes but little reflection to see that Values Clarification contrasts
sharply with our own idea of moral education for the democratic state. What

appears to be the only point on which both theories agree is the claim that values function as guides to action, but even here there are some differences. Our theory maintains that a value consists of an object positively judged according to some relevant standard and fact, whereas Values Clarification contends that a value is nothing but a psychological factor. While our position is concerned with rights just as much as with values, Values Clarification is interested primarily in values. While our view contains a definite set of values for all moral agents, Values Clarification does not; it allows indeterminate sets of values for moral agents. Our theory, therefore, is absolutistic whereas Values Clarification is relativistic. While we have strived to ascertain that the values proposed for moral education in democratic society satisfy an analysis of voluntary action as well as the canons of logic, Values Clarification permits any set of values to be included in such education as long as the set is internally consistent. Finally, while our idea insists that the purpose of moral education in a democracy is to prepare its members to engage in their institutional roles and their noninstitutional activities according to the moral rights and values of voluntary action, Values Clarification contends that the purpose is to help the members develop internally consistent sets of values and to live deliberately by these sets.

There surely are questions to be raised about Values Clarification. For instance, it may be asked if a value is simply a psychological factor, if a set of values is acceptable merely because it is internally consistent, and if moral education in a democracy should not aim at something more than preparing the society's members to live deliberately by internally consistent sets of values. Yet even though it is tempting to discuss these and other questions about Values Clarification, it is more pertinent here to consider some questions posed by this approach to democratic moral education as they relate to our view of the matter. Regardless of any theoretical weakness it might have, Values Clarification makes several quite plausible empirical assumptions: when the members of a democratic society or of any other kind of society are being educated, they might have diverse sets of values; the members might be unconscious or only dimly aware that they operate by values; and the members might not know how to clarify the values that they have. So far, however, our discussion of moral education in a democracy has not addressed any of these points. It has not indicated whether or not students in an actual democracy are likely to be uniform in their values, whether or not the values they have will always be consistent with those we have advocated they should learn, whether or not they should become aware of the values they have that oppose those they ought to learn, and whether or not they ought to learn to clarify their nonestablishment values. It is time, then, to consider how our view of moral education in the democratic state is to be applied under the empirical conditions suggested by these questions.

Having diverse sets of values by the members of an actual democracy is an empirical contingency, as is the opposition of any values held by the members of an actual democracy to the moral values of voluntary action. Given an actual democracy with these conditions, our view of democratic moral education needs to determine whether all or only some of the members' values should be clarified; if only some, whether or not they should include any of those contrary to the moral values of voluntary action; and whether or not the members should be made ready to live by the values that they presently hold. In principle all values unconsciously or dimly held by any member of any democracy should be made clear to that member. Dimly held values will inhibit that person from being cognizant of all aspects of his or her actions and, insofar as they do, will keep him or her from engaging in voluntary action. Moreover, such values will be difficult for the member to relate to his or her other mentals and the objects of his or her experience and, to that extent, will hinder the member in acquiring an educational comprehensive understanding. Circumstances, of course, might prevent a teacher from being able to clarify each and every value that a student barely sees or does not perceive at all. The teacher might be responsible for many students; some students might suffer handicaps that keep them from being clearly aware of some of their values; and there might be no occasions in which the teacher discerns some values unconsciously or dimly held by students or, consequently, the need to clarify those values. Nevertheless, obstructive circumstances do not mean that teachers should ignore the ideal of clarification. What they mean, rather, is that teachers should clarify their students' unconsciously or dimly held values as much as circumstances permit.

It must be emphasized that the clarification of values suggested by our position is remarkably different from that proposed by Values Clarification. One difference concerns the conception of *value* embodied in each view. For Values Clarification, which defines a value as any psychological factor that guides action, getting people to perceive their values clearly consists of getting them to be acutely aware of their desires and other psychological factors guiding their actions. According to our view, which conceives a value as an object positively related to a judgment, getting students to plainly see their values—such as those of material success, popularity, and fun—is getting them to become aware of the objects they value and of the judgments, including the standards and facts, by which they esteem the objects. To be sure, the students' unconscious psychological factors pertinent to their unconsciously and dimly held values are not to be ignored in moral education. But in our view, clarifying what these factors are and how they relate to these values is not one and the same thing as clarifying the values. Another difference concerns the purpose of clarifying a student's values. As far as Values Clarification is concerned, the purpose is to enable the student to live according to an internally consistent set of values that he or she holds. To the extent the values are clarified, the student becomes fully conscious of the psychological forces guiding his or her actions and, thereby, is able to use these forces in guiding the actions; and the student is able to spot and eliminate conflicting psychological forces (e.g., the desire to have a good job versus the desire to have fun) guiding his or her actions and, thus, eliminate conflicts among the actions. With respect to our understanding of the matter, however, the purpose of clarification is not to prepare students to act according to just any internally consistent set of values they might hold. It is, rather, to help them to act according to the moral values and rights of voluntary action. By learning to see clearly their own values (e.g., an esteem of knowledge and freedom and a contempt for mental retardation), values they previously did not perceive or saw only dimly, students will be able to determine which of their values oppose the moral values of voluntary action. They will also be able to examine, through discussion or some other educational learning activity, the justifications they have for their values and those that can be had for the moral values of voluntary action. Thereby, they will be in a position to scrutinize their justifications for opposing the moral rights of voluntary action and those justifications they can have to support these rights. Accordingly, values clarification, far from being the sum and substance of moral education in the democratic state as it is for the Values Clarification approach, is merely a method that might be useful in such education.

For Moral Development the courses of interpersonal action that persons might entertain in a given situation are contingent mainly upon their psychological equipment and the historical milieu in which they live. The moral precepts and rules persons follow in deciding what to do are typically, if not always, products of the culture in which they live. But the standpoints from which they view moral precepts or rules—whether standpoints of self-interest, social authority, moral autonomy, or whatever—are functions of social-psychological stages in which persons are when they consider precepts or rules. A social-psychological stage shaping a person's view of moral precepts and rules is a *moral stage*. According to Moral Development there is evidence indicating sequential and irreversible moral stages through which human beings might go.[11] While the proponents of this approach sometimes disagree over what the specific moral stages are, they tend to classify them as preconventional, conventional, and postconventional. A conventional stage focuses on social authority, such as the authority that might be ascribed to a peer group or to the laws of a society. A preconventional stage centers around some moral viewpoint persons have before entering the conventional period (e.g., power or self-interest). A postconventional stage concentrates on a moral standpoint persons adopt after leaving the conventional period—for instance, the idea of a social contract or of moral autonomy. The members of some cultures develop no farther than the conventional period, but some members of other cultures develop beyond. The task of moral education, consequently, is to guide each student from the moral stage in which he or she presently is to the next stage, until the highest stage possible for each student has been reached. In a modern Western democracy, moral autonomy seems appropriate as an ideal, if not a realistic, goal of moral development.

Moral Development has not been free of criticism. While some objections to it have been limited and internecine, others have come from scholars who are not advocates of the view and have been more challenging.[12] Regardless of any weaknesses the theory might have, however, it poses a serious question for our discussion of moral education, a discussion which has yet to say anything about moral development. We have not determined whether or not morality in democratic society is to be learned through sequential and irreversible stages and, if so, what those stages might be. Why this has not been done can be logically explained. According to our stance, the members of a democratic state ideally are rational agents, and moral agents also are rational agents. Hence, to talk about the moral education of the members of a democracy is to talk about a kind of moral education for rational agents. The moral education of the members of a democratic commonwealth, however, need not be conceived as developmental. According to our conception of the matter, a rational agent does not have to be understood as being subject to an irreversible sequence of moral stages; according to our analysis, the concept of education—in any of its aspects—does not have to be conceived as following an irreversible sequence of stages; and according to our examination of the topic, democratic society does not conceptually require members who undergo development. Yet the fact that logic has not compelled us to take moral development into account in our discussion of moral education does not mean that we should fail to do so. Indeed, the empirical research done in recent decades on the moral development of human beings requires a response. Are we to say that the research is unfounded or irrelevant, or are we to allow that our theory of moral education is compatible with this research?

There are two ways in which our view of moral education in democratic society is amenable to Moral Development. The first is that it allows for postconventional, conventional, and preconventional stages of moral development. For our position, the goal of moral education in the democratic state is the morally educated member of that state; for Moral Development, the postconventional stage that might serve as the goal of moral education in a modern Western democracy is moral autonomy, or a person's ability to conceive and justify his or her own moral precepts and rules. Even though morally educated and morally autonomous persons might seem to be quite different from one another, they are significantly similar; for morally educated persons are morally autonomous. It is a mark of the morally educated person, who has an educational comprehensive understanding of moral matters, to grasp the meaning of the principles of some moral theory and to be able to relate these principles to one another, to his or her other mentals, and to his or her experiential objects. It is another characteristic of the morally educated person that that person can justify the moral principles he or she holds and judgments he or she makes. Insofar as morally educated persons comprehend the meanings of their moral precepts and rules and relate them to each other and other morally relevant matters, they conceive them and thereby satisfy one condition of moral autonomy; and insofar as they can justify their moral principles, they satisfy the other condition.[13] A moraly autonomous person, it should be noted, need not be educated. That people can conceive and justify their own moral percepts and rules does not entail that they have an educational comprehensive cognitive perspective. They might have some deficiencies in the sciences and the arts; they might suffer some deficits in grasping the connections between their ideas and their leisure activities or deportment. Yet there does not have to be an equivalence between being morally educated and being morally autonomous for the state of being morally educated to be regarded by Moral Development as a postconventional stage of moral development. That being morally educated entails being morally autonomous is sufficient for it to fall within the developmental approach's spectrum of postconventional stages.

It is much easier to see that our view of moral education in the democratic commonwealth makes room for a conventional stage. Regarding acts as right or wrong simply because they are in keeping or not in keeping with the laws of a society, it will be remembered, is explicity recognized by Moral Development as an instance of the conventional state of moral development. It is such an instance of the conventional stage that our theory of democratic moral education makes a plain possibility. According to the theory, the members of a democracy are to learn to obey the laws of the society, but they are not to learn to obey the laws blindly; rather, they are to learn to obey them as long as they have good political or moral reasons for obeying them. Up to the time when the members of a democracy learn that the laws of their society are not infallible, they might learn to regard them as ultimate standards of moral right and wrong. We have not discussed peer groups specifically. Nevertheless, in our analysis of the state, reference was made to social groups and their rules in a way broad enough to include peer groups; and in our remarks on the social organization of the democratic state, it was recognized that a member of the state might belong to a variety of social groups, including peer groups. So, while our view of moral education in a democracy has not declared that the society's members have to learn to respect the rules of their peer groups, it has allowed that they should learn to conceive them from the standpoint of rational agency. They ought to learn the rules that are supposed to serve the purposes of the groups and that are morally correct to the extent that they are consistent with the rights of voluntary action. Yet, before the members learn to relate the rules of their peer groups to these moral standards, they might suffer pressure from the peer groups to take the rules as the arbiters of moral propriety. Accordingly, our view of moral education allows that the members of a democracy might enter a peer, as well as a legal, conventional stage of moral development.

Finally, it may be said that our proposal for moral education in a democracy provides for a preconventional stage. For Moral Development, one variety of this stage focuses on self-interest and another on power. People see moral correctness from the standpoint of self-interest when they judge actions to be morally right or wrong simply because the actions favor or oppose their individual interests, enlightened or not. By contrast they see moral rectitude from the viewpoint of power when they judge actions to be morally right or wrong simply because the actions show that their respective agents can do what they individually want to do. While our proposal for democratic moral education has mentioned nothing explicit about self-interested and power-struck persons, it rests upon a theoretical basis that certainly acknowledges the possiblity of such persons. It was mentioned earlier that the members of an actual democracy might be *inter alia* mixtures of rationality and appetite or prospective rational beings. Those who are mixtures might view moral propriety from the position of self-interest or power, whereas those who are prospective rational beings might see it from the standpoint of power but not self-interest. The person who uses his or her intelligence in acting primarily to satisfy personal appetites might adopt a self-interest stance. The person relying mainly upon threats and force rather than intelligence to satisfy his or her appetites might adopt a power morality, but the prospective rational agent who is dependent upon others to satisfy his or her appetites might adopt a power morality too. Thus, infants and very young children might look upon their parents as omnipotent and, therefore, as the source of moral authority.

The second way in which our view of moral education in the democratic state can accommodate the claims of the Developmental Approach is that it permits preconventional, conventional, and postconventional stages to be interpreted as having a sequential order. It is characteristic of a developmental sequence to have an end. For our position on democratic moral education, the end to be attained is the quality of being morally educated. That quality, of course, might not be attained by all members of an actual democracy. Some might suffer irremediable handicaps that allow them to attain it not at all or only partially; others might fall short for other reasons. Even so, the quality may serve as the stage of moral development toward which all other stages may be seen as leading. The preconventional stages may be regarded as leading to the conventional ones; and they, in turn, may be perceived as leading directly, or, if there is more than one postconventional stage, indirectly to the quality. The point can be demonstrated conveniently by reference to Lawrence Kohlberg's schema of moral development stages for human beings.[14]

According to Kohlberg's schema, the first preconventional stage is oriented toward power, whereas the second is centered around self-interest. The first conventional stage focuses upon nonpolitical group rules; the second, upon the laws of political society. The first postconventional stage rests upon the notion of a social contract; the second rests upon the notion of rational autonomy. From the standpoint of our position, a power morality is understandable and might be acceptable for infants and very young children. It is understandable in that such people, being incapable of voluntariness, purposiveness, and evaluativeness and being largely helpless, must depend upon others to provide for them, which suggests that they also must depend upon others for moral directives. The power morality is acceptable if the moral directives given the children respect the goods and rights they have as moral agents, prospective as well as occurrent. A power morality heads toward a morality of self-interest as its subjects become capable of some voluntariness, purposiveness, and evaluativeness and, consequently, of looking after themselves. That their goals and deliberations should become self-centered is comprehensible on the familiar ground that they have not yet learned to put themselves into other people's places and, thus, to recognize that other people have a right to satisfy their interests too. Even though a self-interest morality is far from being entirely satisfactory, it is acceptable to the extent that it provides for an individual's enabling factors of voluntary action and in other ways prepares the individual to become more rational. Although people in the self-interest stage are not concerned with the rights of one another or of others to satisfy their individual interests, they might well have to have intercourse with each other and with others; for in order to look after their respective interests, they might have to seek help, which they would obtain through bargaining. Insofar as a person in the self-interest stage engages in bargaining with others, he or she gains a glimmer of mutual interest, fairness, promise keeping, and social rules. Thereby, the person becomes somewhat prepared to identify his or her interests with nonpolitical group interests and, upon becoming a conscious member of nonpolitical groups, to act from respect for the rules of the groups.

Nonpolitical group morality, which may be found in street gangs, sororities and fraternities, and clubs, suffers deficiencies for a democratic society, the most notable being its tendency to promote mindless conformity, exclusiveness, and intolerance. But nonpolitical group morality might be serviceable to such a society in that it might encourage the society's members to learn about social organization and enable the members to acquire some sense of social justice and of equality among the members of a group. As a developmental stage, nonpolitical group morality is transitory; it contains conditions that encourage its transformation into another kind of morality—that of state law. A member of one nonpolitical group is usually a member of other nonpolitical groups. Moreover, there typically are nonpolitical groups of which he or she is not a member. These two conditions are likely to lead to conflicts. Different groups have different interests and, thus, different and possibly opposing rules. So, when persons are members of various nonpolitical groups, they might find themselves obligated to obey opposing rules; and even if they do not, they might belong to groups whose interests and rules oppose those of nonpolitical groups of which they are not members. The conflicts arising from nonpolitical group morality become motivators for social group rules whereby the conflicts may be reconciled or overridden. The only rules that may do this are those of a social group that comprises all other relevant social groups and has sovereignty over them. Such rules, of course, are the laws of a political society. In a democracy a morality of state law is satisfactory to the extent that the society's laws are in the public interest; nevertheless, such a morality in a state of any kind contains difficulties. Despite the best knowledge and intentions of legislators, some laws of a state might be oppressive; some might conflict with one another; some or all might stand in opposition to the laws of other states; and a standard is needed by which to formulate new laws. When members of a body politic who have a morality of state law become aware of these problems, they well might wonder what the purpose of the society's laws is and, hence, what the substantive and procedural principles of their state are. Once they do this, the members transform their moral viewpoint into one of the social contract, namely, the ideals and procedural principles that they take to explain their state's existence. In a democratic commonwealth the appropriate social contract morality consists of such ideals as order, security, the removal of positive and negative constraints of voluntary action, and the procedural principles of self-government (Chapter 4, Parts II and III). The social contract conceived by any member of any kind of state, however, might have difficulties. The ideals and procedural principles constitutive of the contract might involve conflicts with one another. For instance, the ideal that all violators of the law are to be punished is likely to conflict with the principle of due process. Moreover, the ideals and principles might not be identical with those constituting other members' versions of the state's social contract. For example, one person's version might emphasize liberty over equality while another's stresses the reverse. Finally, the ideals and principles might oppose those that explain the existence of other political societies. Hence, an American finds that the ideals of liberty and property clash with those of totalitarian control and government ownership belonging to the Soviet Union.

Upon seeing such problems, the person with a social contract morality is ready to look for moral principles underlying those of political society and all other forms of social groups—basic moral principles that are to be located in and through moral philosophy. Beyond fundamental moral principles there are, of course, no other moral principles. If, therefore, a person finds contradictions within his or her basic moral principles, the person cannot resolve the conflicts by using deeper moral principles; he or she can only abandon some or all of his or her principles and acquire compatible ones. And if the person learns that his or her set of basic moral principles opposes another, the person cannot eliminate the opposition by utilizing deeper principles; he or she can only determine which of the sets is defensible. To be morally educated, however, it is not enough for the member of a democratic state merely to acquire a moral theory; it is necessary also that the theory be ingredient to an educational cognitive perspective. When, therefore, a member of a democratic commonwealth acquires a defensible moral theory as part of an educational comprehensive understanding, that member has developed, both morally and educationally, as far as he or she can in moral education; the member has reached the highest state of moral educational development.

The lack of conceptual equivalence between being morally educated and being morally developed is worth emphasizing. The former entails a person's having, by virtue of educational learning activities, an educational comprehensive understanding about moral matters. It does not imply the person's attaining this understanding through an irreversible sequence of stages. It is conceivable, in other words, that a person beginning at a level of self-interest morality could attain a moral cognitive perspective without moving through conventional stages or through any other developmental stages. By contrast, moral development does not entail that one is morally educated; it implies only that one views moral matters according to the irreversible sequence of moral stages through which one tends to go. Jesus, for example, may be regarded as morally developed but not morally educated. He appears to have undergone moral growth—from being a quizzical youth to being morally autonomous; but he does not appear to have been very familiar with the theoretical disciplines of his place and time. Thus, a morally educated person need not be morally developed; and a morally developed person need not be educated.[15] Strictly speaking, therefore, the schema of moral development just formulated to show that our conception of moral education in the democratic commonwealth can accommodate the claims of the Developmental Approach should not be described simply as a schema of moral development; it should be described, instead, as one of moral *educational* development. The schema intends that any moral development of the members of a democracy is to be educational. The learning activities that are to assist the members in entering and leaving moral stages are to be educational, and each stage of moral development is to be educational either in the sense of more or less approximating the final stage, which is to be morally educated, or in the sense of being the final stage itself.

That moral educational development in the democratic commonwealth aims ultimately at its members' having an educational cognitive perspective on moral matters does not mean that each and every member of an actual democracy will attain that perspective. Some members might suffer disadvantages as rational beings; and if they do, they might become arrested at a pre-ultimate stage of moral educational development. In truth, the social experience of humankind indicates that the vast majority of an actual democracy's members are likely to become arrested at a pre-ultimate stage, and that a democracy will be lucky if the bulk of its members develop so far as to adopt the state's laws as their viewpoint. This strong possibility does not mean that making a moral educational cognitive perspective the terminal stage of moral educational development is unrealistic. It would mean that only if we hold that every member of any democracy is to become fully educated on moral matters, which we do not. The possibility, however, does post some warnings about moral education in democracies. It suggests that a democratic society must ensure that any check in moral educational development is the result of irremediable conditions rather than of unequal educational opportunity. It intimates further that the educators in a democratic society must work as diligently in helping the vast majority of the society's members to take state law as their moral viewpoint as they do in helping a fortunate few to gain an educational comprehensive understanding on moral matters. It will do the state little good to count moral philosophers among its membership while the majority of its members has no moral respect for its laws.

Democracy in Education

I

WHILE IT IS CLEAR that the citizens of a democracy generally have the duty to help shape the democracy's decisions, it is not readily evident that they have a duty to help form its educational decisions. Being bound to contribute to a society's decision making may or may not be the same as being obligated to take part in each and every decision that the society makes. The question arises, then, as to whether or not the citizens of a democracy have a duty to participate in the society's educational decision making. Another issue also becomes evident: if a democracy's citizens should influence the decision making, what must education do to prepare them for this duty? While the former question has been discussed frequently in educational literature, the latter one typically has been ignored.

It will be argued that the citizens of a democratic commonwealth morally as well politically should participate in the society's educational decision making, and it subsequently will be explained what education may do to ready the citizens for performance of this duty. Before presenting the argument as to why a democracy's educational decision making should be participatory, several views commonly found in the educational literature that bear on the issue, negatively and positively, will be critically examined. This will enable us to identify difficulties that any adequate argument seeking to answer the question must avoid, and to locate the kinds of qualifications with which education must equip a democracy's citizens if they are to help shape the society's educational decisions.

II

OF THE POSITIONS TO BE DISCUSSED, two favor democratic procedures in educational decision making by a democracy and a third opposes them.

One of the positive views appeals to vested interest. In discussions of American education this argument has been used to defend local control of public schools,[1] federal participation by the federal government in public education,[2] teacher control of public school programs,[3] student activism in schools,[4] and other positions.[5] While the argument is rarely, if ever, stated fully and systematically in the educational literature, it can be outlined without much difficulty:

> The things that people value are their interests. Any person whose interests are seriously affected by another has a right to protect his or her interests. In a democratic state different agents are seriously affected by the practice of education, public and private—teachers, students, and others directly involved in the practice; parents, whose children are and will be students; the state itself, because its operations and development are influenced by the practice of education; employers, who depend upon the practice for a source of employees; and so forth. While one person's vested interest in the practice might not be as great as that of another, the former person nevertheless has the right to look after his or her interest. Indeed, because virtually every member of a democracy has a vested interest, occurrent or prospective, in any education within the society, every member may be regarded as having a right to care for his or her interests as they are or might be affected seriously by the practice of education. The way a democracy and its members may protect their vested interests in education in the society is to participate in making the educational decisions relevant to their respective interests. Teachers and school administrators may engage directly in making the decisions. The state may participate through the agency of its governmental officials. Immature students may participate through the agency of elected representatives, through the open discussion of educational problems, and through other democratic forms.

This argument certainly has attractive aspects. That people have a right of some sort—prudential, moral, or political—to look after their vested interests in an activity seems reasonable. Moreover, that people have a right to care for their vested interests by having a say about the object of the interests seems reasonable too. Despite its plausibility, however, the argument suffers difficulties.

The argument fails to distinguish legitimate interests from nonlegitimate ones. A *legitimate* interest here means one that is proper within a democratic state. An interest favoring the basic principles, the ideals, and the policies of the state as a democracy is legitimate; and an interest supporting education's function in the society is legitimate. Why the argument's failure to discriminate between legitimate and nonlegitimate interests is a difficulty is that it calls into question the argument's premise that any party of a commonwealth, including the commonwealth itself, has the right to protect its vested interest in education in the society by participating in educational decision making in the society. Is it reasonable to hold that the members of a democracy who see education in the society as seriously and adversely affecting their interests have the right to engage in democratic practices in order to help form decisions that undermine education within the society? Several reasons for thinking that the members have the right come to mind. Reason *a* is that anybody has the right to do anything to protect his or her interests. Reason *b* is that if a democracy's members do not have the right to act upon any antieducational ideas they might have, they do not have a right distinctive of the members of a democratic society, which is freedom of expression. Reason *c* is that it is practically impossible to screen the members of a democracy according to their beliefs and, therefore, it is practically impossible to treat beliefs as a relevant criterion for having the right to participate in the society's decision-making activities. None of these reasons, however, will stand up to scrutiny. Reason *a* will not because it is false. It is highly questionable, for instance, that one human being has the right to protect a pet by killing an innocent human being. Reason *b* collapses because it fails to recognize that making antieducational decisions vitiates the freedom to express ideas and, therefore, is not an activity to which the members of a democracy have a right. Reason *c* fails even if it is true. All that it tries to show is that *under current existential conditions* the members of a democratic state should have the right to help form public decisions in the society even when they might have beliefs proscribed by what it means to be a member of democratic state. It does not attempt to show that they have this right in view of what it means to be a member of a democratic society. If it ever became possible to screen people according to their beliefs, the reason would become false, of course. This is not to say, however, that the members of a democracy should be screened according to their beliefs in order to determine whether or not they have the right participate in the society's educational decision making. A need to screen beliefs in order to determine who is fit to participate in educational decision making in a democratic commonwealth reflects some flaw in that commonwealth as a democracy and calls for an elimination, certainly not a perpetuation, of the need.

The view appealing to vested interest suffers from more than a failure to discriminate between legitimate and nonlegitimate interests. It is hurt further because it does not clarify which, if any, parties are to have more or less influence in molding educational decisions in the democratic state. Different parties have historically had greater and lesser powers in determining educational decisions in actual democracies. At one time in the United States, for instance, local communities maintained, through school boards, dominant control over decisions affecting schooling; later the individual states of the nation assumed a large share of that control; and since World War II the federal government has had an increasing impact upon decisions affecting schooling. Meanwhile, teachers, administrators, and religious and economic groups have established influences of their own by themselves. But in none of these facts is it clear why one party should have more power than another has in shaping educational decisions. If political power is all that counts, the federal government should dominate decision making; but few have said that it should. If immediate interest is all that counts, then parents, students, teachers, and administrators should prevail; but only radically progressive school reformers have held that they should reign. And if social and economic power counts primarily, then corporations ought to exercise the greatest control; but no one has allowed that they should. It is, then, of practical as well as theoretical importance to determine what measure of control a party is to have in educational decision making in a democratic commonwealth.

The closest that the argument from vested interest comes to settling this issue is an intimated position. According to the argument, different parties may have greater or lesser vested interests in a democracy's educational decision making. This point hints that a party should be able to affect such decision making in proportion to the magnitude of its interest in the decisions. Yet even though this solution is straightforward and consistent with other aspects of the argument, it is too vague to be of use; for it neglects to specify any criterion by which to assess the degree of importance that educational decision making in a democracy has for a given party's interest in the matter. Different sets of criteria do come to mind. Any party whose vested interest in educational decisions in a democracy is of more general significance to the society than is the vested interest of another party should have greater impact in molding those decisions than the other party should. Those parties whose vested interests are directly affected by the decisions ought to have a greater role in determining the decisions than should those whose interests are indirectly influenced. And those whose vested interests are more enduring ought to have more impact upon the decisions than should those whose vested interests are more transitory. When referred to the argument from vested interest, however, none of these criteria provides guidance. For one thing, the argument furnishes no principle for choosing among the criteria if only one is to be used or for weighing them if they are to be used in some combination. Why prefer the criterion of general importance over that of permanence or directness? Should a vested interest that is general but short-lived count more or less than one that is very limited but more enduring? For another thing, the argument does not specify the meanings of the various criteria, and these meanings are not always clear. Is that which is of general importance to the individual members of a democracy identifiable with what is of significance to that particular state? Does the measure of permanence for an individual member count as the measure of permanence also for his or her state?

Still another difficulty with the vested interest theory is that it does not indicate the form or forms of democratic activity in which interested parties are to engage in helping to shape educational decision in a democratic state. Various modes of democratic activity may function to affect such decisions. Direct participation of all interested parties, participation by representation, and public discussion are familiar ones. Voting, directly or by representation, on each and every educational policy, program, and plan also is a common one. Other common modes are direct participation in deciding educational programs and plans, and supervision, which may be undertaken directly or by representation. Presumably, the vested interest argument would advocate whichever form or forms best enable parties to protect their interests; but the argument does not even suggest which form or forms satisfy this condition. Unfortunately, there is nothing self-evident about which form or forms best enable parties to protect their interests. Direct participation has the advantage of ensuring the expression of each party's opinion on a given issue, but it has the drawback of being so time-consuming that it might make educational decision making very inefficient and prevent the involved parties from looking after their interests not related to education. Supervision, if direct, would be very time-consuming too; and supervision by representation, while time-consuming for only a few, has the disadvantage that any representative might have to represent parties with divergent interests and, thus, might not be able to protect all of their interests. Other forms employing representation also have this shortcoming.

The last difficulty to be mentioned is that the vested interest position encourages partial, fragmented, and conflicting educational decisions.[6] One person's interests in any object may concern all or only some facets of the object, may concern its aspects without regard to their relationships to each other, and may oppose some other person's interests in the object. For instance, parents might be concerned with what their schools do for their own children but not with what they do for another's children. They might be impressed with their schools' academic and athletic programs but ignore whether or not one program interferes with the other. And some parents might want their schools to divert funds from vocational programs to expand academic ones, while other parents might want the opposite. Thus, if parties are to shape educational decisions in a democracy with respect to their individual vested interests, they might produce piecemeal, fragmentary, and divided decisions. Because they might have interests in only some facets of education, they might not make decisions about some of its features. Because they might not be interested in the several aspects of education as they relate to one another, they might determine policies, programs, and plans that are without integration. And because they might have conflicting interests in education, they might form educational decisions opposing one another. Historical examples of partial decisions are reflected by the reports of educational commissions, which typically focus upon purposes, curricula, and financial support but ignore administration and teaching activities. Historical instances of fragmentary decisions are found in decisions by legislative enactment, which often mandate educational policies and programs without regard to how those policies and programs are to be fitted with existing ones. And historical examples of conflicting decisions may include some made by social engineers, psychological humanists, and corporation executives, who may respectively treat education simply as a device for solving social problems, merely as a means for self-development, or purely as an instrument for enhancing economic production.

The vested interest view could avoid this difficulty if it set forth an overall framework within which individual interests and education could be interrelated with one another; for if it did this, it would be able to show how individual interests might bear upon all features of education, how they might be coordinated with one another so as to produce integrated educational decisions, and how they might be made harmonious with one another. Far from furnishing such a framework, however, the position views individual interests as the basis of its theoretical framework, which means that the partiality, fragmentation, and conflict encouraged by self-interest could be overcome only by appealing to the type of interest that has encouraged them. At this point, one might propose a Hobbesian solution for the argument: in order to avoid partiality, fragmentation, and conflict in a democracy's educational decisions, self-interest dictates that the state's educational decision making be turned over to an agent with a unified and comprehensive grasp of education whose decisions would be supreme. This way out, however, is not suggested by the argument. Moreover, it opens up a host of difficulties of its own, the most obvious being how the proposal can be reconciled with an advocacy of democracy.

The other theory to be discussed that favors democratic activities for forming educational decisions by a democratic state rests upon a principle of expediency.[7] While the argument is foreshadowed by the thinking of Machiavelli, it did not appear in educational literature until this century; but during its relatively brief existence it has made an impact upon the educational institutions of the United States. Most notably, it has upheld the community public school.[8] According to the argument, officials must do whatever they practically can to fulfill their policies, programs, and plans. Citizens will not support officials in realizing proposals unless the citizens have a positive interest in the proposals. As a matter of empirical fact, the argument continues, people tend to develop a positive interest in policies, programs, and plans only when they participate in deciding upon them. Administrators and other officials, therefore, should encourage the citizenry to help formulate proposals, which means that in a democratic society academic officials should urge citizens to engage in discussions, elections, referenda, committees, and other democratic activities suitable for making educational decisions. This is not to say that officials are to withdraw entirely from decision making and turn it over completely to the citizenry. Indeed, they ought to employ guided democracy; they should retain the initiative in conceiving proposals and guide the citizenry towards agreeing to them.

That this argument is highly questionable is plain. It strongly suggests that the control of educational decision making should rest ultimately with administrative or other academic officials but does nothing to justify the point. While it does contend that this locus of control would enable academic officials to be successful in their roles, it does not clarify why success in their role performance justifies their being the locus of control in educational decision making. Because this argument offers no reason as to why the ultimate control of educational decision making should lie with academic officials, it has no defense for its advocacy of guided democracy. Another criticism is that the argument goes against the normal understanding of democracy. In holding that academic officials should enlist the citizenry to help make educational decisions through democratic activities, the argument indicates that such activities primarily are instruments whereby officials are to accomplish their objectives. By contrast the usual conception of democracy holds that voting, open inquiry, advising, and other democratic modes of participation in decision making are for the purposes of the citizenry as much as they are for those of officials. Finally, the argument does not recognize that it is self-defeating when taken to its extreme. If academic officials should encourage the citizenry to help make decisions favoring their proposals, should not other interested parties encourage the citizenry to participate in democratic activities so as to determine decisions favoring other and, very possibly, opposing educational policies, programs, and plans? Apparently so, for the argument in no way intimates why academic officials should monopolize the recruiting of the citizenry. But if the argument allows that participation by citizens in democratic activities is to be courted by each and every party promoting educational proposals, it means that academic officials might be undone by democratic educational decision making.

The theory opposing democratic decision making on education by the democratic state relies upon the principle of expertise. To some extent the argument is reminiscent of Plato's contention that society should be governed by philosophers, but it is mindful also of the view of the political progressives of early twentieth-century America that decision making on many of the nation's problems should be removed from the public and turned over to experts.[9] According to the argument, an adequate understanding of education, whether for a particular person or for a society's whole membership, requires expert knowledge. Educational goals, curricular content and materials, the evaluation of students, pedagogical methods, the preparation and qualifications of teachers, the performance of administrators, the funding of educational institutions—these and other educational problems are too complex and special to be treated competently by the public at large. They have to be entrusted to those who have expertise about them, namely, educators. Just as lay people entrust their protection to the police and the military, entrust their health to physicians, and entrust their automobiles to mechanics, they should entrust education to educators. This is not to say that the citizenry should not have any role to play in educational decision making in a democratic society. The citizenry is to have the right and duty of advising the experts on how it will be affected by the various proposals being entertained by them. It is to have the right and duty of deciding how much material support it is prepared to contribute to education. And it is to have the right and duty to recommend to educators changes in decisions they have made.

One might be tempted to assume an egalitarian stance in replying to this argument for expertise. For the egalitarian the claim that most problems of education, as well as most other problems of society, can be understood adequately only by experts is open to challenge. Parents do well in rearing their children, and they turn them over to professional teachers not because they do not know how to continue rearing them but because they do not have time to do so. Advanced education, moreover, is not essentially beyond the ken of the public. There is nothing so complicated about vocational educational that it cannot be comprehended by most craftsmen and merchants, nor is there anything so difficult about professional education that it cannot be grasped by the members of the various professions. The contention that decision making in education is mainly for educators is simply a piece of the effort by any group of intellectuals to clothe themselves in self-importance and place themselves beyond public scrutiny.

As interesting as this egalitarian criticism might be, however, it simply will not hold up. Even if most social problems in earlier times could have been understood adequately by the mass of citizens then, which is highly doubtful, those of today surely cannot be grasped thoroughly by the citizenry now. The problems of police work, warfare, health care, urban housing, waste disposal—these and countless other problems confronting people today are often highly technical and can be comprehended fully by experts alone. Moreover, even when it is agreed that many parents can accomplish much toward educating their children, it still may be insisted that many are incapable of determining what has to be learned through what activities for their children to gain comprehensive understandings based on the theoretical disciplines. Even if the parents themselves were educated, they would not necessarily have any specialized knowledge of education. An education well might give one specialized knowledge of some field (e.g., civil law), but that field need not be education. Moreover, it will not do to plead that the citizenry could become fully informed of education if it had the time to do so. It is not known that the mass of citizens could be fully informed of education even with all the time in the world, but it is known that a citizenry never has unlimited time to learn about social problems.

Even though the argument from expertise cannot be challenged successfully by egalitarians, it can be overturned by a position that is quite willing to accord expertise a major place in democratic society. Because any political society has complex and special problems, it requires experts to deal with them. The problems of education often are complex and special. That experts are to dominate decision making about educational problems in a democracy does not mean, however, that their decision making is to be largely beyond the control of the public, as the argument from expertise would have it. Whatever goes on in a democratic state, it has been explained, must be consistent with the fundamental principles, intentions, laws, and public interest of the society. So, even if experts are to be preeminent in making educational decisions in a democracy, they are bound to make only decisions that are in keeping with the society's political constraints. That educators should be trusted to keep their decisions within the limits of democratic propriety is a point conceded, but it is not enough. The effort by educators to constrain their decisions within democratic propriety does not mean that they will succeed; their being experts on education does not assure that they will be fully informed about the democratic qualities of their society and, insofar, does not assure that they will not be mistaken about democratic limits within the society. What is necessary is some mechanism whereby the democratic quality of educators' decisions may be assessed by noneducators. Political philosophers, jurisprudentiallists, judges, legislators, social scientists, and ordinary members of the public should have enough talent to make such a mechanism work effectively. The failure of the argument from expertise, then, is not its advocacy of decision making on education by educators but its assumption that the decisions of educators will not need monitoring as to their consistency with democratic qualities.

III

EVEN THOUGH THE PRECEDING DISCUSSION did not examine any argument that offers explicit grounds for morally justifying democratic participation in a democracy's educational decision making, it did raise a number of difficulties that any acceptable resolution to the issue must avoid. For instance, any such answer must not treat legitimate and nonlegitimate interests indifferently; must not fail to clarify which parties are to have more or less influence in educational decision making; must not neglect to explain which, if any, forms of democratic decision making are to be employed in educational decision making; and must not encourage partial, fragmentary, and conflicting decisions. The theoretical framework within which we have examined education's moral role in the democratic state provides, with respect to this issue, a resolution that is free of these and the other difficulties of concern. The resolution contains two points.

First, participatory decision making in a democracy makes sense only if it involves decision making about education. One reason why is that there logically cannot be a democracy without education (Chapter 6, Part II). Another reason is that education in a democracy morally has the function of preparing its members to engage in its decision making, educational or otherwise, to perform their institutional duties, including those of civil office, and to perform morally acceptable activities outside their institutional lives. Still another reason is that education, by preparing a democracy's members to be voluntary agents, enables the society to promote voluntary action for its members. If participatory decision making in democracy is to make sense, it cannot be restricted to decision making on relatively minor matters; and if it is to bear upon major matters, it certainly should bear upon the most important ones, which include education.

Second, civil participation in a democratic society's educational decision making favors voluntary action for the society's members. Because the participation is voluntary, it in and of itself guarantees voluntary action; and it assures that the decisions will be followed by the members voluntarily.[10] Moreover, by taking part in the state's educational decision making, the members will be in a position to promote educational decisions that are in the public interest and, therefore, compatible with the major features of voluntary action. For instance, the members will be able to encourage decisions that favor equal educational opportunity, that favor teaching students to regard the principle of public interest as a fundamental principle of their society, that favor teaching students to engage in public inquiry, and that favor teaching students to choose their vocations on their own.

With some reflection it will become evident that the argument just set forth avoids the difficulties that we earlier determined must be eluded by any satisfactory answer to the question of whether or not a democracy's members should help shape the educational decisions made by the society. It is easier to see, however, that some of the problems are avoided by the argument than it is to see that others are.

One of the obstacles that readily can be observed to be overcome by the argument above is an inconsistency with the concept of a democracy (i.e., taking a stand on the issue of participation that rests on premises inconsistent with the meaning of democracy). According to the argument, the members of a democracy should engage in the society's educational decision making because their so doing follows from what it means to be a member of the democratic commonwealth. Hence, the argument overcomes the inconsistency obstacle in that it employs the concept of membership in the democratic state as a premise and also in that none of its other premises pertaining to democratic society, which are analytically derived from the concept, is opposed to the meaning of a democracy. Another problem eluded by the argument is a failure to distinguish between legitimate and nonlegitimate interests, or more precisely a failure to distinguish between promoting interests proper in a democratic commonwealth and promoting those not proper. Far from suffering this problem, our argument definitely draws the distinction of concern. By making the public interest (the compatibility of a state's interests with the major traits of the voluntary actions of the society's members) a basic principle of the democratic state, it plainly holds that legitimate interests are those in the public interest—which is to say those compatible with both the state's interests and the major traits of the members' voluntary action—and that nonlegitimate interests are those not in the public interest. The other difficulty that almost immediately can be perceived to be evaded by the argument is the presumption that any vested interest in education qualifies a person to help make decisions about education. Not so much as a hint of this presumption appears in the argument. Indeed, while the argument clearly implies that voluntary agents are qualified to take part in a democracy's decision making only if they possess information and understanding appropriate to the decision making, it does not even allude to vested interest as a qualification.

A problem skirted less obviously by the argument is the encouragement of partial, conflicting, and fragmentary decisions. The reason why readers might not easily see how our argument eludes this difficulty is that they, assuming the members of a democracy to be naturally susceptible to partiality, conflict, and fragmentariness in their decisions, might believe that the difficulty is simply endemic to any advocacy of participatory decision making.

It is agreed that the members of a democracy might arrive at decisions involving partiality, conflict, and fragmentariness; but it is not conceded that their weakness in this respect is engendered by their membership in a democracy. According to our analysis, the decisions made by a democracy are to be in the public interest. Thus, when the members of a democratic society engage in its decision making, they are to aim at decisions in the public interest. If they do, they will reach decisions favorable not only to the state's interests but also to the central features of their voluntary actions and, thus, to their interests as voluntary agents. By relying upon the public interest as a basic principle in shaping state decisions, the members will employ a common ground that, unlike the principle of vested interest, is free of divisiveness and, hence, will not lead to conflicting decisions. In helping to form educational decisions, the members will have to be guided also by an understanding of what education is and what it morally should be doing in the democratic state. With a proper conception of education they will be in a position to recognize all aspects of education, and with a grasp of its moral role in the democratic commonwealth they will have a principle whereby to assess the coherence of the educational decisions they are to help make for their society. How they are to acquire this idea of education and this comprehension of its moral role will be discussed soon. In any event, our argument escapes the trouble at hand in that it—far from regarding the problem as systemic to public decision making—looks upon membership in democratic society as involving principles that lead away from partiality, conflict, and fragmentariness. Thus, insofar as persons who are members of a democracy support partial, conflicting, and fragmentary decisions, they act not as members of a democracy but as aberrations of such members.

The argument does not plainly overcome several other obstacles that pertain to the place of the expert in a democracy's educational decision making. In defending the citizen body's participation in a democracy's educational decision making, the argument does not even hint that experts have a role to play there; it thereby leaves open the possibility that they should have no such role. Surely, however, the argument ought to allow for contributions from educational experts. If it does not, it puts a democracy's educational decision making entirely in the hands of those not equipped to deal with the complex and specialized aspects of education. However, if it does allow for contributions from educational experts, it leaves open the possibility that these experts—who are not necessarily experts on all things relating to education in a democracy but who nevertheless will be making decisions about education in such a society—will be making decisions about something on which they might be only partly expert. This creates doubts about the value of experts in a democracy's educational decision making.

In holding that voluntary agents with greater and lesser qualifications relevant to the possession of certain rights have a claim to those rights in proportion to their qualifications, the Revised Principle of Proportionality (Chapter 2, Part V) recognizes that the members of a democracy might have individual differences with respect to their knowledge, skills, attitudes, and other matters that might justify their having certain rights; and, thus, the members might have greater and lesser qualifications pertinent to the right to take part in the state's decision making, educational and otherwise. Our argument, then, acknowledges that some members of a democratic commonwealth might be experts on education and that to the extent those members are such experts and other members are not, the former have a stronger claim for engaging in decision making on educational matters about which they have expertise than do the latter. Accordingly, our argument proposes that educational experts in a democracy have a prominent place in the society's educational decision making for areas in which they are experts. There are various modes through which they may have a prominent position within a context of civil participation. They may function as advisors to the citizenry, who in turn may reject their advice for good reasons only. They may make all decisions in the special and complex areas of education while the citizenry helps, possibly with the aid of other sorts of experts, to shape the decisions in the other areas of education. They may receive advice from the citizenry but reserve the right to disregard the advice when it conflicts with the decision they reach as experts. And they may be free to make decisions without input from the citizen body even though their decisions may be audited or supervised periodically by those citizens. Which mode or modes should be used is contingent largely upon empirical factors—the traditions and laws of the given society, the number of experts available, the state of communications technology in the society, and, as we shall show soon, the form or forms of civil participation utilized by the society.

By maintaining that educational experts are to be prominent in making decisions in areas where they are experts, our argument obviously does not intend that each educational expert necessarily is to be prominent in making decisions about all aspects of education in a democracy. Thus, a person who is an expert on teaching methods or curricular organization need not have any expertise on the theoretical disciplines, on the existential conditions of a given democracy, on the negative constraints of voluntary action, or on other matters that have to be considered in a democracy's educational decision. By parity of reasoning, however, the argument does intend that in those areas of a democracy's educational decision making where expertise on education is irrelevant and where other expertise is appropriate and present, the latter should be prominent. Hence, a democracy's decision making, educational and other kinds, well might require input from a manifold of experts. The input, of course, would sound much like the speech of the workers at the Tower of Babel if it were not integrated, but it could be integrated through a systematic interaction among experts and through investigations by philosophers, social scientists, and others adept at synthesizing ideas. While experts will be prominent in a democratic state's educational decision making, they are not to impose their will upon the society's members. Their task is to enhance the conditions of voluntary action by the members, and to that end they must take care that the decisions they help bring about not only are in the public interest but are perceived by the members as being in the public interest. So while experts in a democracy must be respected by the members of the public as contributors to the conditions of its voluntary actions, they in turn must recognize that their work will be self-defeating without the free and witting support of the members. It will facilitate this amicable relationship between experts and the members of the public if they all recognize and appreciate that they all share the values of voluntary action; if each expert understands that beyond the limits of his or her expertise he or she might have no special qualifications for decision making; and if the members of the public appreciate individual differences and trust, however critically, the judgment of those with expertise.

The discussion of the place of experts in educational decision making by the democratic state provides a clue as to how our argument gets around the problem of failing to specify which parties are to have greater and lesser degrees of influence in such decision making. In contending that experts are to be prominent in the decision making, the discussion plainly indicates that experts are to have considerable influence; but it also invites one to determine whether or not their influence is to be greater than that of the citizenry or of others. To do this, one should remember that experts may be viewed as a group of individuals or as a collective body. An individual expert may not always have prominence, even in areas where he is an expert. Rather than employing guidance from all available experts in a given area, a society's decision-making process might use guidance from only some experts; and those whose guidance is not employed will not have prominence in that process. The latter, then, well might have no more influence in a democracy's educational decision making than other individual members of the citizen body. However, experts whose individual guidance is utilized will have more influence in the decision making than do other individual members of the citizenry. This will hold whether an expert occupies an official position or not, for he or she might exert influence through unofficial channels and through the impact that his or her ideas have had in shaping the ideas of experts occupying official positions. As a collective body, the experts engaged in a democracy's educational decision making may or may not exert a greater influence than the citizenry exerts as a collective body. Whether or not they do depends upon the mode their prominence assumes. If experts are to be nothing more than advisors to the citizenry, they patently will have less influence in decision making than the citizens will. If the citizens are to be nothing more than advisors to experts, they plainly will exercise less influence than the experts will. If the experts are to have the authority to make whatever decisions they deem appropriate and the citizenry is simply to supervise or audit their work, the experts clearly will have more influence than the citizenry. If the citizen body and the experts are to make decisions in different educational areas independently of each other and those areas are of equal value for education in the state, the citizen body and the experts will have an equal influence upon the state's educational decision making. But if those areas are not of equal value, one of the bodies will exert more influence than the other.

Experts, however, are not the only parties who might have more or less power than the citizenry in determining a democratic commonwealth's educational decisions. As explained in our discussion of the state (Chapter 3, Part II), the members of a body politic may be corporate or noncorporate agents. We often think of the membership of a state as consisting entirely of noncorporate agents. (Sometimes this membership is referred to simply as John Q. Public, who is as baffled and powerless as he is feisty). But business firms, independent universities, churches, labor unions, and charitable foundations may be and frequently are members too. That corporate members may be more powerful than noncorporate members is both a theoretical point and an empirical truth. Because corporations control organized pools of employees, have large amounts of wealth at their disposal, and have ready access to lawyers, public relations experts, lobbyists, and others especially trained in practical affairs, they are in greatly advantageous positions for affecting a state's decision making. Simply a quick survey of any current commonwealth's tax legislation is likely to confirm this point. This power might obtain, moreover, whether corporations oppose noncorporate members acting as individuals or as a collective group. However, it is highly likely to hold when corporations organize themselves as a collective body. There is little point in asking, therefore, whether or not the corporate members of a democracy should have more influence than the noncorporate members in shaping the society's educational decisions. They will have more power. It is appropriate, nevertheless, to ask how corporations morally should use their power in forming the society's educational decisions. In principle, there is nothing morally wrong with a corporate member's attempting to look after its interests. Corporate members too have moral rights. There is something morally wrong, however, with a corporation's promoting its interests by violating the moral rights of other members or by violating a state's interests that are in the public interest. In seeking to help shape a democracy's educational decisions, therefore, corporate members, collectively or individually, are morally bound to try to bring about educational decisions that are in the public interest.

A similar observation can be made about special interest groups. When noncorporate members of a a democratic commonwealth who have a common interest find that their interest is being slighted or neglected by the state's government, they might and frequently do organize themselves into a collective group so as to bring pressure on the government to protect their interest. Thus, American political history in recent years has seen the proliferation of special interest groups, which have promoted such diverse interests as those of the mentally retarded, the aged, the physically handicapped, Vietnam veterans, and homosexuals. The role that special interest groups play has a positive moral importance: they are a mechanism ensuring that noncorporate members can get their government to protect the cardinal features of their voluntary actions even when it slights or neglects the members themselves. To be sure, special interest groups can and sometimes do seek to achieve their respective goals without considering or caring that their goals might conflict with state interests or the central features of the voluntary actions of the state's members. However, they need not act this way. They can and sometimes do act in the public interest, and this is what they morally should do.

Even though our argument advocating participation by a democracy's citizenry in the society's making of decisions on education does not indicate what form or forms that participation should assume, it is capable of meeting this difficulty. Civil participation, it long has been recognized, may be direct or indirect; and the direct and indirect participation may each be total or partial. In direct civil participation all citizens have, occurrently and prospectively, the right to make, discuss, and vote upon proposals for the state. Total direct civil participation (TDCP) differs from partial direct civil participation (PDCP) in that under the former the citizens have the right to make, discuss, *and* vote upon *all* official proposals whereas under the latter the citizens have the right to make, discuss, *or* vote upon *all or only some* official proposals. TDCP is workable under rather limited conditions only, mainly in a face-to-face body politic whose citizens have enough leisure to engage in all of the society's civil affairs. But PDCP is operable in larger states, at least in those whose citizens have enough leisure to participate in some civil affairs. Thus, in some present-day large democracies many, if not all, citizens take part in legislative initiatives, in referenda, and in official discussions of proposals. In total indirect civil participation (TICP) all citizens have the right to elect from among themselves civil representatives who are responsible for making, discussing, and voting on all official proposals, whereas in partial indirect civil participation (PICP) the citizens' representatives are responsible for presenting, discussing, or voting upon all or just some official proposals. While TDCP logically cannot exist in a state with TICP, PDCP logically can exist in a state that has PICP as well. A combination of PDCP and PICP is what the United States and other large democracies have today.

Plainly the form or forms of civil participation that a democracy has are significant for the mode of its experts' prominence. The mode of experts being purely advisory to citizens is compatible with any form of civil participation, but none of the other modes of the prominence of experts is agreeable to all the forms. Restricting the decision making of experts by nothing more than auditing and supervision by citizens, which may be performed directly or indirectly, is consistent with PDCP and PICP but not with TDCP and TICP, which allow the citizen body directly or indirectly to make, discuss, and vote upon all official proposals in a political society. For the same reason, when the prominence of experts is limited by nothing more than advice from citizens, which may be given directly or indirectly, it is compatible with PDCP and PICP but not with TDCP and TICP. When the prominence consists of the experts having complete control over one area of state decision making and citizens having complete control over the remainder, it is agreeable with PDCP and PICP but not with TDCP and TICP.

IV

IN VIEW OF THE FOREGOING DISCUSSION, it becomes clear which qualifications the citizens of a democracy must have in order to engage in the society's educational decision making. First, the citizens have to understand and appreciate education's value for the public interest. Being voluntary agents, the citizens cannot promote education in the public interest unless they, except for instances of whimsicality, esteem it insofar as it does relate to public interest. Second, the citizens also have to understand and appreciate what their society's public interest is and what education is. As voluntary agents the citizens will support the public interest and education only if they understand them and, except for occasions of whimsicality, value them. In order to understand and value their society's public interest, the citizens of a democracy have to understand its interests and, except for cases of whim, appreciate at least those compatible with the major traits of voluntary action; and they have to understand and deem as worthy the main characteristics of voluntary action. Understanding and appreciating the state's interests means understanding and appreciating its basic principles, its intentions, its laws, and its existential conditions (Chapter 4, Part III). In the sense of a practice, it will be remembered, education comprises both objects and activities of learning, including such objects as the ability to search for evidentiary materials and to discuss according to the canons of public argument, the disposition to have an educational comprehensive understanding, and the appreciation of an educational cognitive perspective; and also including such activities as discussion, instruction, training, and rational conditioning. The citizens of a democracy, therefore, have to understand learning objects and activites of these sorts and regard them as valuable. Third, and last, if a democratic society's citizens are to contribute to its educational decision making, they must understand and, except for cases of whimsicality, appreciate its decision-making process; they must also possess the skills and dispositions appropriate to participating in the process. Otherwise, they cannot take part in the process as voluntary agents.

It must be ensured that the citizens learn to understand education from a theoretical standpoint. As a part of their being educated, the members of a democratic society are to become familiar with the theoretical disciplines, which have much relevance for education and democracy. Many of the theoretical disciplines, if not all of them, are sources of curricular content and principles for curricular organization. Thus, the content and organization of arts and sciences curricula sometimes come directly from the theoretical disciplines. Some theoretical disciplines (e.g., psychology, sociology, and anthropology) are notorious for their empirical research on the nature of learning, teaching, and social institutions and organizations. Still others (e.g., political science and economics) have produced much work on the administration and finance of educational institutions in democratic society. Even so, students are not likely to learn much about the theoretical aspects of education in the democratic commonwealth simply by studying the theoretical disciplines. Just by taking a course in mathematics or history one is not likely to perceive mathematics or history as a curricular content or as a source of principles for designing such content. This does not mean that all or even most citizens of a democratic commonwealth have to take theory courses devoted exclusively or mainly to education in the democratic state—courses with such titles as Philosophical Aspects of Education and Democracy, History of Education in Democratic Society, and Psychology of Learning and Instruction in a Democratic Context. Such courses might be very useful, but there is another way to enhance the likelihood that a democracy's members will grasp the theoretical aspects of education in the democratic society. It is that the formal and the informal educational institutions of the society are to include in their presentation of the theoretical disciplines major topics, issues, and problems relevant to education in democracy. The following topics, for example, could be included: equal educational opportunity, individual differences, education and the public interest, enculturation, the impact of economic forces upon educational institutions, and the structure of knowledge.

Second, in order for the citizens of a democracy to be equipped to engage in the society's decison making as it pertains to education, education has to ensure that the members of a democratic commonwealth learn about the society's laws, civil processes, institutions, and existential conditions pertaining to education. To be sure, it is a part of education's moral role in a democratic state to acquaint the members with its laws, civil processes, institutions, and existential conditions. But familiarizing them with these matters apart from their relevance to education will not necessarily prepare them to help make decisions about education in the society. Information on what the society's laws, civil processes, institutions, and existential conditions say about education can be conveyed to the members in diverse ways. Formal educational institutions may offer courses in the society's history, government, social structure, and economic system that deal with its laws, civil processes, institutions, and existential conditions. Thus, schools and colleges in the United States may include in courses on the nation's history and government discussions of the U.S. Constitution's general welfare clause and its first and fourteenth amendments; they may include courses on the nation's social structure and economic system that involve discussions of the relationship between students' educational achievement and their socoeconomic background. In addition to offerings such as these, research reports may be furnished to a democracy's membership on its laws, civil processes, institutions, and existential conditions relevant to education. Appropriate commission studies also may be submitted to its membership. Coursework, research reports, and commission studies of these sorts may not be accessible or appealing to all members; moreover, they might be too intellectual to engender dispositions and values favoring education. However, they may be supplemented by the mass media, especially news reports, talk shows, movies, and books (both fiction and nonfiction). Finally, information, dispositions, and appreciations related to a democracy's laws, civil processes, institutions, and existential conditions bearing on education may be conveyed, instilled, and reinforced by informal face-to-face discussions with family members, neighbors, friends, work associates, school officials, and others.

Third, educational institutions have to make sure that learning objects contributory to the educational cognitive perspectives of a democracy's members are related, where appropriate, to education. Thus, in learning to seek evidentiary materials and draw inferences, to discuss by the rules of public argument, and to grasp and use relational concepts, the members should learn to apply these things to education as well as to other matters. Learning to pursue evidence and draw inferences in mathematics, physical sciences, and military history are important; but by themselves they do not prepare a person as well as possible to pursue evidence and draw inferences about things of educational importance, both abstract and concrete. A similar point may be made about learning to discuss according to the rules of public argument and to grasp and use relational concepts. Hence, courses may and should include discussions of educational issues and problems, concrete as well as abstract, that follow the canons of public argument; and when studying the concepts of justice, equality, public interest, development, and democracy, to name only some obvious matters, students should be encouraged to relate these concepts to education as it is both in theory and in the given society. Along with acquiring these abilities, the members also should gain dispositions to exercise them and appreciation of both the abilities and the dispositions.

Fourth, it has to be ensured that the cognitive perspectives acquired by a democratic society's members cover educational decision making within the state. In effect this means that the members must learn to see whatever connections noneducational theories have with educational ones, whatever relations their theoretical considerations of education have for education as it is in their society, and whatever linkage the practice of education in their society has with the other institutional areas of the society and with the noninstitutional areas of their individual lives. In order to learn to see these connections, students should learn about the theoretical disciplines and practical affairs in certain ways. For one thing, students ought to learn about the disciplines insofar as they are interrelated with one another (e.g., insofar as biology is related to psychology and insofar as anthropology is important for biology). If they learn about the interrelationships among theoretical considerations, they will be in a position to grasp the ties between noneducational theories and theories of educational significance. There are different ways whereby they might learn about these interrelationships. For instance, they may take courses that essentially are in separate theoretical disciplines but that severally show the importance of each discipline of immediate concern for other disciplines; or they may take courses that essentially are interdisciplinary. Moreover, students should study theoretical considerations of education as these considerations apply to educational affairs in their society. They can accomplish this if their courses with theoretical treatments of education use educational affairs in their society as examples and illustrations, and if their courses dealing with the educational affairs of the society treat the educational affairs within some sort of theoretical framework. Also, students should study about educational practice in their society as it relates to noneducational affairs in the society. They can do this if their academic courses and the mass media that address educational practice relate it to noneducational affairs and if those concentrating upon noneducational affairs in the society connect them, where it is relevant to do so, with the society's educational practice. For example, discussions focusing on education in the society might tie it to the society's labor market; and discussions of art in the society might connect it with the society's schools and colleges. Not every course of a theoretical nature necessarily should address the interrelationships of the theoretical disciplines; not every theoretical examination of education has to speak to concrete educational problems; and not every discussion of a democracy's educational affairs has to relate them to noneducational affairs and vice versa. Which courses should do these things and at what point in their lives students ought to take these courses are questions that ultimately have to be answered by empirical investigation.

Fifth, education has to include opportunities for a democracy's members to identify, examine, and assess—according to moral, political, and educational principles—alternative courses of action as means to educational goals for their society. Decision making about anything is a matter of choosing a course of action in view of some goal; and choosing a course of action follows from the identification, inspection, and weighing of different courses of action as means to that goal. If, then, the members of a democratic state do not learn to identify, examine, and assess alternative courses of action as means to educational goals for that society, they will not be qualified in a very significant respect for helping to shape their society's educational decisions. Merely theoretical considerations of education do not seek to instill decision-making abilities in anyone or to teach anyone how to establish goals for a given society; and mere information about the ideals, laws, institutions, and existential conditions pertaining to education in a democracy does not result in anyone having abilities for decision making or for setting purposes for the society. Nevertheless, the study of educational theory and of the educationally significant ideals, laws, institutions, and existential conditions of a given democratic society can help students acquire these decision-making and purpose-setting abilities. If theoretical considerations of education include discussions of simulated educational problems in the democratic state, which necessarily will be abstract, they will enable students to acquire the abilities to some extent. And if study of the society's educationally important ideals, laws, institutions, and existential conditions contains discussions of these facets of the society as they relate to actual or at least likely educational problems in the society, the study will enable students to develop the abilities for use in situations that approximate educational decision-making contexts in their society.

Sixth and last, discussion must be employed as a pedagogical method in its treatment of education in democratic society whenever it is feasible to do so. While discussion—which is an interactive presentation of statements to be learned insofar as they are comprehended by student as well as teacher to be justifiable—is a method suitable for teaching a variety of subject matters, it is especially appropriate for the preparation of citizens for educational decision making. Because it involves a consideration of topics, issues, and problems according to established rules, it will help dispose students to examine educational matters with respect to the canons of public argument. If it is used frequently in teaching and learning about education, it will encourage students to recognize education, whether in the abstract or in their society, as something subject to rational inquiry and debate. Instruction, which assumes that the student has some deficiency in critical thinking, is not as likely as discussion to do so. At any rate, instruction as well as discussion, by emphasizing open-mindedness on the part of teachers and the place of rational understanding by students, will tend to exclude ideological and doctrinaire positions from the education of democracy's members as they prepare to participate in the society's educational decision making.

In holding that education is morally bound to prepare a democracy's members to participate in its educational decision making, we have raised an issue that usually has gone unrecognized by those who have written about education in the democratic state. As the works of Thomas Jefferson, Horace Mann, John Dewey, and others testify, commentators on the topic always have acknowledged that education is vital to the democratic commonwealth and that the citizens of such society should have some part, even if minimal, in shaping its educational decisions; but they typically have failed to state that the citizens do or do not have to be educated so as to perform this civil duty. Jefferson, for instance, never indicated that any of the formal educational institutions that he advocated or that the libraries, newspapers, and other informal educational institutions that he promoted would or would not qualify citizens to engage in educational decision making. Indeed, even after most of his educational proposals were defeated by legislative bodies, he never suggested that the citizenry and its legislators needed to be better qualified to decide upon educational matters.[11] Similarly, while Mann was perfectly aware that public schooling was necessary for citizenship in a democracy, he never questioned whether it was required that American citizens be readied to share in the nation's educational decision making.[12] An irony here is that the position of Mann and the other public school supporters of his era was discussed before the public by virtue of the American Lyceum, an institution that showed thereby the importance of educating citizens for educational decision making.[13] Not even the studies of recent decades that have deplored the quality of American academic institutions have specified that the nation's students do or do not need to be educated for making educational decisions.[14] Considering that such reports have functioned mainly as tools for the nation's citizens to improve, in some sense, their academic institutions, one should think that their authors would have recognized that educating citizens for educational decision making is a vital issue. If commentators on education in the democratic state were to pose this issue, they would be in a position to determine whether or not the programs they recommend for democratic society have to ready citizens for educational decision making.

Yet our contention about the preparation of a democracy's citizens for educational decision making does more than raise a frequently ignored issue; it also indicates that the practical intellectual disciplines are especially important for education in the democratic state. According to its concept, the practice of education does not entail the practical intellectual disciplines, such as prudence, morality, home management, and statesmanship, which aim at right action.

While all schema of the intellectual disciplines include the theoretical disciplines, not all of them embody the practical ones. Comte's schema, for instance, does not. Thus, by conceptually implying only some schema of the intellectual disciplines, education logically implies the theoretical but not the practical disciplines (Chapter 5, Part III). That practical affairs are central to membership in a democracy does not mean that education has to depend upon some schema of the intellectual disciplines including the practical ones in order to perform its moral role in the society. Education conceivably could perform the role by resting upon a schema that excludes what others call "practical intellectual disciplines" on the ground that those disciplines are too little understood to be organized as intellectual disciplines; that they essentially are emotive, not intellectual, matters; or for some other reason. Nevertheless, the importance of practical affairs for the members of the democratic commonwealth does mean that education in that society could be served well by a schema that includes the practical intellectual disciplines. With the aid of such a schema, education would have an articulated source of content for its curriculum, principles for organizing that content, and principles for helping to relate the theoretical disciplines to practical affairs and for relating different practical affairs to one another. All other things being equal, therefore, it is better for education in the democratic state to rest on a schema containing the practical as well as the theoretical disciplines than for it to depend on one that excludes the former.

It follows that some observations ought to be made about the pedagogy and recommendation facets of education as a practical intellectual discipline. Because the practice of education is to prepare the citizens of a democratic state to share in making the society's educational decisions, it requires teachers with the qualifications necessary for achieving this purpose. These qualifications are the knowledge, abilities, dispositions, and appreciations needed in the teaching of educational theory; relationships of educational theory to other disciplines; the significance of educational theory for the society's public good; and the importance for education of the society's basic principles, ideals, laws, institutions, and existential conditions. In a democratic commonwealth, therefore, colleges of education and other pedagogical institutions must ensure that those students learning to teach citizens to participate in educational decision making acquire such qualifications. Because the citizens of a democracy are to take part in its educational decision making, they will be factors in the recommendation aspect of the discipline of education in the society. This means that in a democratic state the recommendation aspect will consist of a large composite of persons (e.g., professional educators, civil officials, and ordinary citizens) engaged in providing educational directives. Such a composite means that it will be as important as it will be difficult to identify and coordinate all the roles of all the persons involved in the recommendation facet of the discipline of education in a democratic society. While this identification and organization will be especially important for the operation of the educational decision-making process in the democratic commonwealth, they will be quite important also for educating students to engage in that process. By articulating what citizens will have to do when participating in the process, the identification and organization will determine specific information, skills, dispositions, and appreciations that students will need to acquire in learning to engage in it.

In view of what has been said on the matter, participatory educational decision making poses a serious difficulty for the democratic state. If educational decisions in a democratic society are to be determined as they morally should be, they have to be shaped by the mass of citizens as well as by officials and experts; and if people are to engage properly in a democracy's educational decision making, they must be educated for the task. But how can the citizens of a democracy be educated for that society's educational decision making unless a suitable education already exists in the state? And how can such an education already exist there unless it already has been decided upon, which is to say, unless the mass of citizens already have been educated to make the society's educational decisions properly? The gravity of this difficulty is apparent. If a democracy does not offer an education suitable to equip its members to make educational decisions, and if the citizens do participate in the society's educational decision making, they may be expected to make wrong decisions on education in the society. Their decisions may even lead to education that again fails to prepare students for educational decision making and, insofar as it does, perpetuates poor educational decision making and thereby enervates or destroys the democratic features of the society. This difficulty is of more than speculative interest; it faces any would-be democracy in its fledgling stage. During its founding as a democracy, the United States was fortunate to have an influential number of citizens who were already prepared for making appropriate educational decisions, but it also had many citizens who were not already prepared but who nevertheless engaged in their respective society's educational decision making. The result was numerous wrong educational decisions that have fostered other wrong decisions and otherwise have thwarted the society's democratic aspirations. Some nations with hopes of becoming full-fledged democracies have been quite unfortunate: those of their citizens already prepared for proper educational decision making were very small in number. The outcome has been poor educational decisions and an increasing tendency for those societies to give up on participatory educational decision making and indeed to abandon their democratic aspirations.

There are several ways by which this difficulty may be overcome, but each of them has a drawback. The first is that the persons who become the initial citizens of a democratic commonwealth might be educated for the society's educational decision making before they became citizens of the society. They might receive such preparation through a program instituted for the purpose,[15] or they might receive the preparation incidentally through programs that were not instituted for the purpose.[16] The former alternative is difficult to organize and rarely has succeeded in history; whereas the latter alternative, which depends upon a lucky confluence of circumstances, is largely beyond anyone's control. The second way is one of guided democracy: the educational decision making of a new democratic state might be left largely to those citizens who are already educated for performing the task properly. In such a guided democracy more and more citizens may become educated for shaping educational decisions, and eventually the society may transform itself into a fully developed democratic state. The problem here is that the history of guided democracies is quite mixed. The leaders of guided democracies sometimes are reluctant to give up their authority and, thus, occasionally restrain the societies from becoming mature democracies. The third way is self-education by trial and error. By this way the citizens of a democracy, even though many of them are not educated for the task, proceed to engage in the society's educational decision making and are likely to make some erroneous decisions; but they will tend to discover and repair their mistakes and in so doing prepare themselves to shape correct educational decisions in the future. This way was the one counted on by the founding fathers of the United States; it certainly reflects their faith in the rule of the people. Its shortcoming is that it presupposes that the initial citizens of a democracy have the ability and inclination to discover and correct their errors in making educational decisions and to improve their decision making talents in the process. A new society with democratic aspirations might have such citizens, but it need not.

None of these different ways of circumventing the obstacle at hand—the difficulty of preparing citizens of a democracy to make decisions about education in the society—is completely satisfactory. This means that the democratic state is difficult to establish in practice. It also means that education's moral role in a democratic society is difficult to institute in practice. Education in a democracy will not perform a moral role unless the citizens of the state help decide that it should; and the citizens are not likely to do this unless they are educated to do so. So, those who want education in a democracy to act according to our conception of its moral role have set themselves a goal that cannot be achieved easily. It must be said, however, that not every ideal that is worthwhile is easy to realize.

Notes

CHAPTER 1

1. James B. Conant, *Education and Liberty: The Role of the Schools in a Modern Democracy* (New York: Vintage Books, 1953).
2. Ibid., pp. viii–ix.
3. Ibid., pp. viii.
4. Ibid., p. ix.
5. Ibid., p. 56.
6. Ibid., pp. 1–2.
7. Ibid., pp. 56 and 86.
8. Ibid., p. 56.
9. Ibid.
10. Ibid., p. 59.
11. Morris Janowitz, *The Reconstruction of Patriotism: Education for Civic Consciousness* (Chicago: The University of Chicago Press, 1983), p. 1.
12. Ibid., p. 2.
13. Ibid.
14. Ibid., p. 10.
15. Ibid., p. x.
16. Ibid., p. xii.
17. Ibid., p. 194. Cf. ibid., p. 12.
18. Ibid., p. x.
19. Ibid., p. 195.
20. Ibid., pp. 196–203.
21. Ibid., p. xii.
22. Ibid., p. xi.

CHAPTER 2

1. Cf. Anthony Kenny, *Action, Emotion and Will* (New York: Humanities Press, 1966), p. 254. "By 'a verb of action' I mean a verb which may occur as the main verb in the answer to a question of the form, What did A do?"
2. Kurt Baier, "Action and Agent," *The Monist* 49 (1965): 183–95. Baier

holds that we refer to some actions as doings of nothing, not as doings of something. It seems to me, however, that when we say that a person is doing nothing, we are not implying that some action is a doing of nothing; rather we are saying that what the person is doing is of no importance ("What is he doing?" "Nothing; he is just pitching pennies") or that it is inappropriate to regard the person as doing anything ("What is he doing?" "Nothing; why do you think he is doing anything at all?").

3. A discussion of some major senses of a free person is provided by Joel Feinberg, "The Idea of a Free Man," in *Rights, Justice, and the Bounds of Liberty: Essays in Social Philosophy* (Princeton, N.J.: Princeton University Press, 1980), pp. 3–29.

4. Aristotle, *N. Ethics* 1109b30–1115a6.

5. For a discussion of the contrast between actions and acts and mere bodily movements, see A. I. Melden, "Bodily Movement, Action and Agent," in *Free Action* (New York: Humanities Press, 1964), pp. 171–98.

6. Alan Gewirth, *Reason and Morality* (Chicago: The University of Chicago Press, 1978), p. 38.

7. Cf. Charner Perry, "Ethics and Democracy," *Ethics* 83 (January 1973): 93–94.

8. Gewirth, *Reason and Morality*, p. 1.

9. Ibid.

10. Ibid., p. 27.

11. Ibid.

12. Ibid., p. 40.

13. Ibid., p. 51.

14. Ibid., p. 49.

15. Ibid., p. 52.

16. Ibid., pp. 53–54.

17. Ibid., pp. 63–64.

18. Ibid., pp. 134.

19. Ibid., p. 135.

20. Ibid., p. 40.

21. Ibid., p. 41.

22. Ibid., p. 50.

23. Ibid, pp. 44, 46–47, 172.

24. The idea of a saucer of mud as an object of desire comes from G. E. M. Anscombe, *Intention* (Oxford: Basil Blackwell, 1958), p. 70.

25. Ibid., p. 71.

26. Gewirth, *Reason and Morality*, p. 49.

27. There are four other arguments by which Gewirth explicitly and implicitly defends the claim. All his arguments have been criticized in Robert D. Heslep, "Gewirth and the Voluntary Agent's Esteem of Purpose," *Philosophy Research Archives* 11 (1986): 379–91.

28. Gewirth, *Reason and Morality*, p. 135.

29. Ibid., p. 134.

30. Ibid., pp. 114–21.

31. Ibid., p. 121.

32. Ibid., p. 120.

CHAPTER 3

1. Indeed, it is commonly recognized that corporate rational agents, sometimes called "artificial" persons, have become increasingly dominant in modern political societies. Cf. James S. Coleman, *The Asymmetric Society* (Syracuse, N.Y.: Syracuse University Press, 1982).

2. Talcott Parsons et al., "Some Fundamental Categories of the Theory of Action: A General Statement," in *Toward a General Theory of Action: Theoretical Foundations for the Social Sciences,* ed. Talcott Parsons and Edward A. Shils (New York: Harper and Row, 1962), pp. 14–15.

3. S. I. Benn and R. S. Peters, *The Principles of Political Thought: Social Foundations of the Democratic State* (New York: The Free Press, 1966), p. 18.

4. Peter A. Facione, Donald Scherer, and Thomas Attig, *Values and Society: An Introduction to Ethics and Social Philosophy* (Englewood Cliffs, N.J.: Prentice-Hall, 1978), p. 199.

5. J. D. Mabbott, *The State and the Citizen: An Introduction to Political Philosophy* (New York: Hutchinson's University Library, 1952), p. 100.

6. There has not always been agreement, of course, on what falls within a state's domain. In the Middle Ages everyone agreed that the state had authority over all within its boundaries and that God had authority over all within His domain, but not everyone agreed what fell within each domain. Souls were definitely within God's domain, but what about the offices and property of the church? Hence, the tragic dispute between Henry II and Thomas Becket.

7. Jacques Maritain distinguishes between a body politic and a state. By the latter he seems to mean the body politic's government. Regardless, his distinction is stipulative, perhaps programmatic. See Jacques Maritain, *Man and the State* (Chicago: The University of Chicago Press, 1956), pp. 9, 12.

8. Benn and Peters, "The State and Other Associations," in *Principles of Political Thought,* pp. 327–49. Also, Mabbott, "The State and Other Associations," in *The State and the Citizen,* pp. 12–38.

9. Benn and Peters, *Principles of Political Thought,* pp. 302–3. In truth, some philosophers regard legal sovereignty as identifiable with state sovereignty. See Iredell Jenkins, *Social Order and the Limits of Law: A Theoretical Essay* (Princeton, N.J.: Princeton University Press, 1980), pp. 107–8.

10. While security and order for its members are the minimum intentions of a state, they also are necessary conditions for the stable existence of such a society. A commonwealth would not endure if its members were long dominated by a foreign power or if domestic turmoil prevailed. The necessary conditions of political society's existence should not be confused with its minimal intentions, however. Another necessary condition is communication, but that condition conceivably can exist for a body politic without the society's intending to establish it.

11. Mabbott, *The State and the Citizen,* pp. 101–3. Also, Thomas Hobbes *Leviathan,* pt. 1, chap. 3; Bernard Bosanquet, *The Philosophical Theory of the State* (New York: St. Martin's Press, 1965), pp. 172–73.

12. It might be that a state will be morally obligated to look after such condi-

tions not for just its own members but for those of foreign groups, including other states. But the conditions under which a state is morally bound to furnish "foreign aid" are too complex to be clarified here.

13. Robert Nozick, *Anarchy, State, and Utopia* (New York: Basic Books, 1974), pp. 333–34.

14. Plato, *The Republic,* bks. 2–5.

15. John Dewey, "Search for the Public," in *The Public and Its Problems* (Denver: Alan Swallow, 1954), pp. 3–36.

16. Alan Gewirth, *Reason and Morality* (Chicago: The University of Chicago Press, 1978), pp. 272–73.

17. Dewey, *The Public and Its Problems,* p. 76.

18. Ibid., p. 77.

19. Cf. Robert D. Heslep, *The Mental in Education: A Philosophical Study* (University, Ala.: The University of Alabama Press, 1981), pp. 57ff.

20. Some philosophers of law maintain that all legal rules, including criminal laws, are primarily indicatives, not imperatives. *Vide,* e.g., Ilmar Tammelo, *Modern Logic in the Service of Law* (New York: Springer-Verlag, 1978). For a criticism of this work, see the review by Philip E. Davis in *Ethics* 91 (July 1981): 671–72. Our view that criminal laws are imperatives does not intend that all legal rules are imperatives. Some may be permissives. Cf. Lawrence Haworth, "The Standard View of the State: A Critique," *Ethics* 73 (July 1963): 271–74. Also, while we recognize that criminal laws usually call for the punishment of violators, we do acknowledge that such laws might require nothing more than the rehabilitation of offenders.

21. Criminal laws calling for rehabilitation exclusive of punishment may be sources of some kind of justice, but they surely are not sources of retributive justice.

22. For a summary discussion of the major reasons, see Benn and Peters, *Principles of Political Thought,* pp. 201–16.

23. Cf. Gewirth, *Reason and Morality,* p. 293.

24. Ibid., pp. 201–4.

25. Ibid., pp. 287–88.

CHAPTER 4

1. Aristotle, *Politics* 1290b18-20.

2. Thomas Aquinas, *On Princely Government,* chap. 3.

3. Thomas Jefferson, *Declaration of Independence.*

4. Joseph H. Schumpeter, *Capitalism, Socialism, and Democracy,* 3rd edition (New York: Harper and Row, 1962), p. 269.

5. Robert A. Dahl, *A Preface to Democratic Theory* (Chicago: The University of Chicago Press, 1956), p. 3.

6. Charles Frankel, *The Democratic Prospect* (New York: Harper and Row, 1962), p. 30.

7. *Encyclopedia Britannica,* 14th ed., s.v. "Democracy."

8. Charner Perry, "Ethics and Democracy," *Ethics* 83 (January 1973): 87.

9. This point is discussed further in this chapter, Part III.

10. Cf. Harry K. Girvetz, "Democracy," in *Democracy and Elitism: Two Essays with Selected Readings,* ed. Harry K. Girvetz (New York: Charles Scribner's Sons, 1967), pp. 4–5.

11. So, the governmental officials of a representative democracy have a dual role as agents. As officials of the state, they are agents of the state (Chapter 3, Part II); as representatives of the people, they are agents of the people. When the officials find the state's interests are compatible with the major characteristics of its members' voluntary actions, they have no inherent conflict in being dual agents; but when they find the state's interests incompatible with the major characteristics, they have an inherent conflict. One way to resolve the conflict is to modify the state's interests (by, for instance, altering its purposes and laws). Another way is to persuade the state's members to make sacrifices for the sake of the state. It is arguable that President Franklin D. Roosevelt pursued the former route during the depression years and the latter route during World War II.

12. Cf. Girvetz, *Democracy and Elitism,* p. 4. "The people are no longer a select society of free individuals. Now we have mass democracy."

13. F. A. Hayek, *Law, Legislation and Liberty,* vol. 3, *The Political Order of a Free People* (Chicago: The University of Chicago Press, 1979), p. 5.

14. T. D. Weldon, *The Vocabulary of Politics* (Baltimore: Penguin Books, 1960), p. 100.

15. S. I. Benn and R. S. Peters, *The Principles of Political Thought: Social Foundations of the Democratic State* (New York: The Free Press, 1966), p. 420.

16. See Jeremy Bentham, *A Fragment on Government,* ed. F. C. Montague (Oxford: The Clarendon Press, 1891), p. 217.

17. Cf. H. L. A. Hart, *Law, Liberty and Morality* (New York: Random House, 1963), p. 79.

18. Cf. Perry, "Ethics and Democracy," pp. 90–91.

19. Hayek, *The Political Order of a Free People,* p. 5.

20. Cf. Aristotle, *Politics* 1281a40-1281b38.

21. Cf. Thomas Jefferson's letter to Peter Carr (August 10, 1787), in vol. 12 of *The Papers of Thomas Jefferson,* ed. Julian P. Boyd et al. (Princeton, N.J.: Princeton University Press, 1950 *et seq.*), p. 15.

22. John Stuart Mill, "Of the Limits to the Authority of Society over the Individual," in *On Liberty;* in John Stuart Mill, *Utilitarianism, Liberty, and Representative Government,* (New York: E. P. Dutton, 1951), pp. 176–200.

23. John Locke, "Of the Ends of Political Society and Government," in *An Essay Concerning the True Original, Extent and End of Civil Government,* bk. 2 of *Of Civil Government, Two Treatises* (New York: E. P. Dutton, 1949), pp. 179–82.

24. A classic discussion of conditions endemic to the modern industrial age that pose obstacles to the accurate perception of the public interest is provided by Graham Wallas, *The Great Society* (n. p., Macmillan, 1914). John Dewey's equally important analysis of these conditions is apparently indebted to Wallas's work. See Dewey, "The Eclipse of the Public," in *The Public and Its Problems* (Denver, Colo.: Alan Swallow, 1954), pp. 110–42.

25. Because the government of any state has moral goods as a characteristic and, hence, has some moral value, even the government of the most despicable state has some moral worth. This does not mean, of course, that the latter government is good in general. That even an evil state is good in some respect is certainly not a novel idea. Thomas Aquinas noted that tyrannies at least maintain order. See *Summa theologica,* 2.2, 42.

26. Cf. Dewey, "Search for the Great Community," in *The Public and Its Problems,* pp. 143–84.

27. This view of political duty is not only commonsensical but is comparable to Plato's view of political justice, which analyzes political justice in the terms of talent and need. Cf. Plato, *The Republic* 369–72, 433, 442–43.

28. Cf. Alan Gewirth, *Reason and Morality* (Chicago: University of Chicago Press, 1978), pp. 290ff, 312ff.

29. John Rawls, *A Theory of Justice* (Cambridge, Mass.: Harvard University Press, 1971), p. 75.

30. Ibid., p. 118.

31. Ibid., p. 75.

32. Ibid., p. 19.

CHAPTER 5

1. For other analyses of the concept of learning, viz. John H. Chambers, *The Achievement of Education: An Examination of Key Concepts in Educational Practice* (New York: Harper and Row, 1983), pp. 47–58. Also, P. H. Hirst and R. S. Peters, *The Logic of Education* (London: Routledge and Kegan Paul, 1970), pp. 74–76.

2. A textbook treatment of education as a discipline is provided by Van Cleve Morris, ed., *Becoming an Educator: An Introduction by Specialists to the Study and Practice of Education* (Boston: Houghton Mifflin, 1963).

3. Cf. Myron Lieberman, *Education as a Profession* (Englewood Cliffs, N.J.: Prentice Hall, 1956).

4. *Phi Delta Kappan* 48 (January 1967), Special Issue, "Big Business Discovers the Education Market."

5. Cf. William M. Cave and Mark A. Chesler, eds., "Introduction," in *Sociology of Education: An Anthology of Issues and Problems* (New York: Macmillan, 1974), p. 3.

6. Cf. John B. Magee, *Philosophical Analysis in Education* (New York: Harper and Row, 1971), pp. 99–103.

7. A view implicitly discussed by Hirst and Peters, *Logic of Education,* p. 21

8. Cf. Alfred North Whitehead, "The Aims of Education," in *The Aims of Education and Other Essays* (New York: New American Library of World Literature, 1955), pp. 13–26.

9. This is a view lying behind the Great Books curriculum.

10. This position seems attributable to many of the education reformers of recent decades (for instance, Paul Goodman, Ivan Illich, and Theodore Rozsak).

11. For an example of the former, see Robert M. Hutchins, *The Conflict in Education in a Democratic Society* (New York: Harper and Brothers, 1953), pp. 67–84, 88–90. For an example of the latter, see J. L. Meriam, *Child Life and the Curriculum* (Yonkers-on-Hudson, N.Y.: World Book, 1921), pp. 147–54, 163–68, 203–204.

12. For example, Herbert Spencer, "What Knowledge Is of Most Worth?" in *Essays on Education and Kindred Subjects* (London: J. M. Dent and Sons, 1963), pp. 1–44. Also, Chambers, *The Achievement of Education*, pp. 18, 24.

13. For a recent defense of the ordinary conception of knowledge, see Marshall Swain, *Reasons and Knowledge* (Ithaca: Cornell University Press, 1981).

14. R. S. Peters, *Ethics and Education* (Boston: George Allen and Unwin, 1978), p. 31.

15. Cf. C. P. Snow, *The Two Cultures and the Scientific Revolution* (New York: Cambridge University Press, 1960).

16. Hirst and Peters, *The Logic of Education*, p. 63.

17. Plato, *The Republic* 509C–511E.

18. Aristotle, *N. Ethics* 1139614–41a8.

19. Auguste Comte, "Estimate of the Results of Positive Doctrine in Its Preparatory Stage," in vol. 3 of *The Positive Philosophy*, trans. Harriet Martineau (London: George Bell & Sons, 1896), pp. 387–400.

20. Thomas Aquinas, *S. Theologic* 1–2, qq. 57–58.

21. A notable contemporary use of the Aristotelian schema in analyzing curricular issues appears in Joseph J. Schwab, "Problems, Topics, and Issues," in Stanley Elam, ed., *Education and the Structure of Knowledge* (Chicago: Rand McNally, 1964), pp. 20–28.

22. Philip H. Phenix, *Realms of Meaning: A Philosophy of Curriculum for General Education* (New York: McGraw-Hill Book Company, 1964).

23. For an examination of teaching that is relevant to the present discussion, see Thomas F. Green, "A Topology of the Teaching Concept," *Studies in Philosophy and Education* 3 (1964–65): 284–319.

24. Giovanni Gentile, *The Reform of Education*, trans. Dion Bigongiari (New York: Harcourt, Brace and World, 1922), pp. 7–17, 27–31.

25. *Contra* Arthur J. Todd. *The Primitive Family as an Educational Agency* (New York: G. P. Putnam's Sons, 1913).

26. John of Salisbury, *Metalogicon* 1.10.33, 1.13.222–23, 4.25.241.

27. Spencer, "What Knowledge Is of Most Worth?"

28. For an anthology of pieces on the subject which have bibliographies, see P. V. Wason and P. N. Johnson-Laird, eds., *Thinking and Reasoning* (Harmondsworth, England: Penguin, 1970).

29. John E. McPeck, *Critical Thinking and Education* (New York: St. Martin's Press, 1981).

30. Peters, *Ethics and Education*, p. 25

31. Hirst and Peters, *The Logic of Education*, p. 21.

CHAPTER 6

1. Alan Gewirth, *Reason and Morality* (Chicago: University of Chicago Press, 1978), p. 274.

2. Talcott Parsons et al., "Some Fundamental Categories of the Theory of Action," in *Toward a General Theory of Action: Theoretical Foundations for the Social Sciences,* ed. Talcott Parsons and Edward A. Shils (New York: Harper and Row, 1962), p. 40.

3. For a touching statement of the egalitarian position on the matter, see the essay by William Manning, "The Key of Libberty" (February 1798), reprinted in *William and Mary Quarterly,* 3d ser., 13 (January 1956): 211–54.

4. S. Alexander Rippa, *Education in a Free Society: An American History,* 3d ed. (New York: David McKay, 1976), pp. 299–305. Edgar B. Gumbert and Joel H. Spring, "War, Machines, and Education," in *The Superschool and the Superstate: American Education in the Twentieth Century, 1918–1970* (New York: John Wiley & Sons, 1974), pp. 51–86. C. A. Bowers, *The Progressive Educator and the Depression: The Radical Years* (New York: Random House, 1969), pp. 116–22.

5. See David Bridges, *Education, Democracy and Discussion* (Windsor, England: NFER, 1979).

6. John Dewey, *The Public and Its Problems* (Denver, Colo.: Allan Swallow, 1954), p. 76.

7. Ibid., pp. 15–16.

8. Ibid., chap. 5, *ad passim.*

9. John Dewey, *Reconstruction in Philosophy* (New York: New American Library, 1954), p. 141. Also, see John Dewey, *Experience and Education* (New York: Macmillan, 1957), pp. 27–29.

10. John Dewey, *Theory of Valuation,* in *International Encyclopedia of Unified Science,* vol 2, no. 4 (Chicago: The University of Chicago Press, 1950), pp. 33–35.

11. Robert D. Heslep, *Thomas Jefferson and Education* (New York: Random House, 1969), pp. 49–51.

CHAPTER 7

1. A classic description of Progressive Education was made by John Dewey, *Experience and Education* (New York: Macmillan, 1938), pp. 4–6.

2. For example, Stanley Elam, ed., *Education and the Structure of Knowledge* (Chicago: Rand McNally, 1964).

3. For example, Paul Goodman, "No Processing Whatever," in *Radical School Reform,* ed. Ronald and Beatrice Gross (New York: Simon and Schuster, 1969), pp. 98–106.

4. For example, Sidney P. Marland, Jr., "The Unfinished Business of Career Education," *Today's Education* 67 (April–May 1978): 57–60, 62.

5. For example: Down A. Graham, "Why Basic Education?" *National Elemen-*

tary Principal 58 (October 1977): 28–32. "What Makes a School Fundamental? These Five Purposes and Four Standards," *American School Board Journal* 158 (February 1976): 30–31.

6. Cf. Goodman, "No Processing Whatever," p. 99.

7. As shown by all the mass media talk about federal aid to education during the Sputnik era.

8. Cf. Tom L. Beauchamp, "The Justification of Reverse Discrimination," in *Social Justice and Preferential Treatment: Women and Racial Minorities in Education and Business,* ed. William T. Blackstone and Robert D. Heslep (Athens, Ga.: The University of Georgia Press, 1977), pp. 84–110.

9. As suggested by the widespread attitude that the point of a high school diploma or a college degree is to assure oneself a good chance to compete for the more lucrative positions in the job market.

10. In order to justify renewed emphasis upon traditional subjects, people tend to cite declines in academic achievement (e.g., as measured by drops in standardized academic test scores). See, for example, The National Commission for Excellence in Education, *A Nation at Risk: The Imperative for Educational Reform* (Washington, D.C.: U.S. Government Printing Office, April 1983), pp. 8–9.

11. Joe Park, "Education: Schooling and Informal," in *Philosophy of Education, 1971: Proceedings of the Twenty-seventh Annual Meeting of the Philosophy of Education Society,* ed. Robert D. Heslep (Edwardsville, Ill.: Philosophy of Education Society, 1971), pp. 1–16.

12. Morris Janowitz, *The Reconstruction of Patriotism: Education for Civic Consciousness* (Chicago: The University of Chicago Press, 1983), pp. 192–203.

13. Arno Bellack, "The Structure of Knowledge and the Structure of the Curriculum," in *Readings in the Philosophy of Education,* 2d ed., ed. John Martin Rich (Belmont, Calif.: Wadsworth, 1972), pp. 239 ff.

14. Cf. Joseph J. Schwab, "Problems, Topics, and Issues," in *Education and the Structure of Knowledge,* ed. Elam, pp. 12–14.

15. Cf. Park, "Education: Schooling and Informal," pp. 12–13.

16. Cf. Robert S. Zais, *Curriculum: Principles and Foundations* (New York: Harper and Row, 1976), pp. 420–29

17. Cf. Park, "Education: Schooling and Informal," pp. 13–14.

18. President's Science Advisory Committee, "Education for the Age of Science" (The White House, Washington, D.C., May 24, 1959, Mimeographed), p. 7.

19. Ibid., p.3.

20. Ibid., p. 2f.

21. Ibid., pp. 7–27.

22. Ibid. pp. 28–33.

23. National Commission on Excellence in Education, *A Nation at Risk,* p.6.

24. Ibid., p.7.

25. Ibid.

26. Ibid.

27. Ibid., p. 18.

28. Ibid., p. 24.

29. Ibid., pp. 26–27.
30. Ibid., pp. 13–14, 24.
31. Ibid., p.8.
32. Ibid., p. 24.
33. Ibid., pp. 13–14.
34. For instance: T. M. Stinnett, *The Teaching Profession* (Washington, D.C.: The Center for Applied Research in Education, 1962). James B. Conant, *The Education of American Teachers* (New York: McGraw-Hill, 1963). Philip L. Smith and Rob Traver, "Program and Prophecy: The Fate of General Studies in Teacher Education," *Educational Theory* 33 (Spring 1983): 73–77.
35. Robert D. Heslep, *The Mental in Education: A Philosophical Study* (University, Ala.: The University of Alabama Press, 1981), p. 120.
36. Ibid., p. 121.
37. Ibid., pp. 106–14.
38. Stanley Elam, *Performance-Based Teacher Education: What Is the State of the Art?* (Washington, D.C.: American Association of Colleges for Teacher Education, 1972).
39. Holmes Group, *Tomorrow's Teachers* (East Lansing, Mich.: Holmes Group, 1986), pp. 15ff.
40. For a good overview of the issue, see Elliot W. Eisner, "The Three Curricula That All Schools Teach," in *The Educational Imagination: On the Design and Evaluation of School Programs* (New York: Macmillian, 1981), pp. 74–92.
41. Ibid., p. 75.
42. Cf. Henry A. Giroux, *Theory and Resistance in Education: A Pedagogy for the Opposition* (South Hadley, Mass.: Bergin and Garvey, 1983). Michael W. Apple, *Education and Power* (Boston: Routledge and Kegan Paul, 1982).

CHAPTER 8

1. Harry K. Girvetz, "Democracy," in *Democracy and Elitism: Two Essays with Selected Readings,* ed. Harry K. Girvetz (New York: Charles Scribner's Sons, 1967), pp. 16ff.
2. For an examination of the distinction, see B. Paul Komisar and Jerrold R. Coombs, "The Concept of Equality in Education," *Studies in Philosophy and Education* 3 (Fall 1964): 223–44.
3. But what if no role commensurate with the talents of the best-qualified is open or otherwise available to the best-qualified? In that case they and the lesser-qualified might share the role for which they are competing; or the former might undergo retraining for other occupations that might help fulfill their life ambitions or, failing all else, alter their life plans.
4. We agree with Fishkin that no moral principle should be, in his meaning of the term, tyrannous; but our insistence that life plans should be restricted by the RPGC does not seem to make the principle tyrannous. Cf. James S. Fishkin, *Tyranny and Le-*

gitimacy: A Critique of Political Theories (Baltimore: Johns Hopkins University Press, 1979), esp. pp. 122–23.

5. So, while we allow with Rawls that the counting of grass leaves in various geometrically shaped areas might count as a life plan, we would insist that it is a life plan that likely consists—if it might consist of voluntary actions at all—of nonevaluative voluntary actions and, thus, all other things being equal, might not be as significant for a rational agent as one consisting of evaluative voluntary actions. See John Rawls, *A Theory of Justice* (Cambridge: Harvard University Press, 1971), p. 432.

6. This case was suggested to me by James M. Giarelli.

7. Accordingly, our position on social equality in the democratic state differs markedly from what Strike calls the "traditional" view espoused by liberal ideology. See Kenneth A. Strike, *Educational Policy and the Just Society* (Urbana, Ill.: University of Illinois Press, 1982), pp. 173ff.

8. Cf. Donald M. Levine and Mary Jo Bane, "Introduction," in *The "Inequality" Controversy: Schooling and Distributive Justice,* ed. Donald M. Levine and Mary Jo Bane (New York: Basic Books, 1975), pp. 3–21.

9. Another way of saying all this is that the scope of the curriculum must include both the necessary and the contingent elements and that these elements, as they appear in the curriculum, must have sequence, continuity, and integration. Cf. Robert S. Zais, *Curriculum: Principles and Foundations* (New York: Harper and Row, 1976), pp. 395ff., 439ff.

10. Rawls, *A Theory of Justice,* p. 106.

11. Ibid.

12. Ibid., p. 107

13. Ibid., p. 60.

14. Cf. Samuel Bowles, "Unequal Education and the Reproduction of the Social Division of Labor," in *Schooling in a Corporate Society: The Political Economy of Education in America,* ed. Martin Carnoy (New York: David McKay, 1972), pp. 36–64.

15. Except for that of genetic educational disorders, all of these conditions were examined in the Coleman Report. See James S. Coleman et al., *Equality of Educational Opportunity: Summary* (Washington, D.C.: U.S. Government Printing Office, 1966).

16. It is problematic as to whether or not a person's willfully not becoming fully educated is morally right. If his or her decision threatens the moral rights of others by depriving other rational agents of a moral resource, it is morally wrong; but if it does not threaten any one's moral rights, it is morally right.

17. Abraham Edel, "Preferential Consideration and Justice," in *Social Justice and Preferential Treatment: Women and Racial Minorities in Education and Business,* ed. William T. Blackstone and Robert D. Heslep (Athens, Ga.: University of Georgia Press, 1975), pp. 111–34.

CHAPTER 9

1. The dispositions and appreciations significant in a moral education may or may not be "genderized." Whether or not they are is an empirical, not a logical, point.

Also, that a system of morality can be constructed satisfactorily around genderized virtues remains to be seen. As the etymology of *virtue* indicates, ancient Romans tried to center their moral beliefs around masculine traits, most notably, courage. Some contemporary writers attempt to place the feminine virtues of caring and responsibility at the heart of morality. See: C. Gilligan, "In a Different Voice: Women's Conceptions of the Self and of Morality," *Harvard Educational Review* 47 (November 1977): 481–517. Nel Noddings, *Caring: A Feminine Approach to Ethics and Moral Education* (Berkeley: University of California Press, 1984).

    2. For a contemporary instance in the sciences, peruse any of the recent publications concerning biomedical ethics, such as Ronald Munson, ed., *Intervention and Reflection: Basic Issues in Medical Ethics,* 2d ed. (Belmont, Calif.: Wadsworth, 1983). For a classical instance in the arts, see Plato, *The Republic* 376–403.

    3. Whether or not the content of a given conception of the theoretical disciplines has a masculine bias, as some have charged, is an empirical rather than a conceptual issue. The important point here is that no schema of the theoretical disciplines should be biased toward either sex without justification. See Jane Roland Martin, "The Ideal of the Educated Person," in *Philosophy of Education, 1981: Proceedings of the Thirty-seventh Annual Meeting of the Philosophy of Education Society,* ed. Daniel DeNicola (Normal, Ill.: Philosophy of Education Society, 1981), pp. 3–20.

    4. Cf. A. J. Ayer, *Language, Truth and Logic,* 2d ed. (New York: Dover Publications, 1946), pp. 107–10. Charles L. Stevenson, *Ethics and Language* (New Haven: Yale University Press, 1944).

    5. Aristotle, *N. Ethics* 1140a24-1140b19.

    6. John Stuart Mill, *Utilitarianism,* in John Stuart Mill, *Utiliatarianism, Liberty, and Representative Government* (New York: E. P. Dutton, 1951), pp. 9–19.

    7. Daniel DeNicola, "The Education of the Emotions," in *Philosophy of Education, 1979: Proceedings of the Thirty-fifth Annual Meeting of the Philosophy of Education Society,* ed. Jerrold B. Coombs et al. (Normal, Ill.: Philosophy of Education Society, 1979), pp. 210–19. For a response to this essay, see in the same volume Robert D. Heslep, "Response to DeNicola," pp. 220–23.

    8. Joan D. Wallace, ed., *Selected Readings in Moral Education* (Philadelphia: Research for Better Schools, 1976).

    9. For example: Louis E. Raths, *Exploring Moral Values* (Pleasantville, N.Y.: Warren Schloat, 1969). Milton Rokeach, "Toward A Philosophy of Value Education," in *Values Education: Theory/Practice/Problems/Prospects,* ed. John Mayer et al. (Waterloo, Ont.: Wilfrid Lauries University Press, 1975), pp. 117–26.

    10. Raths, *Exploring Moral Values,* p. 27.

    11. William M. Kurtines and Jacob L. Gewirtz, eds., *Morality, Moral Behavior and Moral Development* (New York: John Wiley and Sons, 1984).

    12. For example, R. S. Peters, "A Reply to Kohlberg," *Phil Delta Kappan* 56 (June 1975): 678.

    13. Alan Gewirth, "Morality and Autonomy in Education," in *Educational Judgments: Papers in the Philosophy of Education,* ed. James F. Doyle (Boston: Routledge and Kegan Paul, 1973), pp. 39–43.

    14. Lawrence Kohlberg, *The Philosophy of Moral Development: Moral Stages and*

the Idea of Justice, vol. 1 of *Essays on Moral Development* (New York: Harper and Row, 1981), pp. 115–30.

15. Kohlberg and other advocates of the developmental approach make a distinction between moral development and educational development, but they do not distinguish between moral development and moral educational development. Ibid., pp. 49–96.

CHAPTER 10

1. Carl M. Gross et al., "The Control of Teaching: Who Decides What?", in *Readings in School and Society: The Social and Philosophical Foundations of Education,* ed. Carl M. Gross et al. (Boston: D.C. Heath, 1962), p. 352.

2. The Governor's Conference, *Is Education the Business of the Federal Government?* (Raleigh, N.C.: Office of Terry Sanford, Governor, 1964), pp. 83–84.

3. Michael Imber, "Increased Decision Making Involvement for Teachers: Ethical and Practical Considerations," *The Journal of Educational Thought* 17 (April 1983): 36–42. Drew Christie, "Recent Calls for Economic Democracy," *Ethics* 95 (October 1984): 114–115.

4. The Montgomery County Student Alliance, "A Student Voice"; in *Radical School Reform,* ed. Beatrice Gross and Ronald Gross (New York: Simon and Schuster, 1969), pp. 147–60.

5. John Keats, *Schools Without Scholars* (Boston: Houghton Mifflin, 1958), esp. p. 153.

6. Jay D. Scribner, ed., *Seventy-sixth Yearbook of the National Society for the Study of Education, Part II: The Politics of Education* (Chicago: The University of Chicago Press, 1977).

7. Ralph B. Kimbrough, *Political Power and Educational Decision-Making* (Chicago: Rand McNally, 1964), pp. 4ff.

8. American Association of School Administrators, *School Board–Superintendent Relationships: Thirty-fourth Yearbook of the American Association of School Administrators* (Washington, D.C.: American Association of School Administrators, 1956), pp. 26–28.

9. Elisabeth Hansot and David Tyack, "A Usable Past: Using History in Educational Policy"; in *Eighty-first Yearbook of the National Society for the Study of Education, Part I: Policy Making in Education,* ed. Ann Liberman and Milbrey W. McLaughlin (Chicago: University of Chicago Press, 1982), pp. 5–10.

10. In a different but related context Michael Walzer suggests the connection between voluntariness and participation. Cf. Michael Walzer, "Hold the Justice," *The New Republic* 192 (April 8, 1985): 11: "The strongest democratic defense of the right to punish goes roughly like this. When we agree to the laws (participate in making them or in electing representatives who make them) we accept the proposition that if we ever break the law we ought to be punished. Criminals are punished, then, with their own consent."

11. Robert D. Heslep, "Educational Proposals," in *Thomas Jefferson and Education* (New York: Random House, 1969), pp. 87–112.

12. Cf. Horace Mann, vol. 4 of *Life and Works* (Boston: Walker, Fuller, 1868), esp. pp. 345–65.

13. S. Alexander Rippa, *Education in a Free Society: An American History* (New York: Longman, 1984), 5th edition, pp. 110–13.

14. For example: Ernest L. Boyer, *High School: A Report on Secondary Education in America* (New York: Harper and Row, 1983). Linda Darling-Hammond, *Beyond the Commission Reports: The Coming Crisis in Teaching* (Washington, D.C.: Rand, 1984). John I. Goodlad, *A Place Called School: Prospects for the Future* (New York: McGraw-Hill, 1984). Morris Janowitz, *The Reconstruction of Patriotism: Education for Civic Consciousness* (Chicago: The University of Chicago Press, 1983).The National Commission on Excellence in Education, *A Nation at Risk* (Washington, D.C.: U.S. Government Printing Office, 1982). Diane Ravitch, *The Troubled Crusade: American Education, 1948–1980* (New York: Basic Books, 1983). Theodore R. Sizer, *Horace's Compromise: The Dilemma of the American High School* (New York: Houghton Mifflin, 1984).

15. This was Plato's approach to readying persons for membership in his republic. Only children were to be selected for being the initial members of the society, and they were to be subjected to a closely supervised program of learning.

16. This was the way in which members of he Puritan sect were readied for membership in the Massachusetts Bay Colony. They were prepared in England for living in England; and when the opportunity arose, they moved to the colony, where they organized a theocratic society and prospered.

Index

Action: chief characteristics, 17–18; definition of, 15–16; generic and specific traits, 18–19; had, 16; performed, 16; as source of principles for understanding education's moral role in democratic state, 13, 15
Anscombe, G. E. M., 222
Apple, Michael W., 230
Appreciations as objects of education, 93
Aristotle, 55, 68, 89, 91, 174, 177, 222, 224, 225, 227, 232
Attig, Thomas, 223
Ayer, A. J., 232

Baier, Kurt, 221
Bane, Mary Jo, 231
Beauchamp, Tom L., 229
Bellack, Arno, 229
Benn, S. I., 59–61, 223, 224
Bentham, Jeremy, 59–60, 224
Blackstone, William T., 229, 231
Bodily habits as objects of education, 93–94
Bodily skills as objects of education, 94
Bowers, C. A., 228
Bowles, Samuel, 231
Boyer, Ernest L., 234
Bridges, David, 228

Capricious goals, 23–26
Carnoy, Martin, 231
Cave, William M., 226
Chambers, John H., 226, 227
Chesler, Mark A., 226
Christie, Drew, 233

Coleman, James S., 223, 231
Comprehensive understanding, 85–92, 107
Comte, Auguste, 89, 91, 174, 227
Conant, James B., 6–9, 221, 230
Coombs, Jerrold R., 230, 232
Curriculum: academic basics as content, 131–32; appropriate learning activities for curriculum, 132–33; content in democracy, 125–29; hidden, 145ff.; institutions responsible for content, 129–30; organization of theoretical disciplines as content, 130–31; purpose in democracy, 124–25

Dahl, Robert A., 56, 224
Darling-Hammond, Linda, 234
Davis, Philip E., 224
Decision making on education: difficulty in implementation, 219ff.; education of citizens for, 212–17; and expediency, 201–2; and expertise, 202ff., 208–10; participatory, 204ff.; and vested interest, 196–200
Democratic state: definition of, 58; intentions and decisions, 61–67; major principles, 68–69; moral significance, 69–78; noninstitutional activities of members, 116–17; and self-government, 55–58.
DeNicola, Daniel, 232
Desire and valuation, 21–26
Dewey, John, vii, 12, 46, 117, 142, 217, 224, 225, 226, 228
Dispositions as objects of education, 92–93